GLOBAL NEOREALISM

GLOBAL NEOREALISM

The Transnational History of a Film Style

Edited by
Saverio Giovacchini and Robert Sklar

UNIVERSITY PRESS OF MISSISSIPPI • JACKSON

www.upress.state.ms.us

The University Press of Mississippi is a member of the Association
of American University Presses.

Copyright © 2012 by University Press of Mississippi
All rights reserved
Manufactured in the United States of America

First printing 2012

∞

Library of Congress Cataloging-in-Publication Data

Global neorealism : the transnational history of a film style /
edited by Saverio Giovacchini and Robert Sklar.
p. cm.
Includes bibliographical references and index.
ISBN 978-1-61703-122-9 (cloth : alk. paper) —
ISBN 978-1-61703-123-6 (ebook) 1. Realism in motion pictures.
2. Motion pictures—Italy—History—20th century.
I. Giovacchini, Saverio, 1963– II. Sklar, Robert.
PN1995.9.R3G56 2011
791.43'612—dc22   2011015992
British Library Cataloging-in-Publication Data available

For Ingalisa
si vales ego valeo

For Nevona, Nadav, Cedar, and Jake

and

To the memory of Robert Sklar, *maestro e amico*

CONTENTS

ACKNOWLEDGMENTS

We thank the Nathan and Jeanette Miller Center for Historical Studies at the University of Maryland, College Park, for precious help in the organization of the conference that started the process that this book completes. At the University Press of Mississippi, Leila Salisbury admirably shepherded the book and assigned it to very competent readers and an extraordinary copy editor, Ellen D. Goldlust-Gingrich.

Robert Sklar died on July 2, 2011, when *Global Neorealism* was going to press. This book would not have been possible without Bob's unparalleled knowledge of world cinema, his humor, and his commitment to clear and elegant writing. *Global Neorealism* is dedicated to his memory.

GLOBAL NEOREALISM

INTRODUCTION

The Geography and History of Global Neorealism

SAVERIO GIOVACCHINI AND ROBERT SKLAR

Among the terms that cinema scholars, critics, and filmmakers have developed in the course of the twentieth century, few if any have had the staying power of *neorealism*. Since 1943, when Umberto Barbaro took the term from literary analysis and employed it to describe French realist cinema of the 1930s,[1] the term has remained current, widely applied, and hotly debated in its definition. In 2008, after winning the Grand Prix at the Cannes Film Festival for his film, *Gomorra* (Gomorrah), about the Italian Camorra's stranglehold on the harbor of Naples, director Matteo Garrone pointed out that his movie was meant less as a reference to the mob tales of Martin Scorsese than to the neorealist "war trilogy" of Roberto Rossellini—in other words, that it was less indebted to *Mean Streets* (1973), *Goodfellas* (1990), and *Casino* (1995) than to *Roma, città aperta* (Rome, Open City, 1945), *Paisà* (1946), and *Germania anno zero* (Germany Year Zero, 1948).[2] More tragically, in 2010, Iranian authorities arrested Persian filmmaker Jafar Panahi and detained him for three months; they also denied him an exit visa to attend the Venice Film Festival, which he had won in 2000 with his film *Dayereh* (The Circle). International press coverage of Panahi's ordeal, which was related to political conflicts within Iran, invariably referred to him as a "director of neorealist films."[3] Indeed, Panahi has often been asked to speak about Iranian neorealism and its relation to the Italian example (a theme extensively discussed in Hamid Naficy's essay in this volume). In 2001, Panahi told an interviewer, "The Iranian cinema treats social subjects. Because you're showing social problems, you want to be more realistic and give the actual, the real aesthetics of the situation. . . . Whatever shows the truth of the society, in a very artistic way—that will find its own neo-realism."[4]

Panahi's words could serve as the touchstone of the film histories and debates that are the subject of *Global Neorealism: The Transnational History of a Film Style*. This volume seeks primarily to investigate how neorealism has become central to the issues of political cinema in Iran and elsewhere in the world. Our itinerary crosses many nations, starts before the official post–World War II birth of Italian neorealism, and continues after its alleged death at the onset of the 1950s. Examining this long and complex journey, *Global Neorealism* remaps the geography and rewrites the history of neorealism from a transnational perspective. The authors included here conceive of the two as profoundly connected, pushing further three different but intertwined historiographic debates.

The debate about neorealism has often dealt with the issue of defining the term and its style. The discussion recalls the long-lasting arguments about the definition of film noir: everyone from the film critic to the ordinary moviegoer seems to recognize a neorealist or noir film even in the absence of a consensual, unified, critical definition of the genre. Already by the late 1940s, film critics and filmmakers were able to identify the general characteristics of a neorealist film. Writing in 1948, director Stefano "Steno" Vanzina deemed it possible to list the rules that made the "perfect neorealist director [*perfetto regista neorealista*]": for example, he wrote, "if you set your story in the outskirts of the city, you will soon be able to grab [a critical] victory."[5]

Yet scholars and practitioners have encountered problems whenever they have tried to give the term a normative definition. In 1952, the French magazine *Films et documents* listed "the 10 points of neorealism," among which were "topical scripts," "the truth of actors, often nonprofessionals," the "truth of the lighting," a "photography reminiscent of the reportage style," and the "refusal of the studio."[6] In the intervening decades, however, critics have pointed out that Roberto Rossellini cast professionals such as Anna Magnani and Aldo Fabrizi for the central roles of *Rome, Open City*. In his recent *Italian Neorealist Film: An Aesthetic Approach*, Christopher Wagstaff reports that even in *Ladri di biciclette* (Bicycle Thieves, 1948), "only the three leading roles in a very large cast were performed by non-professionals."[7] In those films and many others, technological problems also prevented any consistent direct sound recording, and slow film stock made the use of natural light almost impossible, especially in interior shots.[8]

Responding to the difficulty of finding a shared common denominator among the multiple and at times discordant definitions of neorealism, Lino Micciché and Alberto Farassino attempted two different interpretive strategies to define neorealism in somewhat looser and more capacious terms. For Farassino, neorealism was not a set of rigid norms but rather a stylistic trend ruling over a short-lived moment of Italian cinema from 1945 to 1949. While few true "neorealist films" had been made, almost all films of this period include some elements of the neorealist style, which "infiltrat[ed], cross[ed], ennobl[ed], or even contaminat[ed]" aspects of almost all the Italian films produced in this period.⁹ For Micciché, neorealism was an ethical sensibility animating a generation of diverse filmmakers. In fact, he wrote, neorealism was a shared ethical position "that has characterized a generation [of filmmakers] hungry for reality (to show) and of truths (to tell)."¹⁰

Endeavors to unearth the historical intellectual origins of Italian neorealism have been less multifarious. Commentators now agree with Millicent Marcus's contention that Italian neorealism was an attempt not solely to tell "reality" but also to reveal what makes that "reality" possible. "I accept to be shown the way *banderillas* are made," Cesare Zavattini wrote in 1953, "as long as the entire process of production is also demystified for me, together with all the human and social relations that [this process] implies."¹¹ In the seminal introductory chapter to her *Italian Film in the Light of Neorealism*, Marcus sees neorealism as an attempt to combine classical realism's effort to capture the general laws underlying reality with French nineteenth-century naturalism's notion of dispassionate observation.¹² In a recent essay, Stefania Parigi has looked at the "identity cards" of Italian neorealism and reconstructed the meanings and uses of the term from the 1920s to 1948. She reminds us that before 1948, the term covered a wide array of material in both literature and film.¹³ Neorealism, in fact, defined a variety of phenomena, among which were aspects of Russian, French, and German cinemas; the aesthetics of the German "New Objectivity [*neue Sachlichkeit*]"; postrevolutionary Russian novels; the realist methods of Russian theater director Constantin Stanislavski; and the polemical realism of young Italian novelists such as Alberto Moravia, Elio Vittorini, and Carlo Bernari, who were trying to move away from the precious mannerism of traditional literature.

While accepting the moniker of *Italian neorealism*, these historical analyses highlight that neorealism's origins went beyond the boundaries of the Italian nation. Thus, this volume begins with an interrogation of the complicated geographic origins of neorealism. This point often goes forgotten or uninterrogated in conventional film histories, especially since the movement became a synonym for postwar Italian cinema. Indeed, at its birth, Italian neorealism was often described as a form of nongeneric Italian cinema that was supposed to replace or at least counteract Hollywood's transnational influence. This national aspect, in direct collision with the internationalizing thrust of postwar American cinema, was what Italian leftist intellectuals, after some initial doubts,¹⁴ found appealing: "That cinematic art known as neorealism which has established the name and the triumph of Italian cinema throughout the world," as the communist daily *L'unità* proclaimed in 1955.¹⁵ By that year, the communists and the Left in general had embraced the Italianness of the movement as an antidote to the perceived imperialism of American culture propelled into Italian homes and theaters by the Marshall Plan of 1947 and the Smith-Mundt Act of 1948, which had made American financial help and American culture central elements of the effort to win the hearts and minds of Western Europeans.[16]

As the season of Italian neorealism waned, for example, Moravia, a communist novelist and film critic, saw among the causes of the crisis of Italian cinema "the co-production, with Italian directors and foreign actors or vice versa," which was contaminating even the work of the members of the original neorealist group—for example, the collaboration between director Vittorio De Sica and American producer David O. Selznick, *Stazione termini* (Indiscretion of an American Wife, 1953). Moravia believed that the "national character" of a film was the guarantee of its quality and artistic achievement. On the contrary, "these hybrid films cannot aspire but to a fair commercial success. An Italian director who works with foreign actors is like an Italian writer who writes some of his books in French or English."[17] Sergio Amidei, the communist scriptwriter of *Roma, città aperta*, dropped out of *Ladri di biciclette* because he thought that even that milestone of Italian neorealism "was not Italian enough." An innate Italian sense of solidarity would not have allowed a poor worker to lose his income because his vehicle had been stolen. Another bike would have been found, either by the neighbors or by the party comrades.[18]

As many of the contributors to this volume document, roots in the debate about national rebirth and national cinema did not hamper neorealism's ability to transgress Italian national boundaries. Neorealism soon traveled and acquired an international reputation and an attentive public, winning prizes at Cannes, in New York, and in Hollywood, among other places.[19] This volume gathers together scholarship that explores the "post-Italian" history of neorealism and fits this history in with the recent wave of scholarship that has critically examined the notion of national cinema.[20] Neorealism soon ceased to be Italian—or *only* Italian. In his classic *Storia del cinema italiano*, Gian Piero Brunetta, trying to make sense of all the confusing threads of the neorealist common idiom, invited scholars to study neorealism's "role as modifier of narrative, performative, expressive processes of world cinema."[21] The essays in this volume by Neepa Majumdar, Hamid Naficy, Robert Sklar, Sarah Sarzynski, Paula Halperin, Mariano Mestman, and Sada Niang document the spreading of neorealism in India, Iran, the United States, several Latin American nations, and Francophone Africa, respectively.

The contributors whose work appears here have rarely unearthed the smoking gun of a direct, Italocentric transmission. More interested in echoes, consonances, and similarities, they have avoided what Sklar calls "breezy generalization and common cliché." Nathaniel Brennan brings the power of distributors and exhibitors to bear on the traditional explanation of the post-war success of Italian neorealist films in the United States. He describes the marketing of Italian neorealist films in the United States as a terrain where American exhibitors' interests and advertisement strategies were combined with the Italian government's efforts to promote the image of a postfascist, democratic country. In recovering the intellectual history of the connections between the generation of the Nouvelle Vague and the neorealist filmmakers, Caroline Eades suggests that the connection is "complex," concocted out of similarities rather than direct linkages. In the end, Truffaut, Godard, and company learned from the neorealists to be in a discursive and performative collision with past generations of filmmakers whose work the later filmmakers knew extremely well. "Could we then assume that the influence of neorealism on New Wave directors lies precisely in the realization that it was neither new nor realistic, at least for a younger and restless generation?" Eades provocatively asks.

Majumdar cautions that "the term *influence* only inadequately signals the amorphous forms that the urge toward 'realism' took and to which Italian neorealism gave a name and identity." In many of these essays, the connections are circumstantial. Sklar, for example, discovers a possible response to Italian neorealism outside of mainstream American cinema in the postwar film work of James Agee, Helen Levitt, and Sidney Meyers.

The awareness of neorealism's existence and possibilities seems as current in the cinema of the postcolonial world as it was in the so-called First and Second Cinemas. This book also tells the story of how cinema became truly global in the aftermath of World War II. Mestman, Majumdar, Naficy, and Niang document how the postcolonial cinemas of Africa, Asia, and Latin America were entirely conversant with the tenets of global cinema, among which Italian neorealism stood out. Being conversant, however, did not mean being a tabula rasa, an empty slate to be filled with the styles of the West. Many of these essays point to the transformations that neorealism underwent when it traveled outside of Italy. Niang discovers traces of neorealism in the institutional and aesthetic foundations of the postcolonial cinema of Francophone Africa. His essay also points out the creolization of neorealism in the hands of African filmmakers in the sense that these filmmakers and intellectuals reshaped the themes and character types of the "Italian" film style to render it operative and comprehensible within their context.[22] Covering the New Latin American Cinema, Mestman narrates a story that goes from the 1950s cinema of Fernando Birri to the 1970s films of Glauber Rocha but that also details a sort of declension and transformation—from love to a certain degree of disillusionment. And yet, as he points out, even this rejection finds its echo across the Atlantic. "On either side of the Atlantic," Mestman writes, "these relations acknowledged neorealism as a valid precedent, as a fundamental historical stage, but it was a stage from which these filmmakers had moved on."

Naficy goes back to Georges Sadoul's and Mario Verdone's provocative definition of the neorealist movement as a "school" defined by five characteristics.[23] Naficy's essay detects the similarities and differences between the Iranian New Wave of the 1960s and Iranian art house cinema of the 1980s and the Italian neorealist generation. Much like practitioners of neorealism, Iranian directors are mindful that the "reality effect" is conveyed by limiting the amount of unstaged and unedited "reality" on sets and soundstages. But Naficy also calls attention to the political differences between shooting film in postfascist republican Italy and directing movies within the more direct censorial constraints of the Iran of Reza Pahlavi or of Ayatollah Ruhollah Khomeini.

In her epilogue to this volume, Silvia Carlorosi examines examples of neorealism in recent Italian cinema, highlighting the consonance between the recent, "neo-neorealist" films of the Frazzi brothers and Matteo Garrone and the film aesthetics theorized by Pier Paolo Pasolini. This volume, however, contributes to rewriting both the present and the past of neorealism. Unlike recent volumes that provocatively stress the postwar relationship between *Italian* neorealism and global cinema, we seek to push the internationalization of the geography of neorealism even further back in time.[24] In fact, how "Italian" were the beginnings of neorealism?

The need to push the study of neorealism into the preceding decade is a decision that, as Vito Zagarrio illustrates in the essay that opens this volume, dates to 1974, when, at the Mostra Internazionale del Nuovo Cinema in Pesaro, scholars began to engage "the previous cinema, not only the simplistically defined pre-neorealist cinema . . . but also more generally the entire cinema of the 1930s." Zagarrio, like other scholars of Italian cinema, has argued for a closer look at the cinema of the fascist *ventennio* (the period from the 1922 March on Rome to Benito Mussolini's demise as prime minister of Italy in July 1943) to understand neorealism.[25] Continuities as well as discontinuities are unveiled and the forerunners of postwar neorealism are discovered in the soundstages of Cinecittà (which Mussolini's son, Vittorio, built in 1937), in the hallways of Rome's Centro Sperimentale di Cinematografia (which the regime opened in 1935), and in the pages of *Cinema* (the magazine that Luciano De Feo founded in 1936 and that Vittorio Mussolini directed beginning in 1938).[26] That these connections tended to be obscured should not surprise. The fascist roots of neorealism were an embarrassing legacy willingly left behind by the members of the neorealist generation, some of whom, like Rossellini, were only a few months removed from participation in the regime.

Pushing the roots of the movement back into the Italian 1930s—or even further—runs the risk of renationalizing neorealism. Instead, this volume highlights the beginnings of the global context of neorealism during that decade. After all, among the models for the Cinecittà integrated soundstages were the Hollywood studios; many of the teachers at the Centro Sperimentale worshipped Soviet, French, and American filmmakers; and even *Cinema* counted among the members of its editorial board in 1936 German theorist and refugee Rudolf Arnheim, who had taken temporary shelter in Italy after the Nazi takeover of his home country. In the late 1960s, while reminiscing about his role as one of *Cinema*'s official film critics, Giuseppe De Santis, a communist intellectual and later director of *Riso amaro* (Bitter Rice, 1949), among other films, recalled a 1930s meeting with Vittorio Mussolini. The cinematic styles the two men held as models differed slightly: The young critic was obsessed by French realism, while the fascist editor worshipped at the altar of the American realist cinema of Frank Capra and King Vidor. Yet both men were, in De Santis's words, "bored from within by the termite of realism."[27]

Masha Salazkina's "Soviet-Italian Cinematic Exchanges, 1920s–1950s: From Early Soviet Film Theory to Neorealism" and Luca Caminati's "Role of Documentary Film in the Formation of the Neorealist Cinema" explore the international roots of Italian neorealism. Salazkina's essay provides an in-depth analysis of the relationship between Italian cinema and Soviet cinema in the 1930s, discovering new connections between the filmmaking styles and theoretical writings on films of the two antithetical regimes. Caminati's essay focuses on the documentary films of the 1930s, one of the key elements that would flow into postwar neorealism, discovering the rich, international documentary traditions with which Italian documentary filmmakers communed.

In some sense, the cumulative and broader thrust of these essays may point toward new ways of conceiving not just Italian neorealism but also the debate about realism in the 1930s. It may become impossible to understand the rise of postwar Italian neorealism without conceiving it as the nationalization—engendered in Italy by World War II and the antifascist Resistance, among other factors—of a widely international conversation about realism and political cinema that had been at the center of the 1930s. This conversation had "bored from within" people as ideologically diverse as De Santis and the cultured son of the fascist dictator. At its center was an interest in a definite group of cinematographies—Soviet and American as well as French and to a lesser extent German. In different ways, all of the conversation's participants were concerned with the possibility of making cinema relevant to what they saw as their national realities—that is, all were interested in making cinema political. Seen from another angle, this multisided dialogue may have been connected in oblique and contradictory ways to that "worldwide movement of plebeian artists and writers to create a proletarian culture, a socialist realism" about which Michael Denning has recently written.[28]

In the postwar years, Italian filmmakers imported into this preexisting tradition the images of the war's devastation of the Italian peninsula along with the urgency of dealing with national topics, necessities, and politics. The neorealists were building on and nationalized this 1930s realist tradition. They were thus nationalists and cosmopolites, two terms that, as JoAnne Mancini has recently suggested in regard to American modernism, need not be seen as opposite.[29] In 1989, explaining the adaptation of James M. Cain's hard-boiled American novel, *The Postman Always Rings Twice*, into Luchino Visconti's proto-neorealist film, *Ossessione* (1943), De Santis wrote, "We set this story into [the Italian region of Emilia Romagna] because it seemed that this region could respond to what was the American inspiration [of the film]. But *we did it the Italian way*—that is, we did it like people who, while fully appreciating this culture, while fully charmed by the American literature, intended *to interpret it in a way that was national*. The operation succeeded. The film was important and a turning point for Italian cinema."[30]

Importing Italian neorealism by no means signified the abandonment of a concern with the "national." While our book will contribute to the global and transnational history of cinema, the nation remains central to our—and to cinema's—story. As many studies have ascertained, cinema has had a global calling since its beginnings. Following commercial trends and fluxes, films—even early ones—traveled beyond the boundaries of their nations of origin.[31] Indeed, as Andrew Higson provocatively argues, the "transnational" may be the most precise way to describe "national" cultural phenomena that are rarely, if ever, truly autochthonous but on the contrary are almost "invariably hybrid and impure" because of "the degree of cultural cross-breeding and interpenetrations, not only across borders, but within them."[32] Yet the story of global neorealism also indicates the way that this film style became part of nationally contingent cultural struggles acted out by local historical actors, be they Argentine film critics, young French intellectuals, or Iranian filmmakers. As Valentina Vitali and Paul Willemen wisely suggest, "diverse societies and clusters of films are always inevitably positioned differently within the centrifugal expansion of capitalist modes of production, not least because any given culture encountered cinema in different circumstances."[33] Just as Italian antifascist intellectuals "nationalized" 1930s debates and practices of film realism to tell the stories and the struggles of postwar Italy, filmmakers all over the world soon reshaped the new style and its intellectual slogans to fit their practices, needs, and struggles.

Many of our essays argue that what intrigued Indian, African, or Latin American filmmakers about Italian neorealism was its mode of production, its ability to craft a national cinema without large studio investments. Halperin's essay, a reconnaissance in the making of Mario Soffici's *Barrio gris* (1954), documents how some Argentine critics worried aloud that importing a foreign style could dilute efforts to build a truly national Argentine cinema. Yet while intrigued by neorealism, Soffici used the film to make a direct statement about Argentine national historical contingencies in the midst of Peronism. Similarly, Sarzynski looks at how neorealist techniques consciously employed by the Paraíban documentary school of the Brazilian Northeast served as a building block to construct a particular kind not only of Brazilian cinema but also of Brazilian identity. Sarzynski's essay recovers the story of this little-known movement that played a significant role in fostering the more famous fiction films of Brazil's Cinema Novo.

In postwar Italy, the neorealists coupled drawing on this rich international tradition with an attempt to revitalize Italian cinema by making it speak to local politics and local possibilities in the context of a fragmented market and a destroyed studio system. As in the 1930s, "realist cinema" and "political cinema" again converged. This intertwining and, as many of our contributors recognize, consonance of material conditions made Italian neorealism appealing to other filmmakers searching for their own national, political, and realist idiom. Denning succinctly summarizes the fundamental point: "There is a direct line between the pioneering cinematic alternatives to Hollywood (the Left-inspired Italian neo-realism) and the various Third World cinemas."[34]

The essays in this book continue the process of revising the way we think about neorealism. Far from being "only" Italian, we contend that this film style relinquished its exclusive Italian nationality soon after World War II. Neorealism then acquired many nationalities and became a citizen of the world. Pushing further the effort to expand the geography and the history of neorealism, we have sketched the 1930s origins of this film style as well as their cosmopolitan nature. Emerging from an international conversation about realist cinema in the 1930s, neorealism acquired an exclusive Italian passport only briefly during the war and the antifascist resistance. Finally, the question of neorealism's connection with the intellectual climate of postwar Italy as well as its documented ability to travel thrusts our volume into a third wave of revisionist interventions.

This third historiographic cluster on which this book touches is the connection between Italian cinema, neorealism, and the mythology of the so-called *italiani brava gente* (Italian nice folk).³⁵ In dealing with Italian neorealism, few scholars have strayed from a celebratory tone. Even Marcus's pathbreaking volume on Italian cinema and the Holocaust notes her astonishment that "filmmakers working in a realist tradition known for its courage in facing sociopolitical injustices, past and present, show[ed] a surprising reluctance to confront Mussolini's racial laws and the ensuing genocidal campaign."³⁶ In fact, this reluctance should not be surprising. As one of the pillars of the culture of the new Italian republic, Italian neorealism also supported the nation's attempt to forge a clean break with its troublesome past.

Thus, as Saverio Giovacchini's essay shows, the rise of Italian neorealism was also linked to the self-serving mythology of the Italian as victim rather than perpetrator of World War II. Italian neorealism mostly forgot more than just Italian anti-Semitism: According to Giovacchini, the neorealist mythopoesis also erases the Italian colonialist past, which a new generation of historians are currently unearthing in all its bloody details.

But then, how could such a flawed and politically loaded style be reabsorbed into the avant-garde or the left side of global cinema? The answer may lie in what the contributors to this volume repeatedly stress: Nothing moves, is exported, or is accepted wholesale. In this sense, neorealism worked in the postwar world not unlike American culture, though in the case of neorealism, those at the receiving end had a much larger degree of agency. Some elements were accepted, others were fiercely resisted, and still others were incorporated into the bricolage. Through a process of adaptation and creolization, neorealism—the hybrid, Italianized output of an international conversation about realist cinema that began in the 1930s—was absorbed with varying results into national cinemas, thereby becoming a global style.

Notes

1. Umberto Barbaro, "Neo-realismo," *Film* 6.23 (June 5, 1943), reprinted in Umberto Barbaro, *Neorealismo e realismo*, ed. Gian Piero Brunetta, 2 vols. (Rome: Riuniti, 1976), 501–4.

As some of the essays in this volume document, the debate about the meaning of this term is, in fact, as old as the movement it nominally purports to define. The establishment of a normative definition of the term is not the immediate goal of this volume. For incisive and concise summaries of the debate about the definition of neorealism, see Christopher Wagstaff, *Italian Neorealist Cinema: An Aesthetic Approach* (Toronto: University of Toronto Press, 2007), 30–37; Stefania Parigi, "Le carte d'identità del neorealismo," in *Nuovo cinema (1965–2005): Scritti in onore di Lino Miccichè*, ed. Bruno Torri (Venice: Marsilio, 2005),

80–102; Lino Miccichè, "Per una verifica del *neorealismo*," in *Il neorealismo cinematografico italiano*, 2nd ed., ed. Lino Miccichè (1977; Milan: Marsilio, 1999), 7–28.

2. Geoffrey Macnab, "Gomorrah," *The Independent*, August 8, 2008, http://www.inde pendent.co.uk/arts-entertainment/films/features/gomorrah-the-movie-of-the-real-godfa thers-954292.html (accessed March 9, 2010).

3. See, for example, Borzou Daragahi, "Acclaimed Iranian Filmmaker Arrested in Late-Night Raid," *Los Angeles Times*, March 3, 2010, http://www.latimes.com/news/nation-and-world/la-fg-iran-filmmaker3-2010mar03,0,1962791.story (accessed March 4, 2010).

4. Stephen Teo, "An Interview with the Iranian Director of *The Circle*," *Senses of Cinema* 15 (July–August 2001), http://archive.sensesofcinema.com/contents/01/15/panahi_inter view.html (accessed March 3, 2010).

5. Steno, "Decalogo del perfetto regista neorealista," *Star*, August 24, 1948, reprinted in *Neorealismo: Cinema italiano, 1945–1949*, ed. Alberto Farassino (Turin: EDT, 1989), 130.

6. *Films et documents* 5 (1952), cited in Mia Liehm, *Passion and Defiance: Film in Italy from 1945 to the Present* (Berkeley: University of California Press, 1984), 132.

7. Wagstaff, *Italian Neorealist Cinema*, 31, 313–21.

8. See Stefano Masi, "L'hardware del neorealismo: Ferri del mestiere e strategia della tecnica," in *Neorealismo*, ed. Farassino, 49–52.

9. Alberto Farassino, "Neorealismo: Storia e geografia," in *Neorealismo*, ed. Farassino, 29.

10. Lino Miccichè, "De Santis e il verosimile," in *Non c'è pace tra gli ulivi: Un neoreal ismo postmoderno*, ed. Vito Zagarrio (Rome: Scuola Nazionale di Cinema, 2002), 7. See also Miccichè, "Per una verifica."

11. Cesare Zavattini, "Tesi sul neorealismo," *Emilia* 17 (November 1953), reprinted in Cesare Zavattini, *Neorealismo, ecc.*, ed. Mino Argentieri (Milan: Bompiani, 1979), 112–20.

12. Millicent Marcus, *Italian Film in the Light of Neorealism* (Princeton: Princeton University Press, 1986), 3–29.

13. Stefania Parigi, "Le carte d'identità del neorealismo," in *Nuovo cinema (1965–2005): Scritti in onore di Lino Miccichè*, ed. Bruno Torri (Venice: Marsilio, 2005), 80–102.

14. See Pierre Sorlin, *Italian National Cinema, 1896–1996* (London: Routledge, 1996), 90.

15. *L'unità*, May 20, 1955, cited in ibid., 91.

16. On the Smith-Mundt Act and its cultural mission, see Richard Pells, *Not Like Us* (New York: Basic Books, 1997), 62. For a general study of the Italian communists' reac tion to American culture, see Stephen Gundle, *I comunisti italiani tra Hollywood e Mosca* (Milan: Giunti, 1995). An abridged English version of the book is available as Stephen Gundle, *Between Hollywood and Moscow: The Italian Communists and the Challenge of Mass Culture, 1943–1991* (Durham, N.C.: Duke University Press, 2000).

17. Alberto Moravia, "Il film conformista," *Cinema nuovo* 2.13 (June 15, 1953): 361.

18. Sergio Amidei in Franca Faldini and Goffredo Fofi, *L'avventurosa storia del cinema italiano raccontata dai suoi protagonisti, 1935–1959* (Milan: Feltrinelli, 1979), 135.

19. For example, in 1946, *Rome, Open City* won the Grand Jury Prize at Cannes and the awards for best foreign film of both the American National Board of Review (NBR) and New York Film Critics Circle (NYFCC). In 1947, *Paisà* won both the NYFCC and NBR awards as well as the Japanese Kinema Junpo Award for best foreign film. In 1949, *Bicycle Thieves* garnered the best film award of the British Film Academy (BAFTA), Japanese Kinema Jumpo's best film award, the Grand Jury prize of the Swiss Locarno Film Festival, the Spanish Cinema Writers' Award (CEC), the American Golden Globes and NBR awards for best foreign film, and the NYFCC awards for best film and best director.

20. Andrew Higson and Richard Maltby, eds., *"Film Europe" and "Film America": Cinema, Commerce, and Cultural Exchange, 1920–1939* (Exeter: University of Exeter Press, 1999); Mette Hjort and Scott MacKenzie, eds., *Cinema and Nation* (London: Routledge, 2000); Geoffrey Nowell-Smith and Steven Ricci, eds., *Hollywood and Europe: Economics, Culture, National Identity, 1946–1996* (London: British Film Institute, 1998).

21. Gian Piero Brunetta, *Storia del cinema italiano*, 2nd ed. (Rome: Riuniti, 1993), 3:348.

22. On creolization, see Rob Kroes, *If You've See One, You've Seen the Mall* (Champaign: University of Illinois Press, 1996), 162–77.

23. See Georges Sadoul, *Histoire du cinéma mondial* (Paris: Flammarion, 1966), 326–34. Sadoul's point about the Italian neorealist "école" is formalized in Mario Verdone, *Il cinema neorealista da Rossellini a Pasolini* (Palermo: Celebes, 1977), 27.

24. See Laura E. Ruberto and Kristi M. Wilson, *Italian Neorealism and Global Cinema* (Detroit: Wayne State University Press, 2007).

25. See also Peter Bondanella, "The Making of *Rome, Open City*: The Legacy of Fascism and the Birth of Neorealism," in *Roberto Rossellini's* Rome, Open City, ed. Sidney Gottlieb (Cambridge: Cambridge University Press, 2004), 43–66.

26. See Callisto Cosulich, "Introduzione," in Giuseppe De Santis, *Verso il neorealismo*, ed. Callisto Cosulich (Rome: Bulzoni, 1982), 14–15.

27. See Giuseppe De Santis, "Ripensando ai tempi di *Cinema* prima serie," *Cinema nuovo* 201 (September–October 1969), reprinted in De Santis, *Verso il neorealismo*, 33–39.

28. Michael Denning, *Culture in the Age of the Three Worlds* (New York: Verso, 2004), 32.

29. JoAnne Marie Mancini, *Pre-Modernism* (Princeton: Princeton University Press, 2005), 31.

30. Giuseppe De Santis, "L'influenza della letteratura americana sul neorealismo," in Antonio Vitti, *Peppe De Santis secondo se stesso* (Pesaro: Metauro, 2006), 21–35; emphasis added; translation by authors.

31. For a recent example, see Giorgio Bertellini, *Italy in Early American Cinema: Race, Landscape, and the Picturesque* (Bloomington: Indiana University Press, 2010)

32. Andrew Higson, "The Limiting Imagination of National Cinema," in *Cinema and Nation*, ed. Hjort and MacKenzie, 63–74.

33. Valentina Vitali and Paul Willemen, eds., *Theorising National Cinema* (London: British Film Institute, 2006), 7.

34. Denning, *Culture*, 33.

35. Among the growing literature on the *italiano brava gente*, see Angelo del Boca, *Italiani, brava gente?* (Vicenza: Neri Pozza, 2005); Filippo Focardi, *La guerra della memoria* (Bari: Laterza, 2005); Filippo Focardi, "La memoria della guerra e il mito del 'bravo italiano,'" *Italia contemporanea* 220–21 (September–December 2000): 393–99; Saverio Giovacchini, "Soccer with the Dead: *Mediterraneo* and the Myth of *Italiani Brava Gente*," in *Repicturing the Second World War* (London: Palgrave Macmillan, 2008), ed. Mike Paris, 55–69.

36. Millicent Marcus, *Italian Film in the Shadow of Auschwitz* (Toronto: University of Toronto Press, 2007), 15.

PART 1

BEFORE THE (NEOREALIST) REVOLUTION

VITO ZAGARRIO

Continuity or Rupture?

Continuity or discontinuity? This is the central dilemma of much of twentieth-century Italian history. Is there continuity or discontinuity between fascism and the Christian Democratic regime that followed it? Was fascism a real revolution, just as the *quadrunviri* claimed, or a "revelation," as Giustino Fortunato has argued,[1] that revealed conflicts already present in prefascist Italy? The question of continuity/discontinuity also arises in the political and cultural fields, especially on a terrain as delicate as the analysis of film. Thus, the "Italian" 1930s unfold horizontally onto a cultural geography that is more complex than we initially assumed. The decade also extends vertically, however, into a chronology that projects the cultural presence of the 1930s onto the following decades, belying comfortable definitions and orderly delimitations of history and culture.[2]

The elements of discontinuity between neorealism and fascist cinema are obvious and have been amply emphasized: neorealism's emphasis on the poorer strata of Italian society, its focus on social discomfort, its "direct" take on reality, its move out of the soundstages and into real locations, its use of nonprofessional actors, its "stalking" of ordinary characters, its antifascist glue, and its extolling of the Resistance. But what are the continuities between the two cinemas? And what remains of one period in the next? How much did fascism's "cultural interventionism" in matters of cinema influence the education of the future protagonists of neorealism?

If history does not proceed through jumps, we must acknowledge that the state and industrial policies of fascism contributed—albeit in fairly contradictory and unreflexive ways—to produce skills, technological and linguistic tools, motivations, and theoretical frameworks that became indispensable for the neorealist generation. Roberto Rossellini, Vittorio De Sica, Luchino Visconti, Giuseppe De Santis, Michelangelo Antonioni, Federico Fellini, and

Alberto Lattuada, among others, found a fertile terrain for their ideological and stylistic innovations in the idea of cinema as "the most powerful weapon" (according to Lenin's slogan rephrased by Mussolini); in the state's investments; in the attention paid to pivotal film industries (American, Soviet, German); in the creation of institutions and apparatuses such as Cinecittà, the Centro Sperimentale di Cinematografia, and the Venice Film Festival; and finally in the development of the idea of *skilled* technicians (not just directors, but cinematographers, editors, stage designers, and so forth). Neorealist directors learned their craft and formed their authorial identities either under, during, or in opposition to the fascist regime. Hundreds of electricians, cameramen, stagehands, and other film workers also refined their skills in the Italian *cinecittà* of this very period.

The Generation of the "Redeemed"

At times, continuity may seem opportunism, as it does in Mirella Serri's *I redenti* (The Redeemed), a book whose thesis has become somewhat popular in Italy and with which I disagree.[3] The "redeemed" are those intellectuals of the 1930s and 1940s who lived two lives, the first under and with fascism and the second in the aftermath of the regime's fall and during the cultural hegemony of the Left. Serri places Roberto Rossellini in this group of intellectuals who lived "twice," between continuity with and redemption from fascism. Rossellini's birth as a director certainly does not date to the neorealist "war trilogy" (*Roma, città aperta, Paisà, Germania anno zero*) but predates to the fascist "war trilogy" (*La nave bianca, Un pilota ritorna, L'uomo della croce*). Serri seems taken aback by this ambiguity of Rossellini's: the three fascist films deal strategically with the three branches of the fascist war machine—the navy, the air force, the army; Il Duce's son, Vittorio Mussolini, collaborated on *Un pilota ritorna* (A Pilot Returns, 1942); *L'uomo della croce* (Man with a Cross, 1943) was remarkable for its anticommunism. How can Rossellini, in just about two years, tell first the story of an anticommunist priest (the protagonist of *L'uomo della croce*) and then the story of an antifascist and procommunist priest (Don Pietro/Aldo Fabrizi in *Roma, città aperta* [Rome, Open City, 1945])? Serri's chapter on Rossellini ends with a line that also serves as the chapter's title: "Dall'Odeon all'Odeon [From Odeon to Odeon]." The Odeon Theater exhibited *L'uomo della croce* just a few months before it showed *Roma, città aperta*. "The great artist," Serri writes, "was able to grasp the political reality, as his friend, screenwriter Sergio Amidei remarked, somewhat tongue-in-cheek, after Rossellini's death: 'He was a realist who knew how to live in the real world of politics.' From Odeon to Odeon was a short step."[4] Just like Amidei, Serri smiles knowingly. And the jocular affectionate term *realist*, an attribute that could touch off several long debates, used by the friend sounds just like *cynical* and *opportunist*.

A contradiction certainly exists, but the inconsistency pertains less to the supposed opportunism of Rossellini (who was indeed a tactical man and who cunningly knew how to sell himself, as is demonstrated by his skill and timeliness in putting together *Open City* and the international operation behind *Paisà*), than to the magmatic historical contingency in which he lived and to the subtler ambiguity of art. Rossellini must be examined in a perspective of continuity, but such continuity is not between "fascism" and "antifascism," which would be banal and simplistic, but is both "poetic" and aesthetic. This continuity makes it possible to see no interruption between a first Resistential Rossellini, a second Existentialist Rossellini (the Ingrid Bergman period), a third televisionist Rossellini, and so forth. What really lies at the center of Rossellini's cinema is a coherent itinerary of inward research, an investigation of the soul, an attempt to link the real and the transcendental. Revising (in this case the cliché is most appropriate) Rossellinian cinema means to steer our analysis away from any flattening of Rossellini's work onto an ideology, be it antifascism or Christianity. Indeed, recent studies show that we need to reread the neorealist war trilogy not as a cinema of denunciation or worse as "documentary" cinema (the popular definition of neorealism) but as a universal drama, a complex symbolic operation, a difficult spiritual and aesthetic strategy.[5]

Just as there is little difference between the Rossellini of *Germania anno zero* (Germany Year Zero, 1948) and that of *Europa '51* (Europe '51, 1952), there is no divergence between *L'uomo della croce* and *Open City*. The "fascist" bellicose films and the antifascist and pacifist ones share an ascetic tension, an attention to both history and an individual's story. Of course, *La nave bianca* (The White Ship, 1941) is a film on the Italian navy, but it takes the point of view of those who suffer (the film is about a hospital ship); *Un pilota ritorna* is indeed about the air force, and it even uses some of the narrative codes of the American war film, but its nucleus is the war seen from the victims' position, certainly not from that of the "heroes." The protagonist's feat notwithstanding (captured by the enemy, he steals a plane and flies back home), the center of *Un pilota ritorna* is in fact a journey among the people who are at war with us and who are instead revealed as close to us because of the commonality of humanity and suffering. In this perspective, the two priests of *L'uomo della croce* and *Open City* are not different but instead are linked by the same—albeit ideologically divergent—spiritual tension.

Similar considerations can be made about Rossellini's collaboration with Francesco De Robertis, which Serri seems to see as a sort of military camaraderie: *Uomini sul fondo* (SOS Submarine, 1941) by De Robertis, which was ordered by the secretary of the navy, has long been considered a precursor of neorealism, and it has recently been reread as a model for an alternative, not stereotypical, reading of neorealism.[6] What would then be Serri's judgment of Alessandro Blasetti, the director of fascist cinema with the notorious riding boots (*Vecchia guardia* [Old Guard, 1934]) and then a precursor of neorealism (*Quattro passi tra le nuvole* [Four Steps in the Clouds, 1942]), a man who was both part of the regime and a pacifist (these two souls coexist in *La corona di ferro* [The Iron Crown, 1941]), at first fascist and then antifascist and close to the socialists? Is Blasetti also, in his own way, redeemed or perhaps even forgiven via a sort of communist baptism? (It is well known that Blasetti was held in high esteem by communists De Santis, Pietro Ingrao, and Luchino Visconti.)

I want to avoid any possible misunderstanding of my position about the possible continuity between fascism and the second postwar in Italy. I strongly disagree with the widespread revisionism that tends to reevaluate the fascist regime in its various components (culture, society, mass media) and also logically revises the value of the Resistance.[7] Instead, I seek to identify the elements of formal, filmic, representational, or linguistic continuity between fascism and the post–World War II period in Italy. In this sense, the similarities, or the traces of neorealism in the Italian cinema of the 1930s and early 1940s are surprising.

The "Discovery" of Continuity

This new interpretation of fascist cinema—or, better, of the cinema produced during the fascist regime—began in the middle of the 1970s as part of a broader historiographic revision. The perception of fascism as reactionary mass regime allowed historians to focus on the 1930s as one of the pivotal moments of Italian history and pushed investigations of the tools of fascist consensus building as well as the messages communicated by the various fascist mass media. Alberto Asor Rosa described fascism as "an imperfect totalitarianism"—that is, as a regime efficiently seeking consensus and thus leaving opportunities for autonomy and potential dissent to intellectual sectors.[8] Italian totalitarianism was imperfect because it turned out to be a melting pot of several, sometimes seemingly diverging, tendencies. As examples, one could consider the debate on fascist culture and the diatribes between Roberto Farinacci and Giuseppe Bottai on "fascist art," but it is also interesting to consider the double strategy toward cinema (building a state cinema, as Luigi Freddi would have it, or favoring the private entrepreneurs, as Dino Alfieri ultimately did). The cultural politics of fascism began to attract attention in relation not just to intellectuals but to the entire population. In addition, historians investigated the regime's creation of a "factory of consensus."[9]

It soon became clear that the study of cinema was certainly the best way to analyze the economical-political structures and the sociocultural components of fascist Italy because cinema represented the newest and most efficient way to articulate the regime's propaganda. Thus, at the beginning of the 1970s, cinema became the epicenter of several studies that inexorably engaged the long-standing polemics on the continuity between pre- and postfascism.

Evidence of this historiographic reorientation was the debate that occurred at the Mostra Internazionale del Nuovo Cinema in Pesaro in 1974, a crucial moment in the historiography of Italian cinema and of neorealism in particular.[10] Here, in the aftermath of the ideological interpretations that had characterized the immediate postwar era, numerous prominent scholars questioned the historiographic clichés and engaged the authorial and stylistic dynamics of neorealism. They inevitably also engaged the previous cinema, not only the simplistically defined pre-neorealist cinema (*Quattro passi tra le nuvole*, *Sole*, and *1860* by Blasetti; *I bambini ci guardano* by De Sica; and *Ossessione* by Visconti) but also more generally the entire cinema of the 1930s.

As a logical development, in September 1975, the Pesaro Festival tackled fascist cinema and gathered together film scholars and historians coupling textual analysis of film and historical research into the cultural politics of fascism.[11] And of course this exploration occurred in front of a public of movie buffs who delighted in the projection of the 1930s films. The "fascist" films were seen for the first time by several generations of viewers, who discovered that many of these products were less fascist than they had expected. The new generations applauded the stars and the stories that had previously been labeled the cinema of "white telephones," enjoying films that had been marginalized and even prejudged unseen just because they had been made during the regime.

A wide array of positions and fierce ideological debates emerged during the festival,[12] as many observers also sensed that the rediscovery of "fascist" cinema fit in very well with the broader reinterpretation of the founding moments of national Italian cinema and was bound to modify the normative interpretation of neorealism, which appeared more and more connected with prewar cinema.

Insofar as the filmic texts were concerned, the film meeting at Pesaro identified three authors and three aesthetical lines within the confines of the cinema of the *ventennio*: Blasetti, Mario Camerini, and Ferdinando Maria Poggioli.

Blasetti was an inventor of cinema, a stalwart supporter of the "rebirth" of Italian cinema, and a supporter of neorealism as well as a refined director of sophisticated comedies and a forceful concocter of adventures, even a precursor of neorealism. Camerini was the quintessential craftsman director, a skillful teller of petit bourgeois tales featuring a young actor who would go far, Vittorio De Sica. Poggioli was the refined director who forecast the new authorial moments of postwar cinema.

In October 1976, the most prominent Italian critics gathered at Pesaro to debate fascist cinema while the rediscovery of the lost films of the fascist era continued thanks to their restoration by the Cineteca Nazionale in Rome. Critics analyzed the films' narrative structures, topoi, female characters, oedipal liaisons; ideological and semiotic rereadings alternated. An edited collection published archival documents and analyzed the presence of filmic discourses in the newspapers and magazines of the Gruppi Universitari Fascisti (Fascist University Groups). A sort of ideological blockage seemed broken, making it possible to see fascist cinema without any sort of reticence and with a new sense of discovery. In this perspective, it was possible to see the mythical derivations, the models after which the new fascist imaginary was patterned. And the references could not but be to Hollywood and to Soviet cinema. For example, Sergio G. Germani stressed the influence of American cinema[13] and argued that the Soviet myth remained only a theoretical reference, thus making Italian cinema of the *ventennio* "a minor American cinema . . . at the international level perhaps the closest to American cinema."[14] The idea of an Americanization of Italian cinema became available, something that the evolution of the genres (melodrama, comedy, war film), with the exception of the film noir, would confirm as they began to take shape in the 1930s to constitute the majority of textual codes in postwar Italian cinema: "In Italian cinema under fascism it was difficult to find a model of 'fascist cinema,' the same way as one could indicate fascist architecture or the model of Nazi cinema in the films by [Leni] Riefenstahl. . . . Italian cinema under fascism has been first of all a capitalist cinema, onto which the characteristics of fascism have been grafted."[15]

The Beginnings of De Sica's Neorealism

This "Americanization" of Italian cinema in the 1930s is crucial to understanding not just the comedies by Camerini but the cinema of De Sica. Well before achieving fame with neorealism, the director of *Bicycle Thieves* served his apprenticeship as a young actor in Camerini's films and worked as

Darò un milione (1935): The obsession with food during the Great Depression. The scene refers to *La tavola dei poveri*, by Alessandro Blasetti (1932).

a promising young director in the Italian cinema under fascism. How then can we reconcile the author *engagé* of *Sciuscià* (Shoeshine, 1946), *Ladri di biciclette* (Bicycle Thieves, 1948), and *Umberto D* (1952) with the light touch and escapism of the metteur en scène of *Rose scarlatte* (Red Roses, 1940), *Teresa venerdì* (Do You Like Women?, 1941), *Maddalena zero in condotta* (Maddalena Zero in Conduct, 1940), and *Un garibaldino al convento* (A Garibaldian in the Convent, 1942)? It would be easy to take up the theory of the redeemed or of the opportunist. De Sica, like Rossellini, probably saw the writing on the wall, just like any good self-promoter. But a slow-growing process of evolution also took place as a result of the progress of the war and the crisis of fascism, perhaps aided by encounters such as one with Cesare Zavattini, whom De Sica met on the set of *Darò un milione* (I'll Give a Million, 1935).

How much did these generic films (by an actor and director well versed in generic cinema) owe Hollywood? How organic were they to fascism, or how impervious if not escapist were they in relation to the regime's ideology? These questions concern the entire genre of Italian comedies in the 1930s, including the films by Camerini in which the young De Sica performed.[16] What was surprising was also the total imperviousness of plots, characters, gestures, and situation to the tragedy of the war about to engulf Europe and the world.

Yet comedies, either directed by De Sica or in which he performed (sometimes only in a cameo), appeared to open Italian cinema to international trends (the genres and the subgenres of Hollywood cinema) and to adopt the traditional tropes of the comedy of misunderstanding beside moments of more surreal and bizarre humor. This genre was bound to contain the elements of everyday "realism": the newsstand of *Signor Max* (Mr. Max, 1937); the shop, the bar, the cab, the car, the ads, the Fiera di Milano in *Gli uomini che mascalzoni* (What Scoundrels Men Are!, 1932); and other such elements accounted for a "reality" that was often rebuilt on stage. This kind of comedy was alert, mature, and in tune with the highest international styles, but it was also soon to turn into drama.

Drama was, in fact, at the center of *I bambini ci guardano* (The Children Are Watching Us, 1943), a dark family melodrama that has been rightly interpreted as a clear break from the Italian cinema of the *ventennio*. Lino Micciché's analysis groups *I bambini ci guardano* with Blasetti's *Quattro passi tra le nuvole* and Visconti's *Ossessione* into a triptych of 1942–43 films that can be considered pre-neorealist.[17] Advances in historiography, however, no longer enable us to see these three masterpieces as forerunners of neorealism without critiquing the entire notion of neorealism: *Ossessione* was a dark melodrama, a literature-inspired noir, a crime story that had only a few neorealist elements (the exteriors, the emphasis on landscape, the River Po); *Quattro passi* was a tale à la Frank Capra, endangered only by the well-known parentheses at its beginning and end when the salesman experiences the harsh reality of life. Perhaps *I bambini ci guardano* most clearly forecast the coming new ethical and aesthetical climate. In the desperate story of its young protagonist it was possible to discern the anguished gazes of the children of *Ladri di biciclette* and *Sciuscià* as well as the tragedy of Edmund in *Germania anno zero* and of the old man-child at the center of *Umberto D*. The strong sequence of the train that was about to run over Pricò gestured toward the finale of *Umberto D*, while the neighbors' morbid curiosity, the description of the apartment building, and the anguished gaze of the child somehow echoed Visconti's *Bellissima* (1951).

Compared with *Ossessione* and *Quattro passi*, then, *I bambini ci guardano* was less tied up with literary models, musical references, or generic codes and was much more markedly "realist" even in the description of its contemporary context, the choice of some of the exteriors, and the rough way it treated its theme. If anything, the film's photography and dramaturgy resembled more the melodramas—even the popular ones—of the 1950s—for example, the pivotal final scene in the religious boarding school, when the son refuses to hug his mother, who is in mourning clothes even though she is unable to convey any real feeling of maternal solidarity.

But even leaving aside the issue of whether or not *I bambini* belongs to neorealism, De Sica's film (like Visconti's *Ossessione* and *Quattro passi*) describes a troubled nation oppressed by the shadows of the war and torn apart by family and gender struggles that were no longer likely to be resolved by society's master narratives. To fascism's idealization of wives and mothers who donate their wedding rings to the motherland, Visconti juxtaposes a woman who cuckolds her husband and persuades her lover to kill him, and Blasetti contrasted the protagonist's increasing disinterest in his crude and irascible partner and the unbearable gestures of everyday life. Likewise, De Sica represents a father who is not virile, a weak wife who is able to cause a tragedy, and a child who looks upon adultery and suicide—light years away from the smiling tones of just a few years earlier. The mother's adultery is portrayed in a modern way; its reasons are understood if not justified. Even the lover is not the usual seducer but a man who really suffers because of his love.

I bambini is a tough, uncompromising film with no possible happy ending and marked a clear break from De Sica's prior work. This discontinuity was possible because of the screenwriting of Zavattini, who took part in many of De Sica's future films, becoming almost a coauthor.[18] *I bambini ci guardano* was a film without De Sica as an actor, almost as if the director shied away from impersonating this new representational style. The film also marked a discontinuity in De Sica's directing style—for example, in the dream scene in the train just before the temporary return of the mother and the long sequence of Pricò's escape after he sees his mother embrace her lover. Pricò first risks being run over by the train, then escapes onto the beach during the night. He is followed by a long traveling shot, which may have inspired Truffaut in his *Les 400 coups* (The 400 Blows, 1959).

I bambini ci guardano is a strong, tough, film, a turning point in the history of Italian cinema, even beyond its forecasting of postwar Italian cinema. The film declared that nothing was funny anymore, and comedy was no longer a solution, not even a metaphorical one, for the current troubles. "There are people here who do not want to laugh," the ticket man tells a group of starlets at the Eldorado Theater at the beginning of *La porta del cielo* (The Gate of Heaven, 1945).

I bambini ci guardano carried a concentration of pure pain that was directly transferred into *La porta del cielo*, a film that straddles fascist and postwar Italy[19] and that was part of De Sica's maturation process. *La porta del cielo* is an interesting if not fully successful attempt to mix documentary elements and moments of heavy theatricality. It tells the story of a group of ailing people who make a pilgrimage to the sanctuary of Loreto. It is a sort of travelogue, an account of physical and metaphorical travel through an Italy that remained pained and mournful even from the perspective of Christian hope. Each station adds a car to the train and a character and his or her story to the film.

The simple structure of the script by Zavattini and Diego Fabbri crossed four main story lines: a young crippled person who was "adopted" by a good-hearted woman (Maria Mercader); a woman going to Loreto to pray to avoid a family drama (a widowed man wants to remarry and his sons accuse him of betraying the mother's memory, although we ultimately discover that the mother has sexually betrayed her husband, a thematic obsession with adultery that characterizes this phase of De Sica's career); a pianist who has lost one hand and contemplates suicide; and a man accompanying a friend who has lost his sight because of the man. All the episodes are told in flashback, so that the train becomes a vessel bearing memories and dreams.

All of the stories resolve relatively well: The young cripple befriends an aging disabled person and rebuilds a sort of nuclear family; the blind man restores not his sight but his relationship with his friend; the pianist abandons his suicidal thoughts (the real miracle), and although he does not regain the use of his hand, he is lovingly looked after by a beautiful nurse. There is even a real miracle that excites the crowd—an old lady regains the use of her legs in a scene that echoes the end of Rossellini's *Viaggio in Italia* (Voyage to Italy, 1954), where Ingrid Bergman and George Sanders embrace in the middle of the crowd attending a religious procession. Like Rossellini, De Sica used a hypercinematographic dolly to deny any pseudodocumentary assumption in this sequence. Another sequence oscillated between forecasting the future and referring to the past by resembling a conscious homage to Walter Ruttmann's *Acciaio* (Steel, 1933): The two friends compete for a woman's attention, and the jealous friend (Carlo Ninchi) provokes an accident that costs his friend (Massimo Girotti) his sight. The men are working in an ice factory, and the ice blocks are handled threateningly, just like bars of molten steel in Ruttmann's film.

La porta del cielo confirmed this change in the gaze: The theatrical framework (the mattes showing the exterior landscapes outside the train) does not conceal the moments of crude realism even in some of the railway shots. The film's photography was balanced between realist drama and noir, and as in *I bambini*, the directorial touches and camera movements were inventive and fully developed. For example, in one night shot, the camera wanders around the train, trying to grasp the thoughts and the dreams of the protagonists. Another sequence, remarkable less for its mise-en-scène than for its ideological motif, reveals class conflict: When a train full of wealthy passengers passes by the train carrying the poor ailing people, a well-dressed gentleman deliberately lowers his window curtain. This sequence resembles a more famous one in De Santis's *Riso amaro* (Bitter Rice, 1949) in which the camera pans from the sleeping car to the rice fields where Silvana Mangano is about to begin her dance.

This group of films by De Sica seems to gesture toward both his past and his future as well as toward that of other directors of his generation. This phase illustrates a crossing of inspirations, intuitions, citations, suggestions of future works, a mélange of models and sources, of genres and codes, of art and commerce that hints that the artist of *Ladri di biciclette* was born not all of a sudden but emerged out of a rich array of experiences and experimentations.

More Clues of Continuity

Traces of a vision that later becomes part of neorealism go further than the perhaps obvious discovery of an authorial continuity in Rossellini's and De Sica's works. The broader cultural climate of the 1930s offers clues about what became the poetics of neorealism: During this decade, all of Italy and Europe were coming to terms with the notion of realism, an ambiguous term deployed in Europe by Nazism and Stalinism as well as by the French Popular Front and in America by the realist cinema of Warner Bros. and the New Deal's social documentaries. In Italy, *realism* was a term appropriated in the visual arts by Salvatore Guttuso in his *Crocifissione* (Crucifixion) or by the sort of Nazi-inspired "realism" endorsed by Farinacci; in literature, it was championed by Elio Vittorini as well as by the fascist periodicals; in cinema, it was used by communists Mario Alicata and De Santis as well as by the films of fascist propaganda (*Passaporto rosso* [Red Passport, 1936], *Il grande appello* [The Last Roll Call, 1939], and *L'assedio dell'Alcazar* [The Siege of the Alcazar, 1940]).

A few fascist literary magazines theorized a sort of neorealism in the context of a diverse group of periodicals that offered evidence of far-reaching intellectual debate, especially among the new generations. For example, the magazines linked to the Strapaese group tended to value the province and the earth over the city and the bourgeoisie, represented by Massimo Bontempelli's Stracittà cohort.[20] Other organs of the fascist federations and unions were ideologically organic to the regime yet were characterized by a "purism" that in the end turned into criticism of the fascist state or fit in with the theoretical frameworks proposed by the so-called leftist corporatism.

In 1933, Leo Longanesi's *L'italiano* devoted an entire issue to cinema.[21] Longanesi directly participated with his essay, "Breve storia del cinema italiano" and another attempt at categorization, "Il film italiano." Longanesi's "history" reversed the usual positive view of Italian cinema before World War I, asserting that this petit bourgeois cinema continued after the Great War. While the world was torn apart by class and ideological struggles, Italian cinema lingered on aestheticisms that hid the miserable plots of speculators and profiteers: "Nationalism, heavy industry, the sharks have found their expression in the silent art. . . . To fighting Bolshevism and fascism, they oppose an aesthetics that collapsed during the war in Libya. . . . Cinema is a very good financial investment. To do cinema is a way like any other to break into the banking circles. The silent art is a financial title just like Montecatini. . . . What is called the glorious decade of the Italian cinematographic production is but a decade of rapid industrial fortunes."[22]

Longanesi destroyed the film producer, Pittaluga; the production company, Cines; and even Blasetti. His *Sole* (Sun, 1929) was just "a banal imitation of Soviet cinema, with its *butteri* [Tuscan cowboys] who look like accountants and its peasant women in Via Veneto." The only way out was a clean sweep. "A well known Italian critic wrote . . . that the camera should be replaced by a machine gun. Since then, nothing has changed: We just need to supply the ammunition clip and that critic."[23] But a solution existed. For *L'italiano*, it consisted in the recovery of everyday reality, of those moments of truth offered by the corners of Italian provinces.[24] Longanesi's theoretical declarations, the structure of the dedicated issue of the magazine (with the selected excerpts by Chaplin, Grosz, Fulop-Muller, and Kerr), the very revealing choice of published scripts, with their plots drawn from reality and everyday life, all pointed in this direction. "I do not think that in Italy we need set designers to build a movie. We should put together films as simple and as poor of set design as possible—films without artifices, shot as often as possible from the real. It is indeed reality which is lacking in our films. We need to go into the streets, bring our cameras in the streets, the courtyards, the barracks, the stations. It would be sufficient to go out in the street, stop anywhere, and observe what goes on during any half hour, but with alert eyes and no stylistic bias, to make an Italian film which is natural and logical."[25]

This radically innovative hypothesis went against the notion of Italian film "as a linear series of glossy postcards."[26] Even the state's intervention was useless: "Now, what can the state do in Italy? What can it lead? The decaying passive and banal Italian cinema? Does it want to defend the aesthetic and morals of a petit bourgeois cinema, the offspring of French *pochades* [sketches]? Whatever it does, nothing will come out of it: It is not a matter of organizing."[27]

Longanesi concluded that "Italian cinema is a corpse in the holds of a sailing ship." Other types of films had been rescued: comic cinema "could not help but throw itself in the arms of life" after literature had rejected it; American cinema reproduced the reality of the nation along with its peculiar types and situations in its topoi and in its standardized characters; Russian cinema "does not make reality but mirrors it as [cinema] has remade [reality] earlier." Russian cinema had a collective nature, reflecting the nation's character and seeking characters in life, in the streets: "Indeed, often [these characters] are *men from the street*," a formula that was to become characteristic of neorealism.[28]

Before neorealism: *1860*, by
Alessandro Blasetti (1934).

Neorealism found in this issue of *L'italiano* its term *ante quem*, its first unconscious theoretical formulation. Longanesi's propositions, his *film dal vero* and his *motivi per un film italiano*, contain elements of neorealism: the bicycle, the railroad, the pension. The accompanying photographs are of documentary type (the fair, the social club, the conference, the marketplace, and even the Neapolitan shoe shiner) and document the exigency of this "new realism." Some of Longanesi's words seem to forecast Zavattini. Longanesi's notion of a "reality which is lacking in our films," the idea "to go into the streets . . . and observe what goes on during any half hour" was what Fellini recalled about the filmmakers who did not need subjects in the immediate aftermath of the war: They could find their subjects around any corner.[29]

This issue of *L'italiano* also presaged all the limits of the future neorealism: the populism, the paternalism, the tendency for the sketch. In 1939, in *Corrente di vita giovanile* (one of the trendsetting magazines of the last phase of fascism), Luigi Comencini echoed the themes of *L'italiano* with regard to Camerini's *Batticuore* (Heartbeat, 1939), which Longanesi had scripted. According to Comencini, "The first impression was that of an effort to demonstrate what is well known, that in Italy there is an abundance of types and environments to offer material for a film, while nothing really good comes out of the false way of the conventional dramas and comedies. . . . What did we get from the issue of *L'italiano*? The certainty that Longanesi was a smart man, that he had some taste . . . that he could 'see' some scenes with a cinematic eye, but ultimately that he was not capable of composing a film and, even worse, that he was not aware of the flaws of his sketches."[30]

Fascism—or at least parts of it—thus tended to favor a new realism, since the regime was not monolithic. As far as cinema was concerned, clues—or desires—of a neo "realism" can be traced to Blasetti: in the exteriors of *1860* and in the direct recording of the dialogue in the original dialects in that film; in *Sole* and its use of a "documentary style," which Bazin identifies in neorealism;

in *Terra madre* (Mother Earth, 1931) and its referencing of the Strapaese ideology of the healthy countryside against the corrupted city.

Terra madre depicts the countryside as the difficult but virile environment, lacking in comforts but rich in ethical values, and it is there that the protagonist returns. The city is the easier environment, with a swinging rhythm that tempted and corrupted the protagonist via the femme fatale. This theme recurred in much of the Italian cinema of the 1930s as well as in many American films of the early part of the decade. Even *Vecchia guardia*, one of the few films dealing with the March on Rome, was openly fascist but was also concerned with the recovery of life outside the big city, with the atmosphere of village life, with everyday characters gathered in the barbershop, the bar.[31] But *1860* in particular serves as a huge reservoir of moments of future cinema: Leda Gloria wrapped up in a black shawl echoes Visconti's *La terra trema* (The Earth Trembles, 1948); the rosary recited by the priest and the shepherds arrested by the Swiss-Bourbon soldiers forecast Aldo Vergano's *Il sole sorge ancora* (Outcry, 1946); the death of the *garibaldino* calling for his mother in the arms of Gesuzza is echoed in the Florence episode of *Paisà*. For this reason, even aside from *Quattro passi*, Blasetti has been considered pre-neorealist.

Strong clues of a new realism can perhaps paradoxically be found in the cinema of the regime's fellow travelers, those who were closer to the fascist ideology. *Acciaio*, for example, insists on the complementary elements of tradition and modernization: the inn, the street, the ancient faces of the people across from the steel factory. Surprising moments of realism occur in apparently propagandistic films (*Il grande appello*, *Squadrone bianco*) and especially in De Robertis's semidocumentary films, most notably *Uomini sul fondo*, which linked some stereotypes of the Hollywood film with the style of Soviet cinema and with this new desire for *verismo* that permeated society and media.

De Robertis was making films with a realistic and documentary eye that could objectively grasp technical or psychological details. The director provides a wealth of details about the technology employed in the rescue of the submarine in *Uomini sul fondo*, about family dynamics, about the anthropological context of the individual sailor both in this film and in *Alfa tau!* (1942). De Robertis's cinema is a crucial document, an excellent historical source for recovering not just the contemporary technologies of war but also bourgeois domesticity and the social contexts of people not directly involved in the fighting. De Robertis placed humanity at the center of his films, just as Visconti had suggested in writing of "anthropomorphic cinema."[32] But like most pre-neorealist works, De Robertis's films must now be seen in the context of their contemporary cinematic models and in light of the models of filmic imaginary that permeated that cultural moment. In *Uomini sul fondo*,

The credits for *La nave bianca*, by Roberto Rossellini (1941).

an invaluable source on the Italian social reality of the early 1940s as well as a synthesis of myths and collective imaginaries of those years, are flavors from Hollywood as well as France and Russia. In this sense, *Alfa tau!*, which proposes the same ambiguities as *Uomini sul fondo* in an even more hybridized context, is outstanding. If *Uomini* was about prewar maneuvers, *Alfa* was about the real war action; if the latter was a reassuring message about the efficacy of Italy's military means, the former provided reassurance that life goes on normally even during wartime. The film begins and ends like a war movie, the story first filtered from the headquarters on the ground and told through protagonists' narrations, then shown in the most classical of fictional reconstructions. In between, just like a parenthetical moment, is another movie that narrates various parallel episodes on the pretext of the brief furlough of some officers.

As it emerges from these two films, De Robertis's work was an often unresolved and always interesting pastiche, but it should not be read solely from the perspective of neorealism, which it forecast. On the contrary, thanks to the multifaceted filmic legacies embedded into them, De Robertis's films offer a hybrid poetics that enabled them to offer diverse images of Italy and sketch a gallery of characters that were in turn dramatic or comical, rhetorical or antirhetorical, realistic or antirealistic. In representing characters and situations, De Robertis struck a balance between two different registers, a schematically theorized realism and the most artificial of fictional representations. Thus we find the most stereotypical generic conventions (Hollywood submarine war films, war films, comedy, melodrama) as well as gestures that point toward the cinema of Zavattini. From this perspective, the opening titles of *Alfa tau!* are worth considering: "In this story, all elements respond to a historical and environmental *verismo*. The humble sailor who is the central character has in fact lived the event that he lives again in this story. Likewise, the role of each character in the story corresponds to the role each of them has in real life." Here is the most extreme form of neorealism, also expressed in *Umberto D*: historical and environmental *verismo*, reality of life, nonprofessional actors who performed as themselves.

De Robertis's former assistant, Rossellini, used similar opening titles in *La nave bianca*, and they shed new light on the Rossellini of *Paisà*: "In this sea story as in *Uomini sul fondo*, all characters are placed in their environment and their real life and are followed through the spontaneous *verismo* of their expression and the simple humanity of those feelings that constitute our ideological universe. Volunteer nurses, officers, noncommissioned officers, and the crews participated in this film. This story has been made on the hospital ship *Arno* and on one of our warships."

In sum, the young Rossellini stressed, the characters interpreted themselves and the film had been shot on location. It was already neorealism.

Notes

1. Giustino Fortunato, *Carteggio, 1927–1932* (Bari/Rome: Laterza, 1981), 185.

2. On the continuity between neorealism and the cinema of fascism, see also Peter Bondanella, "The Making of *Roma, Città Aperta*: The Legacy of Fascism and the Birth of Neorealism," in *Roberto Rossellini's* Rome, Open City, ed. Sidney Gottlieb (Cambridge: Cambridge University Press, 2004), 43–66; Ennio di Nolfo, "Intimations of Neorealism in the Fascist *Ventennio*," in *Re-Viewing Fascism: Italian Cinema, 1922–1943*, ed. Jacqueline Reich and Piero Garofalo (Bloomington: Indiana University Press, 2002), 83–104.

3. Mirella Serri, *I redenti: Gli intellettuali che vissero due volte, 1938–1948* (Milan: Corbaccio, 2005).

4. Ibid., 233.

5. See Stefania Parigi, ed., *Paisà* (Venice: Marsilio, 2005), esp. Vito Zagarrio, "Uscire dal tunnel: Il quarto episodio," 85.

6. See Lino Micciché, ed., *Il neorealismo cinematografico italiano* (Venice: Marsilio, 1976); Lino Micciché, *Nuovi materiali sul cinema italiano, 1929–1943* (Ancona: Mostra Internazionale del Nuovo Cinema, 1976). For a less stereotypical reading of the film, see Vito Zagarrio, "Bassifondi: Appunti su due film 'fascisti' di De Robertis," in *In fondo al mare: Il cinema di Francesco De Robertis* (Bari: Edizioni del Sud, 1996), 41.

7. See esp. Gian Paolo Pansa, *Il sangue dei vinti* (Milan: Sperling and Kupfer, 2003), which has been recently turned into a movie directed by Michele Soavi (*Il sangue dei vinti* [The Blood of the Vanquished, 2008]); Gian Paolo Pansa, *Sconosciuto 1945* (Milan: Sperling and Kupfer, 2004). These two best-sellers equate—at the levels both of memory and of historical judgment—partisans and supporters of the fascist Salò Republic.

8. See Alberto Asor Rosa, *Storia d'Italia Einaudi*, vol. 4, *Dall'unità ad oggi* (Turin: Einaudi, 1975), 1502.

9. Philip Cannistraro, *La fabbrica del consenso: Fascismo e mass media* (Bari: Laterza, 1975).

10. See Micciché, *Neorealismo*.

11. *Materiali sul cinema italiano, 1929–1943: Blasetti, Camerini, Poggioli* (Pesaro: 11th Mostra Internazionale del Nuovo Cinema, 1975).

12. See Steven Ricci, *Cinema and Fascism* (Berkeley: University of California Press, 2007).

13. Sergio Grmek Germani, "Cinema italiano sotto il fascismo: Proposta di periodizzazione," in *Materiali sul cinema italiano*, 333.

14. Ibid., 339.

15. Ibid., 359.

16. Micciché, *Neorealismo*; *Materiali sul cinema italiano*. One line of interpretation has stressed comedy's fascist leanings insofar as it was organic to the regime's consensus; another interpretation has seen the comedy of the 1930s as "a-fascist" because of its inability to adhere to the regime's rhetoric and provincialism. See Mino Argentieri, ed., *Risate di regime: La commedia italiana, 1930–1944* (Venice: Marsilio, 1991); Andrea Martini, ed., *La bella forma* (Venice: Marsilio, 1992).

17. See Micciché, *Neorealismo*.

18. *I bambini* was based on *Pricò*, a novel by Cesare Giulio Viola, and in addition to Viola and De Sica, the screenwriters were Aldo Franci, Gherardo Gherardi, Margherita Maglione, and Zavattini.

19. The title that accompanies the initial traveling shot shows that the film belongs to the period of the liberation: "During the occupation of Rome, struggling against all kinds of obstacles, a few men of the Italian cinema realized this film, sustained by their desire to serve, with their art, the Christian faith."

20. Examples of these journals include Mino Maccari's *Il selvaggio*, Longanesi's *L'italiano*, and, although it did not completely subscribe to the Strapaese position, Malaparte's *Prospettive*.

21. *L'italiano* 17–18 (1933).

22. Ibid., 23–24.

23. Ibid., 28.

24. On Longanesi, see also Bondanella, "Making," 46.

25. *L'italiano* 17–18 (1933): 35.

26. Longanesi cited in Vito Zagarrio, "Tra intervento e tendenza: Le riviste culturali e il cinema del fascismo," in *Nuovi materiali sul cinema italiano, 1929–1943* (Ancona: Mostra Internazionale del Nuovo Cinema, 1976), 1:219.

27. *L'italiano* 17–18 (1933): 60.

28. Ibid.

29. See Federico Fellini, *Intervista sul cinema* (Bari: Laterza, 1976).

30. Luigi Comencini, "Il cinematografo a riposo," *Corrente di vita giovanile* 4 (1939), cited in Zagarrio, "Tra intervento e tendenza," 211.

31. Even Blasetti's comedies describe contemporary society in a realistic way, though from the perspective of the upper classes (for example, *La contessa di Parma* [The Dutchess of Parma, 1938] with the fashion atelier, the professional soccer, the cars, and the racing horses).

32. Luchino Visconti, "Cinema antropomorfico," *Cinema* 173–74 (Fall 1941): 109.

SOVIET-ITALIAN CINEMATIC EXCHANGES, 1920s–1950s

From Early Soviet Film Theory to Neorealism

MASHA SALAZKINA

Introduction

In the *Soviet Dictionary of Film* (Sovetskii kinoslovar', 1970), the entry on Italian neorealism concludes, "Having emerged under the influence of Soviet cinema (theoretical works by Eisenstein and Pudovkin, and cinematic works by Dovzhenko, among others), neorealism in its turn influenced the work of the young Soviet filmmakers of the 1950s."[1] In a similar vein, a recent Russian book on documentary contends, "The painstaking study of the films of Pudovkin and Donskoi at the Roman Experimental Center, which influenced the formation of neorealism, is well known."[2]

Yet what is "well known" in Russia is less so among film scholars brought up on the version of film history and aesthetics (from André Bazin to Gilles Deleuze) that places Soviet avant-garde cinema in stylistic and ideological opposition to neorealism. Thus, such canonical English-language accounts of neorealism as, for example, Peter Bondanella's *Italian Cinema: From Neorealism to the Present*, report that "while there is little reason to believe that Russian cinema itself was a major influence upon this young generation of Italians, Russian film theory certainly helped to move the focus of Italian film-makers toward a penchant for realism."[3] In Italy, conversely, Gian Piero Brunetta's classic four-volume history of Italian cinema is clearer about the Soviet-Italian interchange, pointing to theoretical and cinematic influences of early Soviet avant-garde cinema on the Italian cinematic theory and practice of the 1930s and 1940s.[4] In Brunetta's wake, specialists in fascist cinema[5] and neorealism have slowly started to challenge the Bazin-influenced thesis that Soviet film and neorealism were opposites. In his recent book on neorealism, Mark Shiel begins his account of the genesis of the movement by highlighting

Umberto Barbaro's translations of Russian film theorists and "the teaching of the Russian film-making techniques at the Centro Sperimentale."[6] Still, Shiel takes the point no farther, leaving us with a fragment and a puzzle: How and why did the future neorealists turn to the Russians? What was attractive about the film practices of Pudovkin and Eisenstein? How were these practices incorporated into the formulations of neorealism as they emerged in the 1930s and 1940s? This essay answers these questions but does not do so by closely reading neorealist films and adducing the cinematic influence or a specific set of techniques that may have been "borrowed" from the Soviets. Rather, I am more interested in the relationship between the conceptual framework of the early Soviet avant-garde (of which cinema formed a vital part) and that of neorealism, bringing out the moments of concrete mediation in the dialectical relationship between avant-garde and realism in cinematic history. Ultimately, this essay points to the need to retrace the genealogy of neorealism by placing it in an international context in which ideological and national barriers—in this case, those created by the opposition between fascism and communism—are seen to be much more porous than many historians suppose. I make my historical case by presenting a broad outline of the dissemination of early Soviet film theory in 1930s–40s Italy (a period encompassing the rise and fall of fascism) and showing how this dissemination helped initiate the formulation of the neorealist discourse. The dissemination of Soviet film culture was not haphazard but radiated out from certain agents and institutional centers, most notably the Centro Sperimentale di Cinematografia. Within the Centro, we find a key figure, film critic and writer Umberto Barbaro, who operated as the indispensable intermediary between Soviet and Italian film circles. Although the opposition between fascist Italy and the Soviet Union did not foreclose the aesthetic interchange between the two, on the official level, the relationship was politically fraught, ultimately hostile, and inflected the reception of Soviet film in Italy.

In conclusion, I briefly point to the presence of Italian neorealism in the Soviet film of the postwar and post-Stalin period, asserting an aesthetic interdependence between the Cinema of the Thaw in the Soviet Union and Italian neorealism. Both were caught up in a tangled dialogue with early Soviet film theory and practice as mediated by its reception during the foundational period of Italian neorealism. In this way, the germinal period of neorealism came to play a role in the formation of two of the great postwar cinemas.

Soviet-Italian Cinematic Relations, 1920s–1930s

The ideas surrounding the emergence of neorealism as a new way of thinking about cinema were developed by 1930s Italian intellectuals who were engaged in active dialogue with non-Italian contemporary film theory and practice. This dialogue both reflected and subverted the fascist culture of the time. It reflected some fascist preoccupations and positions—for example, the meliorist modernizing agenda that saw cinema as a sophisticated instrument penetrating the archaic spheres of Italian society, particularly the agricultural sector, to disseminate modern attitudes to the peasantry under the patronage of a cohesive nationalist ideology. Thus, according to fascist theory, cinema, particularly documentary cinema, was fundamentally a tool of propaganda rather than an entertainment industry. The latter posed a problem for the fascists, because entertainment was dominated by the Hollywood model of filmmaking, which gave a geopolitical advantage to the Anglosphere. But these concerns were shared by the Soviet Union and formed the basis for the precarious compact between the two national film industries. The fascists were impressed by the size and prestige of the Soviet film industry, seeing it as a model for developing one of modernity's key industries along alternative, non-Hollywood lines.[7] While the fascist state was officially resistant to communist ideology and even found its raison d'être in a militant anti-Bolshevism, future neorealists did not feel the same way. They found much to admire in Soviet cinema, not only for the level of its technological advances but also for its ideology. Many neorealists first engaged with Marxism through film, using it as a resource to mount a sub rosa polemic against official fascism. Some of the polemics were in fact a continuation of the debates that had gone on in the 1920s, when the Italian artistic scene had been less subject to fascist interference than was the case in the 1930s. The closure of civic society to artistic pluralism put an end to the public exposure of points of view antipathetic to fascism. This change had the paradoxical effect of shifting the locus of the aesthetic discussion to the cinematic domain, which was defined by new constituencies and new techniques. From the point of view of cinema technique, Soviet film theory and practice could be accommodated to the fascist norms governing art, and fascism itself was searching for an alternative to Hollywood-style film production. In this way, Soviet cinema entered the fascist sphere as a proposed model for the development of Italian cinema.

Thus was formed the institutional vector through which Italy and the USSR enacted a heterogeneous series of artistic—and specifically cinematic—exchanges in the 1920s and early 1930s. These exchanges took various forms, ranging from official and personal visits to participation in film festivals, translations, and screenings. Such interchanges made the intervention of Soviet film theory and practice a defining catalyst for avant-garde Italian film.

This story of the convergence of fascist Italy's film aesthetic and the film practice of the early Soviet film industry may seem unexpected, but if we look at the institutional commonalities between the two national cinemas, we can understand the logic of the Soviet film effect on the beginning of neorealism.

- In both countries, the film industry was nationalized under the premise that cinema was too important to remain outside state control.
- In both countries, the state supported the creation of a centralized film institute as an academic setting for critical and creative cinematic expression outside of the commercial sphere.
- In Italy, as leftist activity was suppressed, left-leaning personalities in Italian avant-garde cultures often sought ways to remain viable, some by becoming advocates of the official fascist ideology and others by finding ways to express their "internal exile" while remaining involved with Italian cultural life. Both sorts gravitated to the Centro as a primary forum for cultural activity. This process bears some similarities to the dynamic inside Soviet film circles in the Stalinist period.
- The government in both the Soviet Union and Italy had ideological reasons for at least officially proclaiming its resistance to the Hollywood model of filmmaking (and de facto competing with it). Documentaries, which made up for their lack of production values by their greater authenticity, early on became central to the creation of the anti-Hollywood aesthetic in both countries, further contributing to the discourse on greater "realism."
- Finally, both the Soviet and Italian regimes turned away from the formal experimentation that had attached itself to revolutionary or fascist ideology in the 1920s (the formalists and futurists in the USSR, and the futurists in Italy). Instead, both states sought to promote varied models of realism and entertainment as part of the official cultural discourse and patronage of the 1930s.

To explore this dynamic in more depth, I will now briefly outline the institutional relationship between the two film industries and then highlight the particular engagement of the neorealist circles with Soviet film theory.

Between 1924, when Italy recognized the Soviet Union, and 1933, when the two countries signed a nonaggression pact, both states encouraged a great deal of cultural interaction. At the outbreak of the Spanish Civil War in 1936, these relations were abruptly terminated. By that time, however, most of Italy's major cinematographic institutions were well established and had already incorporated and reworked Soviet models. These institutions included the industrial (film production), pedagogical (film education and noncommercial distribution), and critical (film journals and publishing) aspects of the Italian film industry. Although the anti-Soviet line hardened after 1936, the models in place were not significantly changed.

Thus, from the late 1920s to the mid-1930s, Italians were encouraged to look at Soviet Russia as a state with many affinities to Italy. Pietro Sessa's 1934 study *Fascismo e bolscevismo* touted the many similarities between the two nations' ideology and governance, allied as they were in the rejection of the logic of the plutocracy, identified with France, England and the United States, that dominated the world and had shown, in the crash of 1929, the degeneration of the forms of capitalism to which they owed their imperial roles.[8] As Ruth Ben-Ghiat, Piero Garofalo, and Vito Zagarrio note, the press of the time was ready to exploit the various similarities between the Soviet and Italian situation: *Critica fascista*, an ideologically influential journal, often underlined the connections that it saw in the fact that both countries lagged behind the modernization of France, Germany, and the United Kingdom and in the fact that both countries adopted state-led programs to liquidate archaic customs and traditions to create a modern economy organized around industrialization and science. From this point of view, Bolshevism could be claimed as the precursor of fascism. Of course, this rhetoric was a screen for Mussolini's realpolitik, which was motivated by the desire to use the threat of a strategic alliance with the Soviet state as a negotiating tactic that would allow Italy to pursue its African and Balkan policy undisturbed. Moreover, Italian industry could benefit from the Soviet market. At the same time, members of the fascist intelligentsia commonly believed that the Soviet Union needed to be saved from itself by abandoning the Bolshevik doctrine in favor of the fascist one (as journalist Renzo Bertone suggested in his *Il trionfo del fascismo nell'URSS* [1934] and *Russia: Trionfo del fascismo* [1937]).[9] But despite this triumphalist note, the Soviet Union remained an object of admiration for many among the fascist elite as well as many artists and filmmakers. In the period before fascism arrived in Italy, members of leftist circles, from futurists to Gramsci's Ordine Nuovo, commonly visited Russia and then the Soviet Union, and while the fascists disbanded many of these circles, some remained (at least informally) in place within Italy throughout the 1920s. Thus, by the late 1920s, Italian intellectuals were very familiar with Soviet literature, theater, and visual arts—and above all with Soviet cinema.

Both nations openly assigned priority to the film industry in their state projects: Lenin's dictum, "Cinema is the most important of the arts," was rephrased by Mussolini as "Cinema is the strongest weapon!" The Soviet film industry by the 1930s was world renowned for its experimentation, its technical advances, and its production values. It was consciously cultivated as a Soviet showcase, so it is not surprising that cinema became the focus of the official cultural relations between the two countries during the period of their rapprochement, especially as Italy was aggressively pursuing the goal of modernizing its own rather underdeveloped film production. Another tie—this time an aesthetic one—was the privileged place accorded to documentary by both the Soviet and Italian film industries. Many Soviet filmmakers experienced the civil war in the Soviet Union as reporters of one type or another; consequently, when they moved into the cinematic arena, they brought with them a documentary mind-set. In Italy, the mind-set was a matter of professional training: All directors by the 1930s had to start by making documentaries at the Istituto LUCE (see Luca Caminati's essay in this volume).

The debates about Soviet cinema in Italy preceded Soviet films themselves, which were hardly shown before the 1930s. Of course, Soviet cinema provoked intense debate on the issue of cinema as an autonomous and independent art across Europe, particularly in France, which was most influential for Italian intellectuals. Starting from the second half of the 1920s, Italian journals (both those specifically dedicated to cinema, such as *Cinemalia*; *Lo schermo*, which became *Cinematografo*; and *Lo spettacolo d'Italia*, and literary and cultural journals, such as *La fiera letteraria/L'Italia letteraria* and *Occidente*) often featured articles about Soviet cinema. In the early 1930s, the first translations of works by Soviet film theorists started to appear in these venues as well. Italian intellectuals followed other European critics in seeing Soviet cinema from the perspective of its most celebrated innovation, montage, which demonstrated the unique capabilities of cinema in creating works of art unlike any other. At the same time, the socially and politically explicit nature of Soviet films began to be recognized in the emerging Italian discourse on realism in cinema. However, despite a great number of references to specific films and directors, many writers on Soviet cinema in Italy at the time were experiencing these films only secondhand via the French media, since Soviet films were not being shown at the time in Italy but were available in France largely as a result of the efforts of Leon Moussinac, whose Ciné-Club de France regularly screened Eisenstein, Pudovkin, and Dovzhenko in the late 1920s and early 1930s.

In July 1932, Luciano De Feo, a former director of LUCE and then director of the International Institute of Educational Film (Istituto Internazionale della Cinematografia Educativa), set off on an official trip to "study the organization of film business" in the Soviet Union, visiting Moscow and Leningrad film studios and viewing a number of films by Eisenstein, Dovzhenko, and Vertov.[10] This trip was part of a long-term exchange between De Feo and the Soviet

All-Union Society for Cultural Ties Abroad on the subject of the educational potential of cinema[11] that had two immediate consequences for the Italian film industry. The first was the increasing centralization of the industry as a whole, most notably in the founding of the National Cinema School (Scuola Nazionale di Cinematografia, known after 1935 as the Centro Sperimentale di Cinematografia), which was modeled directly on the All-Union State Cinema Institute (VGIK). Many of the future neorealists were educated at the Centro. Second, two Soviet films—Dovzhenko's *Zemlya* (Earth, 1930) and Nikolai Ekk's *Putiovka v zhizn'* (The Road to Life, 1931)—were included in the first Venice International Film Festival, which De Feo organized in 1932. At the festival, the Soviet film industry (rather than any individual film) received an award for achievement in cinematographic production.[12] Consequently, in 1934 Stalin permitted a group of Soviet filmmakers and functionaries to attend the Venice festival, where they presented more than ten films, including documentaries (Vertov's *Tri pesni o Lenine* [Three Songs of Lenin, 1934] and Arkady Shafron and Mark Troyanovsky's *Cheliuskin* [Chelyuskin, Heroes of the Arctic, 1934]); literary adaptations (Vladimir Petrov's *Groza* [Thunderstorm, 1934], and Mikhail Romm's *Pyshka* [1934]); and musical comedies (Grigori Aleksandrov's *Veselye Rebyata* [Jolly Fellows, 1934]).[13] Apart from the festival screenings, few of the films garnered wide distribution; most of the films were projected in private clubs and before university groups, which formed a widespread network of venues for noncommercial film exhibition. But while Soviet films lacked a popular Italian audience, especially in contrast with the much more popular American cinema (despite the government-imposed limitations on the exhibition of U.S. films), among the inner circle of filmmakers, Soviet films became the cornerstone of cinematic education, an integral part of the curriculum of the Centro Sperimentale di Cinematografia.

Centro Sperimentale di Cinematografia and Umberto Barbaro

While the Centro was created "to make film production one hundred percent Italian," as Luigi Chiarini, its first director, declared in his inaugural speech, it quickly became the major site of international cultural dialogue.[14] Beginning in 1936, each course of study was designed to last two years and encompass an impressive range of both practical and theoretical subjects. The structure and curriculum were directly borrowed from VGIK, the Moscow film institute founded in 1919. While Chiarini served as the Centro's public face, the real intellectual influence was wielded by Barbaro, who promoted cultural (and, although never directly stated, ideological) diversity at the Center. A fervent communist, Barbaro translated Sergei Eisenstein, Vsevolod Pudovkin, and Semyon Timoshenko, along with Béla Balázs and Rudolph Arnheim (who also briefly taught aesthetics at the Centro), and was an active participant in the critical debates in *Cinematografo* and *L'Italia letteraria*, journals active in disseminating a vision of Soviet cinema as a model for Italian filmmaking. Barbaro understood Soviet cinema to be "the starting point and . . . example for the rebirth of Italian cinema."[15] As one of the Centro's first professors, Barbaro used Soviet cinema both in his teaching and in his writings. His influence reached beyond the classroom through his post as the coeditor of *Bianco e nero*, the Centro's journal, which quickly became Italy's most important source of film scholarship.

The key moment in Barbaro's theoretical trajectory remains his discovery in the late 1920s of the writings of Pudovkin, whose theories henceforward remained at the center of Barbaro's theoretical work. While he translated the works of other Soviet theorists (Eisenstein and Timoshenko), Barbaro's translations of Pudovkin and his introductions and commentaries to those works contain clusters of the most important aspects of Barbaro's theoretical thought. For him, the key issue was the necessity of a materialist approach to cinema and the derivative notion of realism. This issue eventually led Barbaro to formulate the proto-agenda of Italian neorealism in his writings and teaching at the Centro Sperimentale.

The debate on realism found its most explicit forum in relation to cinema in *Bianco e nero* and *Cinema*, the two journals associated with the Centro Sperimentale. Barbaro was involved with their editorial direction from their inception, using them to effect a subtle subversion of the fascist ideology by means of a formal and aesthetic critique as the fascist state hardened its attitude toward the open discussion of leftist art and politics in the late 1930s. From 1940 onward, *Cinema* in particular became the preeminent journal for explicitly formulating the aesthetic and political program of neorealism through essays by Barbaro and his students, Michelangelo Antonioni and Giuseppe De Santis, as well as critics such as Guido Aristarco and Carlo Lizzani. The term *neorealism* appeared in a 1943 article by Barbaro addressing the need for new truly realist art.[16] Barbaro apparently borrowed this term, which had been put into circulation in relation to Soviet literature, in a series of articles (particularly in *L'Italia letteraria*) in which he defined postrevolutionary Soviet literature as "neorealist." Barbaro meant that it was made in the spirit of Dostoevsky with characteristics of "Proust, Joyce, and the most lively examples of the new European literature" superimposed on it.[17] Barbaro evidently saw neorealism as rooted in literature not only in the Russian/Soviet sphere but also in the modernist and therefore antirealist aesthetic of bourgeois Europe. Similarly,

Soviet montage, which has been associated with the avant-garde (and therefore antirealist) techniques since Bazin's famous opposition of directors who place faith in reality with those who place faith in the image, was for Barbaro (writing before Bazin) not an opposition but rather an adjunct to a truly realist work of art. This view explains why Barbaro considered Pudovkin the greatest realist.

Barbaro's realism, then, should not be understood through its opposition to the avant-garde (see the Brecht-Lukács debate) but rather as the materialist articulation of the relation of cinema and its apparatus to the social and political both in the sense of the conditions of production and reception and in terms of the relationship between the subject matter and social and political reality. Most important for Barbaro, the rhetoric of realism (or neorealism) functioned in opposition to philosophical idealism and its accompanying aesthetic as propounded by Benedetto Croce and his followers. Croce's antipositivist philosophy insisted that "reality" was subordinate to and derivative from "the spirit," thus locating artistic production in the realm of the subjective. While Croce was not in favor with the fascist regime, Giovanni Gentile, the fascist regime's semiofficial philosopher and another neo-idealist whose vocabulary infused much of the official fascist doctrine, was daringly targeted. Barbaro's preface to Pudovkin's *Il soggetto cinematografico* provides great insight into this debate.[18] Here Barbaro not only calls Pudovkin the "best filmmaker ever" but also explicitly uses Pudovkin's pragmatic approach to filmmaking and his realist filmmaking style as a weapon against the Crocean orthodoxy in academia and important cultural circles. As his rhetoric shows, Barbaro is performing a balancing act symptomatic of the neorealist movement in general. He stays within an acceptable national(ist) discourse while aligning himself with a fundamentally internationalist phenomenon. Barbaro's call to go back to Italian nineteenth-century naturalist writers must be understood in this "empiricist" vein, leading to Luchino Visconti's adaptation of Giovanni Verga's novel *I malavoglia* (The House by the Medlar Tree) in *La terra trema* (The Earth Trembles, 1948). This apparent contradiction (neorealism supposedly was an antiliterary movement) signals that the problem of the "literary" was a matter not of the adaptation of books to the screen but of the kind of books that ought to be adapted to the screen. For the neorealist Barbaro, Verga's *verismo*, his painstakingly accurate description of Sicilian fishermen's daily lives, performs an exemplary confrontation with social and class issues. Barbaro's reference to a certain literary lineage is coherent with the rewriting of the Italian literary canon started by Luigi Russo in 1941, which broke with Croce's simplistic reading of naturalism to review Italian literature under a materialist ideological lens. In effect, far from being antiliterature, literature was being made pro-neorealist, as the canon of the nation's literature was re-configured. In this way, Barbaro transposed Pudovkin's theory away from the Soviet context to the Italian arena, where it could provide a framework for reanimating materialism in its old debate with Crocean idealism.[19] Thus, in materialist terms, the "reality" that becomes the central concept for neorealism is not so much a matter of realism as an artistic style, with its psychologistic tendencies, but an affirmation of the primacy of social and political reality in the content of film and in providing the material conditions of film produc-tion. For Barbaro, then, the natural consequence of this understanding of realism was to impose not a mimetic function on cinema but a transformative one: as Brunetta affirms, Barbaro's understanding of realism and the binomy of art/life "is not limited to making an interpretation of the world but intends to actively transform reality."[20]

However, the first aspect of the notion of realism as broadly rooted in so-cial reality while governed by the power of individual artistic (self) expression defined the broader ideological self-understanding of neorealism as a form of making the facts "speak." Chiarini appropriated Barbaro's clearly Marxist materialist understanding of realism and adapted it for a discourse that was acceptable to both fascism and liberal humanism. In this way, the antibour-geois aesthetic of neorealism was gilded with an idealistic gloss, "the cinemato-graphic realism . . . in the sense of spiritual reality of the people."[21]

Italian film scholars and filmmakers took the lesson of Soviet film theory to be the radical materialist conception of cinematic reality, opposing it to the then dominant orthodoxy of idealism in educational institutions, film journals, and film production. Yet Chiarini's compromised neorealism, taking on a liberal and humanist rhetoric, resonated most prominently in postwar European society, from Bazin to the Soviet filmmakers of the Thaw period. However, while Bazin saw neorealism as a matter of valorizing the set of tech-niques, for the postwar Soviet film community it became a code word for the specific anti-Stalinist tendencies of the Cinema of the Thaw.

Thus, critics need to remove the postwar humanist grid to see the real in-tellectual understandings in place in the Italian film industry as the country plunged into World War II. These understandings framed the way in which the neorealists responded to the postwar situation and were understood—and misunderstood. While the general trend of the neorealist movement was strongly antifascist, the original neorealist themes were worked out within the parameters of the fascist era: the openness to material reality even up to the use of nonactors, the encounter between traditional society and modernity, and the self-consciousness of the role of film itself as it actively enters and ex-ists as a polarizing presence in the social and political sphere.

In conclusion, I now turn to the neorealist effect on the Cinema of the Thaw, which is an instance of a national tradition being reencoded by its inheritors from an exterior national tradition. This process imparts a dialectical tension to the concept of a "national" cinema, installing a cosmopolitan Other at the heart of the process of tradition.

Italian Neorealism in the Postwar Soviet Union

At the end of World War II, a large contingent of young future filmmakers came into the All-Union State Cinema Institute (VGIK), bringing with them a very different background from that of their elders, who personally remembered non-Soviet Russian culture. Many of the film students had been veterans of the front. The fruits of this generational change can be seen in the emergence of a new Soviet cinema, usually referred to as Cinema of the Thaw.[22] The Thaw was the nickname of the shift of direction in cultural policy under Khrushchev: From around 1956 to 1964, the official denunciation of Stalin and the cult of personality resulted in the loosening of state censorship of cinema. Many correspondences between the Soviet aesthetics of this period and Italian neorealism are the result of both direct influence (as the Italian cinema was the most watched by these emerging filmmakers during their formative years) and of these young filmmakers' particular understanding of the ideological implications of the term *neorealism* (as a form of socialist humanism). In an ironic reversal of the situation in prewar Italy, the critical discourse on Italian neorealism in the 1950s and 1960s Soviet Union functioned as a coded polemic regarding the changes within Soviet cinema—and ideology at large—during Khrushchev's years.

Soviet officials never took an overtly hostile line with regard to neorealism, unlike Poland, where Italian neorealism came under direct attack. The level of that attack is shown by an outburst by Włodzimierz Sokorski, the Polish minister of culture, who called neorealism a "primitive exhibitionism of mankind's lowest instincts, the most hideous forms of cruelty, sadism, and superstition" that "has nothing to do with scientific analysis of life; it has to do with employing (what we have observed in Fascist art) a naturalistic method to promote false insolent arguments."[23] In the Soviet Union, the official line pointed out "shortcomings" but laid the general emphasis on the neorealists' antifascist stance and on their connections to the Communist Party and the tradition of socialist realism. Consequently, films by Giuseppe De Santis, an active communist and a regular visitor to the Soviet Union, especially after 1948, were widely distributed, as were most of Rossellini's and De Sica's films.

The new Italian films were also incorporated into the curriculum for all film students.

Several of the most iconic Soviet films from the late 1950s–early 1960s were perceived at the time of their release as extensions of and reactions to postwar Italian cinema. This group includes the first Soviet film seen inside the country as a break with Stalinist filmmaking, Marlen Khutsiev's *Vesna na Zarechnoy ulitse* (Spring on Zarechnaia Street, 1956), which initiated wild debates both within and outside of the VGIK.[24] This film, which now looks extremely conventional, was seen as a sign of a real revolution in the postwar Soviet cinema primarily because of its attention to the details of everyday life. From the time of its release, Khutsiev was accused of imitating Italian neorealism. The one macrofeature that most struck an audience raised on Stalinist film conventions was this overt emphasis on the authenticity of personal human interactions rather than on action didactically derived from an ideologically correct standpoint. This ethos of authenticity, a hallmark of the postwar culture worldwide, was much valued by the neorealists and later by post-Stalinist generations of filmmakers. It functioned oppositionally as an implicit critique of the official Stalinist culture of the previous years.[25] Thus, the official Soviet version of neorealism could accommodate it to the reigning ideology by emphasizing its use as a cognitive tool of social and political analysis for exposing structures of exploitation and class struggle. But another tendency—the seemingly unstructured attention to the everyday aspect of reality—attracted the attention of postwar Soviet filmmakers. They saw the return to realism largely in terms of a renewed sense of humanism (connected to the contemporary notion of "socialism with a human face") emphasizing the importance of the lives of "common people [*riadovoi chelovek*]," the private sphere, the ambivalence of emotional responses to historical traumas instead of their petrifaction in heroic and monumental gestures, the fragility of the human psyche and of human life itself.[26] However, because of a significant temporal delay, Soviet Cinema of the Thaw, which was so closely associated with neorealism, coincided with neorealism's decline, and the term *neoromanticism* might seem more appropriate to these Soviet films. The term was actually coined by Pier Paolo Pasolini in 1962 after Grigorii Chukhrai's *Ballada o soladate* (The Ballad of a Soldier, 1959) was shown at the 1960 Cannes Film Festival, where it competed against Fellini's *La dolce vita* (1960), Antonioni's *L'avventura* (1960), and Bergman's *Jungfrukällan* (The Virgin Spring, 1960).[27] Observers both in the Soviet Union and abroad noticed that *Ballada o soladate* differed a great deal from the cinematic masterpieces of the Stalinist era, most notably in its refusal to construct a heroic framework for the action. Chukhrai's film is about a very young common soldier who in the first scene runs in panic during a battle sequence and in subsequent scenes is shown on his short leave, at the end of which he dies an accidental, absurd death, thus foreclosing on his "balladic" potential to redeem himself as a war hero. The Soviet reception was sensitive to the "unexceptionality" and "humanity" of the main character. This "greater realism" was regularly linked to the "neorealist influences," functioning as the code word for the Thaw's humanistic ideology, which promoted a new form of socialism that would overcome the familiar disconnect between the state and the people to address the ordinary problem of the people in an age of rising affluence. From Pasolini's vantage point in post-neorealist 1960s Italy, this position was romantic. Moreover, he compared the film to the "miraculous ruins of a great ancient building" appearing among the gray modern blocs.[28] This metaphor may seem counterintuitive since what distinguished the Soviet film was precisely its simplicity compared to the other films at the festival—"a calming note in a discordant symphony," in the words of the British press, representing "normal and healthy people," according to *Le Monde*.[29] The ancient ruins to which Pasolini was referring, however, are precisely those of neorealism, which had by that time become remote and disconnected from the contemporary Italian political and cultural situation.

Conclusion

I began this account by posing the problem of sorting out the relationship between Soviet and Italian cinema of the 1930s–50s, proposing that we see it as a relationship of mutual influences. A closer look at the history of this dialogue, however, demonstrates the inadequacy of the term *influence* to capture the real transnational history of neorealism, in which different nationally specific film cultures responded to a shared history of the political, intellectual, and artistic developments of the twentieth century and swapped motifs, methods, and attitudes. In presenting this narrative, we sought implicitly to answer a question inevitably raised in relation to Italian neorealism: Is it best approached in terms of its formal innovations? In other words, is its novelty defined by its use of those radically new techniques that make it a style or even a genre that can be reappropriated by other cinemas? Is it a different way of relating the cinematic image to its ontological source, a kind of cinema typologically different from other cinemas inasmuch as it self-consciously constructs this relationship outside of aesthetics, in an openness to unprocessed social reality itself? Or is it a moment in Italian cultural history and therefore unique and specific to it? One of the key reasons for Italian neorealism's remarkable worldwide impact on cinema is precisely in its synthesis of these three questions, in its conscious tie to a sociopolitical and cultural reality by means of the most effective stylistic techniques, representing a reality that is both specific to its chronotope and yet always articulated in relationship to its outside, making it a transnational phenomenon.

Notes

1. *Sovetskii kinoslovar'*, ed. S.Iu. Iutkevich (Moscow: Sovetskaia Enciklopediia, 1970), 2:205; translations by author.

2. Liudmila Dzhulai, *Dokumental'nyi illuzion* (Moscow: Materik, 2005), 11.

3. Peter Bondanella, *Italian Cinema: From Neorealism to the Present* (New York: Continuum, 2003), 24.

4. Gian Piero Brunetta, *Cent'anni di cinema italiano*, vol. 1, *Dalle origini alla seconda guerra mondiale* (Rome: Laterza, 2004). See the recent English-language translation of Brunetta's work, *The History of Italian Cinema: A Guide to Italian Film from Its Origins to the Twenty-first Century* (Princeton: Princeton University Press, 2009). Although the English version is much condensed, chapters 2 and 3 frequently mention Soviet cinema.

5. Soviet influences on fascist cinema are discussed in Piero Garofalo, "Seeing Red: The Soviet Influence on Italian Cinema in the Thirties," in *Re-Viewing Fascism: Italian Cinema, 1922–1943*, ed. Jacqueline Reich and Piero Garofalo (Bloomington: Indiana University Press, 2002).

6. Mark Shiel, *Italian Neorealism: Rebuilding the Cinematic City* (London: Wallflower, 2006), 17.

7. For a detailed discussion of this topic, see Ruth Ben-Ghiat, *Fascist Modernities: Italy, 1922–1945* (Berkeley: University of California Press, 2001).

8. Pietro Sessa, *Fascismo e bolscevismo* (Milan: Mondadori, 1934).

9. Garofalo, "Seeing Red," 227. For a recent exploration of this topic, see Wolfgang Schivelbusch, *Three New Deals: Reflections on Roosevelt's America, Mussolini's Italy, and Hitler's Germany, 1933–1939* (London: Metropolitan, 2006), 201.

10. GARF (State Archive of the Russian Federation), f. 5283, op. 7, d. 664.

11. GARF, f. 5283, op. 7, d. 543.

12. Garofalo, "Seeing Red," 232.

13. Aleksandr Deriabin, ed., *Letopis' Rossiiskogo Kino, 1930–1945* (Moscow: Materik, 2007), 285.

14. Quoted in Ben-Ghiat, *Fascist Modernities*, 90.

15. Gian Piero Brunetta, *Storia del cinema italiano* (Rome: Riuniti, 1993), 170; translation by author.

16. Umberto Barbaro, *Neorealismo e realismo* (Rome: Riuniti, 1976), 2:500–504.

17. Umberto Barbaro, "Letteratura russa a volo d'uccello," *L'Italia letteraria* 7 (January 4, 1931): 6.

18. V. I. Pudovkin, *Il soggetto cinematografico* (Rome: Edizioni d'Italia, 1932).

19. See Gian Piero Brunetta, *Umberto Barbaro e l'idea di neorealismo, 1930–1943* (Padua: Liviana, 1969), 32.

20. Ibid., 28.

21. Cited in ibid., 44.

22. For a thorough account of Soviet cinema of the postwar period in its relationship to the politics and culture of the Thaw, see Josephine Woll, *Real Images: Soviet Cinema and the Thaw* (London: Taurus, 2000).

23. Quoted in Marek Haltof, *Polish National Cinema* (New York: Berghahn, 2002), 58.

24. On the impact of the film in the VGIK circles and in Soviet culture in general, see, for example, Armen Medvedev, *Territoria kino* (Moscow: Vagrius, 2001); Woll, *Real Images*, 47–51.

25. On the relationship between socialist realism and Cinema of the Thaw, see Alexander Prokhorov, "Inherited Discourse: Stalinist Tropes in Thaw Culture" (Ph.D. diss., University of Pittsburgh, 2002); Alexander Prokhorov, "Soviet Family Melodrama of the 1940s and 1950s: From *Wait for Me* to *The Cranes Are Flying*," in *Imitations of Life: Two Centuries of Melodrama in Russia*, ed. Louise McReynolds and Joan Neuberger (Durham, N.C.: Duke University Press, 2002), 208–31.

26. For the most thorough account of these aspects of the Soviet Thaw cinema in Russian, see Evgenii Margolit, "Dialog pokolenii," in *Kinematograf ottepeli: Kniga pervaia*, ed. Vitalii Troianovskii (Moscow: Materik, 1996), 118–31; Evgenii Margolit, "Kinematograf 'ottepeli': K portretu fenomena," *Kinovedcheskie zapiski* 61 (2002): 195–230; Evgenii Margolit, "Proshchanie s 'ukhodiashchei naturoi,'" in *Kinematograf ottepeli: Kniga vtoraia*, ed. Vitalii Troianovskii (Moscow: Materik, 2002), 211–27.

27. For a longer discussion of the reactions to *Ballada o soladate*, see, for example, Woll, *Real Images*, 96–97.

28. Quoted in N. Zorkaya, *Portrety* (Moskva: Iskusstvo, 1966), 274–75.

29. Quoted in Woll, *Real Images*, 97.

THE ROLE OF DOCUMENTARY FILM IN THE FORMATION OF THE NEOREALIST CINEMA

LUCA CAMINATI

The importance of the debates on the nature of realism in art and mass culture and on the role of nonfiction films in the formation of the fascist culture forces scholars not only to reevaluate the role of the documentary in the Italian context but also to rewrite the narrative of the genesis of neorealism as part of the evolving discourses on Italian modernity.[1] Documentary and newsreels played a key role in the process of modernization brought forward by the Italian fascist regime, both as documentations of the successes of governmental initiatives (the images of Il Duce leading the way in all fields of modernization are a staple of this period) and as integral parts of a thrust toward a more direct engagement with reality.[2] On both the formal and ideological levels, the bond between neorealism and documentary form has been considered self-evident, a point of view that is reflected in the scholarship: Even a quick survey of histories of Italian cinema immediately points to the documentary quality of neorealist filmmaking, making a tie between the two on the basis of their shared "realist" ambitions.[3] Bill Nichols's account of this relationship, Mariano Mestman notes,[4] sounds attractive because it is reminiscent of the historical order of things: The realism that characterizes the documentary dates back to the Lumière brothers, turning into an aesthetic and political motif in the hands of Dziga Vertov, Robert Flaherty, and John Grierson. In his discussion of the shared qualities of the two modes of filmmaking, Nichols enumerates the fictional representation of "time and space in experience as it is lived," the combination between "the searching eye of the documentary and the inter-subjective, identifying strategies of fiction, and the prioritisation of victims as subject-matter."[5] The notion of a predominant "social mission" separated the documentary from fiction and show business, "but thanks to the Neo-realist movement in postwar Italy, documentary realism found an ally to its ethic call in the field of fiction, as a form of responsible and often committed representation of history."[6]

While it is widely acknowledged that neorealism shows strong documentary qualities, the exact nature of this relationship (in terms of the history of reception of documentary by neorealist practitioners and mutual influence between fiction and nonfiction filmmaking) has never been fully explored.[7] Many reasons account for this historiographical lacuna. Many postwar film and cultural critics (those who first wrote the history of neorealism) certainly were fully committed to differentiating both the new cinema and themselves from any cultural product tainted by the ideology of the fascist era.[8] Rather than looking back at fascist cinema—or more generally, films produced during the fascist period (following Steven Ricci's distinction)—all intellectuals looked geographically outside of Italy and temporally to an antecedent period to systematize the cultural milieu of the new postwar cinema.[9] Moreover, film historians have associated prewar documentary with LUCE newsreels, known for their didactic and/or propagandist overtones, without taking into consideration the rich production of other types of nonfiction films.[10] On a more complex ideological/cultural level, this omission may reflect the cultural bias, established by criticism derived from Benedetto Croce's idealist aesthetics, against documentary as "nonartistic." And given neorealism's status as modernist cinema par excellence, this omission may reflect a particular—liberal—reading of neorealism as above all a form of art cinema, uncontaminated by such "low" forms as documentary. The insistence of early Italian film historians (such as Umberto Barbaro and Carlo Lizzani) on literary and painterly indigenous sources reflects precisely this anxiety regarding artistic hybridity and miscegenation.[11]

My research shows that a lively Italian cinematic culture in the 1930s and 1940s generated an interesting though small body of documentary films and a very dynamic cultural debate on the issue of realism in the arts and in cinema in particular. This essay addresses the historical connections between the rise of the documentary in the 1920s–30s, its reception in Italy and its effects on both critical discourse and filmmaking practices, and the formation of neorealism. Thus the structure of this essay is twofold. First, it is concerned with the ideological and political implications of the post-facto narrative of the genesis of neorealism as a way of re-creating a nationalist historiography of cinema. The standard narrative of the genesis of neorealism emphasizes Italian literary and foreign cinematic influences, while domestic film production, embarrassingly associated with fascism, is forgotten. This essay, then, places the standard account in its historical context. Second, this work ascertains the alternative genealogies of neorealism by reconstructing the historical connections between fiction and nonfiction filmmaking in Italy in the 1930s, the emergence of Italian documentary filmmaking and the Istituto LUCE, and the larger international history of prewar documentary cinema and its impact on the stylistic changes in fiction films of that period. This shift from documentary to fiction is particularly significant for the artistic trajectory of Italian directors working at the Centro Sperimentale and of those, like Roberto Rossellini, who started their careers as documentary filmmakers. Thus, this body of material forces us to shift the inception in Italy of a realist mode in cinema (and in the arts in general) to an earlier date and further renegotiate the nexus of fiction/nonfiction as pertinent exclusively to the neorealist movement.

In addition to the cinematic practices, I address the critical discussions of realism and documentary in Italian film journals. While the debate surrounding documentary disappears in the flowering of post-1945 neorealism (for political and ideological reasons that I discuss later), this conversation was indeed very animated from circa 1930 until the end of the war. Most writers for *Cinema* (culturally gravitating around the Istituto LUCE under the directorship of Vittorio Mussolini, Il Duce's son) and *Bianco e nero* (published by the Centro Sperimentale beginning in January 1937), the two most influential film journals of the time, discuss the impact on Italian cinema of documentary filmmakers John Grierson, Alberto Cavalcanti, and Joris Ivens; American filmmaker Robert Flaherty; and American photographer Walker Evans, highlighting the importance of this genre for the development of contemporary cinema. Among various discussions on the documentary as a genre, what stands out most is the debate on *documentario narrativo* (narrative documentary, as Cavalcanti defines this type of film that blends fiction and nonfiction.)[12] I focus on this hybrid genre of *documentario narrativo* as a cultural battlefield between these two modes of filmmaking and as a progenitor to neorealism. Moreover, the highly sophisticated critical discussions this genre engendered can greatly contribute to the ever-evolving history of critical discourse on documentary cinema and on the complex relationship between fiction and documentary modes.[13] But before delving into the history of documentary practice and its reception in Italy, we must confront its absence from most of the historiographies of neorealism and the historical context for this important omission.

The Neorealist Narrative Redux

There are two major strands in the narratives of the formation of neorealism. The first is the original foundational narrative that emphasizes the movement's Italian roots—in particular, its literary antecedents. This story originated in the Italian critical discourse of the late 1930s and was further strengthened by national sentiment that firmly associated neorealism with the nation's new (antifascist) identity. Because neorealism was seen as a liberal embodiment of the new "liberated" Italy in need of overcoming its tainted past, it is hardly surprising that much of the discussion of the origins of neorealism traced them back to the prefascist literary sources as a way to reconstruct a foundational national narrative that bypassed the recent cultural heritage. In this sense, André Bazin's unapologetic critical enthusiasm played well into this "springtime in Italy" narrative. According to the French critic, "Some components of the new Italian school existed before the Liberation," but "in Italy Liberation did not signify a return to the old and recent freedom; it meant political revolution, Allied occupation, economic and social upheaval."[14] Traces of this conception of neorealism persisted in critical literature as late as the 1970s and 1980s—for example, in Peter Bondanella's widely popular textbook on Italian cinema.[15]

The more recent work on neorealism seems to give greater weight to international sources (French realism, the American novel, and so forth) in an attempt to counter the perception of Italian cultural exceptionalism bringing both its fascist and postwar periods in closer contact to the contemporary (largely European) movements. For example, in Gian Piero Brunetta's authoritative *Storia del cinema italiano*, a brief mention of the European avant-garde (and in particular the *neue Sachlichkeit*) as a model artistic context for the emergence of neorealism stands out as one of the first major attempts to look outside of the culture of the peninsula.[16] But this is a fairly recent development in the foundational narrative of neorealism. In the 1930s and 1940s, when the discourse of neorealism was being formed, its critical discussions were usually shaped by a clearly nationalist framework and thus strongly emphasized Italian national literary and cultural sources.[17] This return to realism in cinema is solidly linked to the autarchic Giovanni Verga and the Italian *verismo* tradition as best exemplified by Mario Alicata and Giuseppe De Santis's often-quoted 1941 articles, "Verità e poesia: Verga e il cinema italiano" and "Ancora di Verga e del cinema italiano."[18] What sutures together these two schools of interpretation is a willful attempt to disconnect the neorealists from the institutions in which they operated, inasmuch as these institutions were fascist creations. Thus, the origin is sought either in a moment of institutional rupture (the war) or in the influence of institutional moments outside Italian cinema (the literature and film cultures of other countries). Both schools, then, swerve around the institutional context of Italian cinema under the fascists. Political and ideological reasons obviously underlie this swerve, as does the assumption that propaganda is inherently antiaesthetic and somewhat nonartistic (very much in the Crocean ideological mode). The Alicata/De Santis articles have been instrumental in triggering a narrative that connected neorealism to southern realism, pointing to that mostly painterly and literary tradition of the Italian *meridione* and the towering figure of Verga.

Why does the Sicilian-born writer Giovanni Verga sit at the top of Italian realist art? Indeed, it is not a surprise to find him in the title of De Santis's and Alicata's call to arms and subsequently anthologized and quickly incorporated as the patron saint of the *école italienne*.[19] Alicata and De Santis followed in the footsteps of a new interest in Verga, triggered by a new 1941 edition of Luigi Russo's *Giovanni Verga* (1919).[20] In "Verga e noi" ("Verga and Us," 1929), even Luigi Pirandello notes how the Sicilian writer had already been singled out as a Janus-like figure that different camps could use to support their visions.[21] Croce's ambiguous role in fascist Italian culture as a cornerstone for all intellectual debate, a liberal asserting "individuality" and autonomy of the artwork, foundational for Giovanni Gentile's educational programs (and therefore accepted by the fascist culture at large), and target of materialist philosophers, is transposed and applied to Verga's realist art. As Verga becomes a key protagonist in Croce's liberal/idealist philosophy, realism becomes a key concept for Croce's opponents, both positivists and materialists, such as Barbaro and Alicata, who reclaim Verga as a precursor in their genealogy of realist art in Italy.[22] The southern realist vein of Italian art singled out by Barbaro became a master narrative that was sure to please Crocean idealists (including the heretical Russo); materialist philologists such as Sapegno and his protégé, Alicata; and the more progressive Barbaro, who regularly praised Verga in *L'Italia letteraria*. This "imaginary" Verga becomes the flag that all parties can follow without losing face: it is national/popular, it is realist, and Croce liked it! Moreover, by incorporating Verga and his southern characters into a national narrative, the fascist regime sought to complete the process of full integration of the South of Italy into the Italian polity as an integral part of the new fascist nation, thus eliminating the North-South divide that had haunted the nation from its inception.[23]

What would become a seminal first attempt to theorize more broadly the origins of neorealism and to escape the narrow nationalistic narrative did not take place until 1950. In *Bianco e nero* (Nuova Serie), Franco Venturini attempts a comprehensive systematization of the elements in the cultural milieu that originated the neorealist movement. Venturini singles out six key factors: the regional traditions, calligraphisms, the influence of French realism, Mario Camerini and Alessandro Blasetti, Luchino Visconti, and the documentary.[24] Venturini was the first Italian critic to recognize the neglect of the institutional context of much of the debate up to this point, denouncing the idea that the realist tendency in Italian cinema arose perforce from a pictorial and literary

tradition that was a way of domesticating neorealism by "grafting it to the indigenous tradition of Giotto, Dante, Verga, Caravaggio and Masaccio in hopes
of obtaining the quintessence of the genius of the race so as to inject it directly
in the vein of Italian cinema."[25] Venturini was also one of the only critics to
deal directly with the legacy of documentary cinema. His section on documentary focuses in particular on the war documentary and the experiments
of Francesco De Robertis and Rossellini's *Uomini sul fondo* (SOS Submarine,
1941), the rescue story of sailors trapped in a submarine, as a hybrid fiction/
nonfiction experiment. For Venturini, the combination of documentary and
fiction, the lack of professional actors, and the abandonment of fascist rhetoric
characterize this new Italian cinema, which finds its highest manifestation in
neorealism. He further claims that while *Ossessione* (1943) was an end point of
an earlier era of Italian cinema (in terms of a coalescence of different styles of
fiction cinema—mainly French realism and classic Hollywood), *Uomini sul
fondo* is a "new event,"[26] thus shifting the status of proto-neorealist film away
from Visconti's *Ossessione* and toward the ideologically more problematic film
by De Robertis. Venturini's article went largely unnoticed at the time, however, and had little effect on the evolving narrative of origins. In fact, Venturini's
claims have not been fully explored until fairly recently, when the question of
the relationship between neorealism and prewar Italian cinema and culture
has begun to be thoroughly reevaluated in both Italian and Anglo-American
scholarship.[27]

Whether or not we should follow Venturini in finding Visconti's *Ossessione*
more an end point than the beginning of a "realist" movement in the arts,
many critics have already addressed the inconsistencies of an absolute rebirth
of Italian cinema ex novo in 1945 and incorporated it into a larger vein of realism.[28] Likewise, many documentary filmmakers and scholars of the fascist era
were involved in a conversation centered on the issue of nonfiction film. The
role of nonfiction film during the late fascist period is signaled by the translation in the first issue of *Bianco e nero* of an ample selection from Paul Rotha's
1936 book *Movie Parade*. In addition, the Centro's interest in the *documentario
narrativo*, as Cavalcanti defines these films à la Flaherty, seems to be an inten-
tionally neglected missing link in the history of neorealism.

This connection between cinema *dal vero* and neorealism can now be
tracked backward. When the term *neorealism* was first applied in Italy—previous to its "late" inclusion in film magazines around 1948—the term was used
in the context of a reference to the documentary. In her genealogy of the word
neorealism, Stefania Parigi states that from the mid-1930s onward, Italians applied the term to various aesthetic experiences—for example, to Grierson's
British Post Office documentary film unit.[29] Alberto Cavalcanti suggested that

Grierson use the same word for his documentary work.[30] The fact that neorealism is an elastic term from the 1930s thus signifies a general philosophical and societal trend of return to a more stringent engagement with reality. The historic neorealism (the actual cinematic movement) is a culmination of a long process of rapprochement between art and reality in the Italian and European *weltanschauung*.

The *Documentario Narrativo*

Even a cursory look at the documentaries produced during the second decade of the fascist regime (roughly 1933–43), excepting the propagandist LUCE newsreels, shows that this new foreign genre presented exciting possibilities to Italian filmmakers. In magazines and journals of the time, the great popularity of John Grierson's social investigations (*The Drifters*, 1939), Flaherty's narrative documentaries (*Nanook of the North*, 1922; *Moana*, 1926; and *Man of Aran*, 1934), and similar docufiction experiments, such as F. W. Murnau's *Tabu* (1931), helped to set off a wave of Italian filmmakers working on the same lines, creating the *documentario narrativo*, a hybrid fiction à la Nanook.

The real shift in interest toward new documentary forms must be attributed to the cosmopolitan figure of Alberto Cavalcanti, a Brazilian-born, French-educated intellectual of Italian origin who moved to Paris in the late 1920s and started a career in cinema as a set decorator. His first feature film is an experimental documentary, *Rien que les heures* (Nothing but the Hours, 1930), a sort of city symphony film depicting twenty-four hours in the life of members of the Parisian lumpenproletariat. Cavalcanti joined Grierson's Empire Marketing Board in 1934, subsequently moving on to the General Post Office (GPO) Film Unit, where he became one of the driving forces behind the British documentary movement and directly worked on such GPO masterpieces as *Coalface* (1935). Cavalcanti also taught at the Centro Sperimentale in Rome and contributed regularly to *Bianco e nero*. One 1938 article, "Documentari di propaganda," sets up a genealogy for the *documentario narrativo* (not to be confused, in Cavalcanti's taxonomy, with the *documentario puro* of Grierson).[31] The *documentario narrativo*, sometimes dubbed the *documentario poetico* (poetic documentary), had its precursors in Flaherty's *Nanook* and *Moana*, Ernest Schoedsack and Merian C. Cooper's *Grass: A Battle for Life* (1925) and *Chang: A Drama of the Wilderness* (1927), and Leon Poirier's *La croisière noire* (The Black Journey, 1927). A short unsigned article in *Bianco e nero* attests to Cavalcanti's role as an intermediary between London and Rome and as an active participant in the life of the Centro:

We saw a private screening of some documentaries produced in Great Britain by Alberto Cavalcanti. Short films made on the cheap, but realized by people with great enthusiasm and with a great sense of cinema. What interested us the most was the way in which sound was used: noises, words, and music. Instead, in our Italian documentaries, which are rarely shown in our theaters, there is not much to be impressed by because of the use of sound. Almost always it consists simply of a generic and banal music which comments on one image after the other. And by the way, individuals whose names are not shown on the film title cards produce the great majority of Italian documentaries.[32]

Cavalcanti's role as "modernizer" of the Italian documentary scene has not yet been fully appreciated. He played a key role at the Centro Sperimentale until 1942, when he had to leave Italy because his citizenship was deemed suspicious.[33] The issue of sound raised by the editors of *Bianco e nero* points in the direction of a "creative use of sound"—in particular, toward the handling of diegetic and nondiegetic elements. Grierson's emphasis on "noises" and "words" impressed the Italian directors, probably for their realism. In *The British Documentary Film Movement, 1926–1946*, Paul Swann singles out a key issue in the Cavalcanti-Grierson relationship. When Grierson resigned from the GPO in June 1937, Cavalcanti stayed on, leading "the GPO Film Unit away from theoretical discussions about public education and 'art' and towards films that relied heavily upon the narrative techniques of the commercial film industry. . . . The story-documentary made its first appearance while Grierson was still at the Post Office."[34] In the same new populist tone, Harry Watt produced *The Saving of Bill Blewitt* (1936), which had scripted dialogue, some studio sets, and most significantly was built around a wholly fictional story. However, it also was made largely on location and employed nonprofessional actors, who were real people acting out events that might happen to them during their day-to-day lives. As Swann points out, this film "in some respects anticipated the production techniques and the aesthetic of Italian neorealism." *Bill Blewitt* was indeed a rejection of the earlier Griersonian tradition of didacticism in favor of a much more humanistic approach that was less intimidating to film subjects and audiences alike.[35] "The story-documentary," Swann writes, "in contrast to this other tradition, relied primarily upon conventional feature film continuity editing. In this type of film the burden of the film was carried within the narrative and the performances of the actors. Watt had learned how to treat people in films from his apprenticeship under Robert Flaherty."[36] The direction in which Cavalcanti was taking the GPO was also very evident in his insistence on having nonprofessional actors act a script.[37]

The influential figure of Cavalcanti in the development of the *documentario narrativo* must have found an eager audience among the Centro's students, teachers, and hangers-on.[38] More generally, Italian filmmakers and film critics shared the worldwide interest in the new genre of documentary, as proven by *Bianco e nero's* publication of Paul Rotha's interventions and of the entire translation of Raymond J. Spottiswoode's *A Grammar of Film* in 1938.[39]

Cavalcanti found at the Centro a fertile ground, even though the Italian way to *documentario narrativo* did not achieve the results of other countries. This said, however, it was certainly conceived as a possible venue of expression and explored by some directors in the early 1930s. One of the first experiments with mixing reality and fiction predating Cavalcanti's arrival at the Centro could be *Palio* (1932), directed by Alessandro Blasetti with Anchise Brizzi as director of photography. The film is described as a "a mix of documentary and narration. . . . [N]ot prone to quick cuts and Russian-style montage, [Blasetti] often uses tracking shots and pan shots since he is interested in giving narrative consistency and fluidity to his films."[40] Another such experiment, *Camicia nera* (Black Shirt, 1933, produced by LUCE and directed by Giovacchino Forzano), was shot partially in the Maremma with nonprofessional actors. It impressed the contemporary reviewers, including the one who wrote in the March 1933 issue of *Scenario* that the film was

> anti-literary and anti-intellectual, careless of particulars, scornful of technical bravura, sworn enemy of decorativeness and calligraphy, totally devoted to description . . . fundamentally unaware of photography and lighting effects, the film has a naturalist, positive character, all substance and no form. What one can say, in a word, is an ingenious thing. . . . The dominant light of the film is . . . obscurity. All the shots are immersed in shadow, in dark and wide gray areas, so that there is, then, an anti-elegant but genuine tone of spontaneity. The photography is verist [*verista*], without excessive softness, little worked and absolutely lacking final polish.[41]

Other documentaries of the time were picking up on different European traditions, such as the city symphony films or the humanistic study of a particular event or location.[42] Examples include *Acciaio* (Steel, 1933), directed by Walter Ruttmann and loosely based on a script by Pirandello; Francesco Pasinetti's *Il canale degli angeli* (The Canal of the Angels, 1934); Francesco Di Cocco's *Il ventre della città* (The Belly of the City, 1933); and Umberto Barbaro's *Cantieri dell'Adriatico* (The Shipyards of the Adriatic, 1933). But according to Barbaro, writing in 1936, documentary film was spearheaded by the production house Cines under the direction of Ludovico Toeplitz del Ry and Emilio Cecchi[43] and culminated with the great critical reception of Giacomo Pozzi-Bellini's *Il pianto delle zitelle* (The Crying of the Spinsters, 1939).[44] This documentary, shot in the Simbruini Mountains in Lazio, describes the pilgrimage to honor the Vallepietra icon by hundreds of anonymous people from Lazio, Abruzzo, and Campania. Bertozzi notices the interesting use of sound, a blend of narrating voice-over and diegetic noises.[45] Although the film won a prize at Venice, it was quickly censored by the regime.

Italian filmmakers' particular interest in narrative and poetic documentary is proven by Jacopo Comin's short essay in *Bianco e nero*, "I volti della realtà" (Faces of Reality).[46] This piece is symptomatic of the contemporary debate in Italian film circles operating under the pressure of the political establishment. While this article might seem to be a simple acknowledgment of the medium's intrinsic limitations, it operates on two levels: it establishes the yardstick of the value of documentary cinema in its inability to "objectively represent reality" and therefore subtracts from the pressure of being used as mere propaganda; and it elevates documentary to that celestial place where the art of the Crocean tradition resides. "If the reality of things . . . didn't have but one face, a single aspect and almost a single surface, we might be ready to concede that cinema is not an art. . . . In documentary, as in every art, there is the intervention of a strictly subjective element, a interpretative element of reality, hence an artistic element: the choice of point of view which acquires function and character of a creative act . . . and the choice of subject."[47]

Comin lists Barbaro's *Cantieri dell'Adriatico*, Marco Elter's *Miniere di Cogne* (The Mines of Cogne, 1934), Matarazzo's *Littoria* (1933) and *Sabaudia*, and Di Cocco's *Il ventre della città* as examples of this "artistic" documentary[48] where the artistry is defined by both form and content: the choice of point of view of the director of the film, and the topic chosen to be filmed. In "Appunti sul cinema d'avanguardia," Comin mentions Flaherty, Joris Ivens, and in Italy, Barbaro, Matarazzo, Di Cocco, and *Paestum* (1932) by Luciani as documentaries that push the boundary of mere documentation.[49]

The general interest in realism and how much the *Bianco e nero* crowd pushed for it is summed up in an article by Giuseppe Prezzolini, "L'uomo comune, personaggio del cinema e delle radio" (The Common Man, Character in Cinema and the Radio), that originally appeared in *La gazzetta del popolo* and was reprinted in *Bianco e nero*: "The latest character of American films is the man in the crowd, or, as they say over there, the average American."[50] The influence of American culture—in particular, in the realist vein of American writers on Italian culture—is well known.[51] What is of interest here is how Italian critics picked up certain aspects of American cinema. The general interest in the "common man" is also a major point of the fascist propaganda in its double attempt to modernize and fascistize the country. In an article, "Il cinema per i rurali" (Cinema for the Peasants), that appeared in *Il lavoro fascista* and was later reprinted in *Bianco e nero*, Vittorio Cardinali claims that the Confederazione Fascista dei Lavoratori dell'Agricoltura (the Fascist Confederation of Agricultural Workers) is preparing to shoot films with real peasants—one in the rice fields, the second in Puglia—to promote both the *battaglia demografica* (the demographic battle) and *battaglia per il grano* (the corn battle).[52]

The Gioventù Italiana del Littorio was also responsible for some documentaries beyond the mere celebration of the Fascist Youth. In 1937, Ivo Perilli made *Ragazzo* (The Boy), which follows the descent of a Neapolitan street urchin into the criminal underworld. The film, destroyed by the Nazis in late 1943, was personally censored by Il Duce himself, and the only viewers were the students of the Centro Sperimentale.[53]

The Way of Rossellini

The most critically successful *documentario narrativo* is De Robertis's *Uomini sul fondo*. Produced by the Marina Militare Italiana (the Italian navy), it uses only nonprofessional actors to tell the story of the rescue of a military submarine off the coast of La Spezia. While the film is meant to enable the navy to impress the Italian audience with cutting-edge technological equipment, it turns very quickly into a gripping story of humanistic values. Roberto Rossellini (with Ivo Perilli, subsequently in the writing teams of both Giuseppe De Santis's *Riso amaro* [Bitter Rice, 1949], and Rossellini's *Europa '51* [1952]), who visited the set,[54] might be one of the reasons behind the striking resemblances of *Uomini sul fondo* to the postwar realist films. The combination of highly dramatic moments (Will the ships find the submarine in the fog?) alternating with long takes that painstakingly show the suffering of the sailors because of lack of oxygen and undersea pressure in the sunken submarine. The sailors are both anonymous (all of them wear the same clothes and the same expression) and identified by some specific qualities: their accents, pictures of their mothers, food hidden in their pockets. The narrative structure, while less episodic or "elliptical" (to use Bazin's terminology in "An Aesthetic of Reality")[55] than in *Roma, città aperta* (Rome, Open City, 1945) or *Ladri di biciclette* (Bicycle Thieves, 1948), certainly lends itself to detours that have no primary narrative motivation. While the film has a clear teleology (Will the ships rescue our heroes?), the many asides enrich the humanity of the story while augmenting the film's documentary value. One such episode is the scene in which the mother of one of the sailors trapped in the submarine has a conversation with an official of the Italian navy. She claims that her sixth sense is telling her that her son is dead and that the navy therefore must be hiding information from her. To prove her wrong, the high-ranking official does not hesitate to create a radio connection with the submarine, allowing mother and son to have a brief but very emotional conversation. This scene exemplifies the modus operandi of De Robertis and Rossellini. On the one hand, it shows off the great technological advances of the Italian navy and its absolute commitment to its sailors in the most difficult circumstances; on the other hand, it inserts a melodramatic and almost comedic tone (the actual conversation of mother and son). Similarly, in *Rome, Open City*, we see Don Pietro playing both a comedic and a dramatic role (as in the search for rebels in Pina's building ending with Don Pietro banging a frying pan on an old man's head). As Venturini noted in 1950, *Uomini sul fondo* disappeared from the official history of neorealism, replaced by more illustrious literary predecessors.

While the long *cammino della critica verso il neorealismo* (march of criticism toward neorealism), as Brunetta titles his chapter devoted to the cultural milieu that produced the Italian return to reality, was indeed rich with national and international stimuli, I seek to relocate documentary cinema on the map of Italian cinema. Understanding both theory and praxis of nonfiction filmmaking in Italy in the late 1930s is indeed vital to understanding the postwar phenomena of neorealism's mixed origins. Any history of Italian cinema would certainly lack a very important piece of the puzzle without the lively Italian documentary scene of the late 1930s.

Notes

1. This essay is very much in debt to Ruth Ben-Ghiat's seminal *Fascist Modernities* (Berkeley: University of California Press, 2001), which reassesses the influence of European "realist" trends on Italian modernism.

2. As Francesco Casetti has recently pointed out, cinema represents the true eye of the twentieth century not simply as a representational device but more importantly in the way in which it influenced the outlook of the arts on reality. On the relationship between cinema and modernity, out of a possible very long bibliography, I suggest Francesco Casetti, *Eye of the Century: Film, Experience, Modernity* (New York: Columbia University Press, 2008); Tom Gunning, "The Cinema of Attraction: Early Film, Its Spectator, and the Avant-Garde," *Wide Angle* 8.3–4 (1986): 63–70; Miriam Hansen, "America, Paris, the

Alps: Kracauer (and Benjamin) on Cinema and Modernity," in *Cinema and the Invention of Modern Life*, ed. Leo Charney and Vanessa R. Schwartz (Berkeley: University of California Press, 1995), 362–402.

3. See, for example, Gian Piero Brunetta, *Storia del cinema italiano* (Rome: Riuniti, 1993); Gianni Rondolino, *Storia del cinema italiano* (Turin: UTET, 1996); Millicent Marcus, *Italian Film in the Light of Neorealism* (Princeton: Princeton University Press, 1987).

4. See Mariano Mestman, "The World of Labor and Social Conflict: From Italian Neorealism to New Latin American Cinema," paper presented at "*Neorealismo*: A Workshop on Cinema, History, and National Culture," University of Maryland, College Park, October 4–5, 2007. See also Mestman, this volume.

5. Bill Nichols, *Introduction to Documentary* (Bloomington: Indiana University Press, 2001), 92.

6. Ibid.

7. As far as I know, the only essay that tangentially touches on this topic is Ivelise Perniola, "Documentari fuori regime," in *Storia del cinema italiano*, ed. Orio Caldiron (Venice: Marsilio, 2006), 5:372–80.

8. See Ennio Di Nolfo, "Intimations of Neorealism in the Fascist *Ventennio*," in *Re-Viewing Fascism: Italian Cinema, 1922–1943*, ed. Jacqueline Reich and Piero Garofalo (Bloomington: Indiana University Press, 2002), 83.

9. See Steven Ricci, *Cinema and Fascism: Italian Film and Society, 1922–1943* (Berkeley: University of California Press, 2008), 20. Historians have written extensively on the many elements of political and ideological continuity between the pre- and postwar period. Probably the most thorough and insightful study remains Claudio Pavone, *Una guerra civile: Saggio storico sulla moralità nella resistenza* (Turin: Bollati Boringhieri, 1991). As far as cinema studies, Alan O'Leary brilliantly summarizes the issues at stake: "The assertion of a definitive split between the cinema of the fascist period and that which followed the war has regularly been challenged since the 1970s. The perception of a strict division tends, however, to reassert itself. It might be suggested that the short span allotted to SCI vii (1945–1948) [*Storia del cinema italiano*, coordinated by Lino Micciché] inevitably sunders the neorealist moment from that which preceded it. More generally, many tenaciously maintain an ideological stake in insisting that the cinema of the nascent democracy and republic is ethically and aesthetically distinct from that produced by or under fascism. Conversely, the commitment to neorealism as the ethical or aesthetic core of Italian cinema has the paradoxical effect of asserting that anything of quality, including that which comes before, centrifugally derives from it" ("After Brunetta: Italian Cinema Studies in Italy, 2000 to 2007," *Italian Studies* 63. [2008]: 284). This continuity is very cogently reasserted by the thorough study on Italian spectatorship by Mariagrazia Fanchi and Elena Mosconi, who assert the existence of a "spectatorial continuum" in terms of visual experience between the pre- and postwar audiences (*Spettatori: Forme di consumo e pubblici del cinema in Italia, 1930–1960* [Rome: Biblioteca di *Bianco e nero*, 2002], 9). Motivated by a similar intent "to

circumvent certain historical prejudices" (O'Leary, "After Brunetta," 305) is the fifteen-volume *Storia del cinema italiano* (conceived by the late Lino Miccichè for the Centro Sperimentale and currently being published by Marsilio). Each volume tackles roughly a five-year period.

10. On LUCE and fascist propaganda, see Mino Argentieri, *L'occhio del regime* (Rome: Bulzoni, 2003).

11. See Umberto Barbaro, "Piccola storia del film documentario in Italia," in *Neorealismo e realismo* (Rome: Riuniti, 1976), 471–76; Carlo Lizzani, *Storia del cinema italiano* (Florence: Parenti, 1961).

12. "Documentari di propaganda," *Bianco e nero*, 10.2 (October 1938): 3–7.

13. On the nexus between fiction and nonfiction, see the current debates in Gary Rhodes and John Parris Springer, eds., *Docufictions: Essays on the Intersection of Documentary and Fictional Filmmaking* (London: McFarland, 2006); Alexandra Juhasz and Jesse Lerner, eds., *F Is for Phony: Fake Documentary and Truth's Undoing* (Minneapolis: University of Minnesota Press, 2006).

14. André Bazin, *What Is Cinema?*, trans. Hugh Gray (Berkeley: University of California Press, 1971), 2:17.

15. Peter Bondanella, *Italian Cinema: From Neorealism to the Present* (New York: Continuum, 1997).

16. Gian Piero Brunetta, "Il cammino della critica verso il Neorealismo," in *Storia del cinema italiano, 1895–1945* (Rome: Riuniti, 1979), 441.

17. According to the Regio Decreto Legge no. 1121, an "Italian film" has the following characteristics: it is shot on Italian soil, by an Italian crew, and, if of foreign source, it is adapted by an Italian. See Reich and Garofalo, eds., *Re-Viewing Fascism*, 8.

18. Mario Alicata and Giuseppe De Santis, "Verità e poesia: Verga e il cinema italiano," *Cinema* 127 (October 10, 1941), 216–17; Mario Alicata and Giuseppe De Santis, "Ancora di Verga e del cinema italiano," *Cinema* 130 (November 10, 1941), 50–53.

19. See David Overbey, ed., *Springtime in Italy: A Reader of Neo-Realism* (London: Talisman, 1978).

20. Luigi Russo, *Giovanni Verga* (1919; Bari: Laterza, 1941). Russo (1892–1961), a Sicilian-born critic, was a heretical Crocean who blended historicism and idealism. Throughout his career, he kept a very intense intellectual relationship with Benedetto Croce.

21. Luigi Pirandello, "Verga e noi," in *Studi verghiani* (Palermo: Edizioni del Sud, 1929), no. 1, reprinted in Lina Perroni, *Studi critici su Giovanni Verga* (Rome: Edizioni Bibliotheca, 1934).

22. Mario Alicata, assistant to Natalino Sapegno, chair of Italian literature at the University La Sapienza in Rome beginning in 1940, remembered that for Sapegno, "Verga in 1945 looks like the prodigal son, and his work a 'home coming'" (Orio Caldiron, ed., *Il lungo viaggio del cinema italiano: Antologia di "Cinema," 1936–1943* [Padua: Marsilio, 1965], lxv; translation by author).

23. Giorgio Amendola, *Fascismo e Mezzogiorno* (Rome: Riuniti, 1973).

24. Franco Venturini, "Origini del Neorealismo," *Bianco e nero* 11.2 (February 1950): 31–32.

25. Ibid., 34.

26. Ibid., 42.

27. See Reich and Garofalo, *Re-Viewing Fascism*, a collection that fully exemplifies this trend.

28. Carlo Celli, for example, has aptly investigated what he defines as the "Camerini–De Sica continuity" in terms of both style and content: "Camerini's films, like De Sica's efforts in the neorealist style, were part of a current of realism or *verismo* that appeared as a reaction to the D'Annunzian rhetoric that dominated Italian culture early in the century and was associated with centuries-old mimetic traditions in Italian artistic expression" (Carlo Celli, "The Legacy of Mario Camerini in Vittorio De Sica's *Bicycle Thieves* [1948]," *Cinema Journal* 40.4 [Summer 2001]: 4).

29. Stefania Parigi, "Le carte d'identità del neorealismo," in *Nuovo Cinema (1965–2005): Scritti in onore di Lino Micciché*, ed. Bruno Torri (Venice: Marsilio, 2005), 80–102.

30. "Was Cavalcanti in some way undermining Grierson's work? What exactly was the difference of opinion between them? 'The only fundamental difference was that I maintained that *documentary* was a silly denomination,' says Cavalcanti. . . . 'I had a very serious conversation in the early, rosy days with Grierson about this label *documentary* because I insisted that it should be called, funnily enough (it's only coincidence, but it made a fortune in Italy), *Neorealism*. The Grierson argument—and I remember it exceedingly well—was just to laugh and say, "You are really a very innocent character. I have to deal with the Government, and the word documentary impresses them as something serious"'" (Elizabeth Sussex, "Cavalcanti in England," *Sight and Sound*, August 1975, reprinted in *The Documentary Film Movement: An Anthology*, ed. Ian Aitken [Edinburgh: Edinburgh University Press, 1998], 188).

31. "Documentari di propaganda," *Bianco e nero* 10.2 (October 1938): 3–7.

32. *Bianco e nero* 7.2 (February 1940): 67.

33. Ian Aitken, *Alberto Cavalcanti: Realism, Surrealism, and National Cinema* (Trowbridge: Flick, 2000), 82.

34. Paul Swann, *The British Documentary Film Movement, 1926–1946* (Cambridge: Cambridge University Press, 1989), 85–86.

35. Ibid., 86.

36. Ibid., 88.

37. "Cavalcanti once cabled David MacDonald, a commercial director who had been brought in to direct *Men of the Lightship* (1940), to tell him to reshoot all the 'totally unconvincing' footage where he had used professional actors, while the footage he had shot with real people was 'splendid'" (ibid., 163).

38. The list of students enrolled or affiliated with the Centro Sperimentale in 1940 is quite interesting: Michelangelo Antonioni, Giuseppe De Santis, Stefano Vanzina (Steno), Gabriel Garcia Marquez, Pasqualino De Santis, Gianni Di Venanzo, Pietro Fermi, Dino De Laurentiis, Pietro Ingrao, and Francesco Pasinetti. Among the teachers were Umberto Barbaro, Alessandro Blasetti, and Pietro Sharoff.

39. The chapter "Origin of the Documentary Movement in the Class Struggle" is translated into Italian omitting the reference to class struggle, and throughout the article, *USSR* is translated as "Russia."

40. Barbaro, "Piccola storia," 474; translation by author.

41. Cited in Elaine Mancini, *Struggles of the Italian Film Industry during Fascism, 1930–1935* (Ann Arbor, Mich.: UMI Research Press, 1981), 134.

42. Marco Bertozzi discusses with a certain depth these documentaries in a chapter, "Un regime in luce," in his *Storia del documentario italiano* (Venice: Marsilio, 2008), 59–95.

43. Barbaro, "Piccola storia," 471–76.

44. Emilio Cecchi wrote the film's text. The director of photography was LUCE's Angelo Jannarelli, and the music was by Luigi Colcicchi. It won a medal at the Venice Film Festival in 1939. See Mancini, *Struggles*, 154.

45. Bertozzi, *Storia*, 81.

46. Jacopo Comin, "I volti della realtà," *Bianco e nero* 2.8 (1938): 123–24.

47. Ibid., 123.

48. The article erroneously attributes the film by Di Cocco to Luciani.

49. Jacopo Comin, "Appunti sul cinema d'avanguardia," *Bianco e nero* 1.6 (1937):6.

50. Giuseppe Prezzolini, "L'uomo comune personaggio del cinema e della radio," *Bianco e nero* 1.1 (1937): 115; translation by author.

51. Gian Piero Brunetta, *Il cinema italiano di regime* (Bari: Laterza, 2009), 186–87.

52. *Bianco e nero* 2.1 (1937): 119–21.

53. The same article mentions *Viviamo* by Francolini and *Chiostri e cortili* by Ubaldo Magnaghi.

54. See Tag Gallagher, *The Adventures of Roberto Rossellini* (New York: Da Capo, 1998), 67.

55. Bazin, *What Is Cinema?* 2:35.

PART 2

"THE EXALTED SPIRIT OF THE ACTUAL"

James Agee, Critic and Filmmaker, and the
U.S. Response to Neorealism

ROBERT SKLAR

Credit the U.S. film industry with early and powerful recognition of post–World War II Italian cinema. The Hollywood Motion Picture Academy in 1947 awarded its first-ever special Oscar for a non-English-language film to *Sciuscià* (Shoeshine, 1946), stating that "the high quality of this Italian-made motion picture, brought to eloquent life in a country scarred by war, is proof to the world that the creative spirit can triumph over adversity." Two years later the Academy's board gave another Oscar to *Ladri di biciclette* (Bicycle Thieves, 1948), "the most outstanding foreign language film released in the United States during 1949" (a prelude to the establishment in 1956 of an annual foreign-language film award). More remarkably, Academy members—most of whom were capable of reading only the films' English-language subtitles—gave Oscar nominations to the screenplays of these two films as well as to Rossellini's *Paisà*. *Bicycle Thieves* also became a cause célèbre in the struggle over Hollywood censorship, with several major theater circuits releasing an uncut version in defiance of the movie industry's production code.[1]

In the 1950s, as Italian cinema of the immediate postwar years came to be regarded as a distinct historical movement, U.S. film culture adopted the name that Europeans applied to those Italian films: neorealism. It was becoming clear that neorealism's legacy to world cinema had outlived its brief Italian reign. As a mode of film production and perhaps as a model for representing contemporary social life, neorealism inspired filmmakers in Latin America, Asia, and elsewhere, offering a template for filmmaking practices that could succeed apart from or in opposition to U.S. global market dominance and Hollywood's industrial style. Even in the United States, filmmakers working outside the dominant commercial paradigms—most notably the black independent film movement of the 1970s, with works such as Charles Burnett's *Killer of Sheep* (1976)—took heart from neorealism's example. Filmmakers as disparate as Stan Brakhage and Robert Frank have acknowledged neorealism among their influences.[2]

More recently, commentators have begun retrospectively to assert that neorealism made an immediate impact on postwar mainstream U.S. moviemaking as well. In his "official" history of the Oscars, for example, Robert Osborne writes, "The gritty, realistic look of [*Shoeshine*], coming at it did on the heels of Rossellini's *Open City* and other post-war European pictures, was to have a major effect on altering the glossy, glamorized look of Hollywood movies in the next decade." Scholars search the film noir canon for resemblances to the harsh, barren cityscapes of neorealist films. Perhaps most frequently cited as the apotheosis of neorealism's impact on postwar Hollywood cinema is the multiple Academy Award–winning 1954 film *On the Waterfront*. Director Elia Kazan "was heavily influenced by Italian Neorealism," states the *Encyclopedia Britannica*, one of many similar accounts, "and became an advocate of location shooting because of its greater realism."[3]

These expansive claims for neorealism's importance to postwar Hollywood rank among the mysteries of historiographic fashion. No doubt systematic research may yet produce intriguing and perhaps significant nodes of specific affinities and practical interactions. For the present, however, most such assertions remain unexamined, undocumented, and generally improbable. Kazan seems to have made only one published remark concerning neorealism, referring to his casting of a nonactor in the lead role for his 1964 film, *America America*. In commenting on *On the Waterfront*, he emphasized Marlon Brando's performance and Budd Schulberg's screenplay—not surprisingly, for a director whose aesthetics were formed by live theater work. More broadly, location work in postwar Hollywood has been regarded as a sure sign of neorealism's influence and as a guarantor of heightened "realism." Both are contestable propositions.[4]

As for grit versus gloss, one could argue that with greater utilization of color and the advent of widescreen technologies, glamour thrived as never before in the postwar era. On the subject of realism, critic Manny Farber lamented in 1952 that postwar Hollywood movies had become "mannerist" and no longer offered an "intelligible, structured image of reality." This is rather too large a debate to take on adequately here, but it indicates how much the questions of neorealism's place in critical thinking about cinema in the United States and in the aesthetic practices of U.S. filmmakers in the immediate postwar years remain in the realm of breezy generalization and common cliché.[5]

The historian's task at this point involves pursuing the historical traces and laying the groundwork for analysis with evidence. The questions "What is neorealism?" and, more broadly, "What is realism?" take on relevance in this context as part of the discursive framework of a past historical era. As André Bazin cautioned in his essay on *Bicycle Thieves*, "'Realism' can only occupy in art a dialectical position—it is more a reaction than a truth." In searching for a dialectical response to neorealism in the postwar United States, this preliminary inquiry discovers it first outside the precincts of Hollywood, in the practices of film criticism and independent nonfiction filmmaking. The figure who inaugurates the critical discourse and serves as a link between aesthetic theory and production is James Agee, a journalist, poet, novelist, and film critic.[6]

Agee wrote the first prominent critiques of neorealist films in the United States with his reviews in *The Nation* magazine of *Roma, città aperta* (Rome, Open City, 1945) in 1946 and *Sciuscià* (*Shoeshine*, 1946) in 1947. But his endeavors concerning film reach considerably beyond his role as a reviewer. Before and during his years as a critic—which encompassed 1942–48 for *The Nation* as well as 1941–48 for *Time* magazine, which printed his reviews anonymously— he published several screen treatments in literary periodicals. His career trajectory from the 1930s through the 1950s—he died of a heart attack in 1955, at age forty-five—suggests that an appraisal of neorealism's reception in the United States requires exploring its archaeological and genealogical foundations in the formations of practices and personnel in place before films such as *Open City* and *Shoeshine* appeared in U.S. theaters.[7]

During the 1930s, Agee's friendship with photographer Walker Evans, with whom he collaborated on the classic nonfiction work of reportage and reflection on southern sharecroppers, *Let Us Now Praise Famous Men* (1941), carried him beyond New York journalistic and literary circles into the milieu of visual media, of photography and cinema. Although Agee seems never to have been more than a sentimental leftist, many of his colleagues in that world were veterans of the communist-initiated documentary film movement stemming from the Workers Film and Photo league and its successor organizations, which evolved during the 1930s out of ideological schisms and personal rivalries. Some of Agee's links to this community have been obscured by a propensity of U.S. communists of that era to utilize pseudonyms. "Robert Stebbins" and "Eugene Hill," the on-screen credited codirectors of *People of the Cumberland*, a 1937 Frontier Films documentary about the Highlander Folk School in Tennessee, were in fact, respectively, Sidney Meyers and Jay Leyda, the latter one of Agee's friends and a potential filmmaking collaborator.[8]

At some point around the end of World War II, Agee became involved in two independent nonfiction film projects, *The Quiet One* and *In the Street*, both of which were released in 1948. Agee's participation in these two productions came about through his friendship with the photographer Helen Levitt, who once had been Evans's assistant, and Janice Loeb, a painter of private means who, according to some accounts, financed the making of both works. Loeb produced *The Quiet One* and brought on Meyers as director; she and Levitt served as cinematographers on parts of the film, with Agee enlisted to write the voice-over commentary and dialogue. Around the same time, Levitt invited Agee (and later Loeb) to help her add a filmmaking component to her project of taking still photographs of New York street scenes, primarily of children; Agee spent a day shooting 16mm footage for the resulting short film, *In the Street*. In the same year that these two films gave him his first screen credits—as a writer on one, as a cocinematographer on the other—Agee quit his film reviewing jobs and began to explore the possibilities of becoming a screenwriter on Hollywood fiction films.

Before looking more closely at these two films, we need to consider Agee's critiques of *Open City* and *Shoeshine*, written around the same time that he was contributing to *The Quiet One* and *In the Street*, with an eye to how one pair of films may have inflected the making or the perception of the other. Agee at this time was widely regarded as the preeminent U.S. film critic. His status in literary circles gave respectability to his reviewing for *The Nation* if not to the film medium itself, which many intellectuals of the era continued to deplore. His influence even expanded posthumously, with the 1958 publication of his collected film reviews and essays, *Agee on Film* (which appeared in the same year that he was awarded the Pulitzer Prize for fiction for his novel, *A Death in the Family*, also published posthumously).[9]

He began his March 23, 1946, *Nation* column with an unusual teaser, remarking that he had just seen a motion picture, *Open City*, "so much worth talking about that I am still unable to review it," and adding, "I can say only that I am at once extremely respectful and rather suspicious of it." He devoted his next column, on April 13, to the film, writing one of his rare lengthy commentaries on a single work. After some plot summary, he launched into his suspicions, which centered on the film's representation of an affinity between a priest and an underground leader united in the anti-Nazi struggle. "I cannot help doubting that the basic and ultimate practicing motives of institutional Christianity and leftism can be adequately represented by the most magnanimous individuals of each kind," he wrote, and in that sense, the film is selling spectators "something of a bill of goods."[10]

Beyond that suspicion, he had little other than praise for the film. What he valued most was its "immediacy." This freshness and vitality, "the exalted spirit of the actual experience," he contrasted with "the WPA-mural sentimentality and utter inability to know, love, or honor people to which American leftists are liable." He noted the production circumstances: a miniscule budget, no sets or studio lighting, sound including dialogue added later, professionals behind the camera but mainly amateurs in front. The performances, especially that of Anna Magnani, "somewhere near perfectly define the poetic-realistic root of attitude from which the grand trunk of movies at their best would have to grow." Inevitably, the film offered him a stick with which to beat Hollywood: "The result is worthless to those who think very highly of so-called production valyahs. . . . Others may find this one of the most heartening pictures in years, as well as one of the best."[11]

In his 1946 retrospective, Agee restated many of his views about *Open City* and named it the best film of the year. Discussing also a film released in the United States as *The Raider* (originally *Western Approaches*, a 1944 British Crown Film Unit Technicolor film that had nonprofessionals re-creating scenes of merchant seamen at war), Agee elaborated on the aesthetic values he drew from these films. It was not their use of nonactors, or their documentary aspects, or because they were "realistic" (his quotes); "it is, rather, that they show a livelier aesthetic and moral respect for reality—which 'realism' can as readily smother as liberate." In sum, "The films that I most eagerly look forward to will not be documentaries but works of pure fiction, played against, and into, and in collaboration with unrehearsed and uninvented reality."[12]

Agee's response to *Shoeshine* repeated his approach to *Open City*: A brief notice in the September 13, 1947, issue of *The Nation*—"The Italian-made *Shoeshine* is about as beautiful, moving, and heartening a film as you are ever likely to see. I will review it when I am capable of getting any more than that into coherent language and feasible space"—was followed by an October 11 review devoted solely to the film. This time, however, instead of opening with plot summary, as he did with *Open City*, Agee spent a lengthy first paragraph musing in disjointed fashion on the current status of what he called "the humanistic attitude." What followed were several more long paragraphs of high if often rambling praise, coupled with qualifications and reservations. The review leaves the impression of a critic so deeply moved by a work that he is unable to find, even after nearly a month of reflection, the coherent language that had eluded him on first viewing.[13]

Agee saw *Shoeshine* as simultaneously "one of the few fully alive, fully rational films ever made" and "not a great or for that matter a wholly well-realized work of art." As he elaborates on the film's achievements and vacillates on its status in the field of art, the retrospective reader—looking back on the review in a biographical context—cannot but wonder how strongly in Agee's mind was the context of his own work on the commentary and dialogue for *The Quiet One*, another film concerned with troubled youth. Describing *Shoeshine* as a "true tragedy," he writes of its boy protagonists, "The heroes would not have been destroyed unless they had been caught into an imposed predicament; but they are destroyed not by the predicament but by their inability under absolutely difficult circumstances to preserve faith and reason toward themselves and toward each other, and by their best traits and noblest needs as well as by their worst traits and ignoblest needs." Perhaps also thinking about the youths who perform fictional scenes in *The Quiet One*, he marvels that *Shoeshine* director Vittorio De Sica "had to put his amateurs through as many as thirty-nine takes for one scene." The film's "illusion of spontaneity," Agee writes, "is one of the pure miracles of fifty years of movies."[14]

Agee had reviewed *Shoeshine* anonymously in the September 8, 1947, issue of *Time* with all the crisp coherence that his *Nation* treatment lacked. He tells the plot, he calls the film a "masterpiece," there are no caveats, and he makes a similar point, even more succinctly, about why the boys are "true tragic heroes." The review opens, "*Shoeshine* . . . may strengthen a suspicion that the best movies in the world are being made, just now, in Italy."[15]

If Agee may have been thinking of *The Quiet One* when writing about *Shoeshine*, a reviewer of the U.S. film made the comparison explicit. Calling *The Quiet One* "a genuine masterpiece in the way of a documentary drama," Bosley Crowther of the *New York Times* went on to link the film with "those stark film dramas which we have had from Italy since the war." He pointed to its nonprofessional actors and location shooting. But as a critic who often regarded moral issues as paramount, he gave greater emphasis to the connection in ethical terms, relating the two films on the grounds of "a clear and candid eye," "compassion but utter clarity," and "an honest conclusion." *The Quiet One*, he wrote, "might be reckoned the 'Shoe Shine' of American urban life, with the fade-out less fatal and tragic because of our more fortunate state."[16]

In a 1950 issue of *Hollywood Quarterly*, a liberal scholarly/critical journal published by University of California Press, a Los Angeles–based Brazilian writer, Vinicius de Moraes, also matched the two films in a detailed treatment of *The Quiet One*. In his view, the U.S. film comes out ahead. "More beautiful than *Shoeshine*, to which it is related in some respects, it is also a more excruciating social document," de Moraes wrote. "The young delinquents of Vittorio De Sica's picture do not suffer like the children of *The Quiet One* from the impossibility of seeing their own faces in the mirror. For De Sica's children loneliness will come later, but at present their poverty is cheered by freedom to pursue vicious adventures through the sunlit streets of Rome." De Moraes goes on to describe in detail the isolation and "infinite loneliness" of *The Quiet*

One's protagonist, which he clearly regards as a condition more dire than the "freedom to pursue vicious adventures" enjoyed by *Shoeshine*'s youths.[17]

Some obvious further contrasts exist. Loeb's financing and producing of *The Quiet One* have been described as at least in part motivated by her desire to support and publicize the Wiltwyck School, a private residential treatment center for boys in Upstate New York. As she, Levitt, and Meyers developed the story and screenplay—and Agee wrote his commentary and dialogue based on the completed image track—all those involved no doubt understood that a central goal of the film was to valorize the work of the school's counselors and psychologists in an artistic framework that could be positive and uplifting for spectators without appearing too obviously promotional or unduly optimistic about easy cures. Though Agee's commentary emphasizes—and Crowther's review echoes—that the story does not have a "happy ending," the trajectory of *The Quiet One* ineluctably if cautiously leads to the future healing of its protagonist's mental troubles. *The Quiet One* is not a "true tragedy," in the sense that Agee regarded *Shoeshine*. The *Quiet One*'s main character, the fictional ten-year-old Donald Peters, portrayed by nonactor Donald Thompson, is not, as Agee found De Sica's Italian youths, a true tragic hero. In de Moraes's terms, Donald lacks the freedom to pursue vicious adventures; his adventures, vicious or not, are imposed by his predicament. He is a waif amid forces.

Donald's predicament, one might say, is that he is black. How race is acknowledged is a curious aspect of the contemporary commentary on the film. Crowther's *New York Times* review refers to "sleazy Harlem apartments" and to Thompson as a "Harlem youngster," presumably sufficient clues for any reader. Crowther stresses the point of universality: "The race of the boy is a circumstance. For this is essentially the story of any child who has hungered for love, and, in the misery of that hunger, has rebelled in some unsocial way." The Brazilian de Moraes locates this color blindness, as it were, or apparent color indifference more clearly than does Crowther in the filmmakers' intentions. "For the makers of the film," de Moraes writes, "the [racial] problem did not exist at all. The fact that they chose a Negro boy as the hero of their film, however sly as strategy, is incidental to the finished work. The little boy might equally well have been white, yellow, red, or even blue."[18]

But it is de Moraes's goal to see the film differently. "The message of *The Quiet One* [transcends] the intent of its producers without their being conscious of the fact," he continues. "The film attacks the racial problem with the most powerful and precise of weapons—poetry. Instead of exposing the problem it disguises it with the outer appearance of the misery in which it hides." A further viewpoint on the film was briefly stated in a 1950 article,

Donald Thompson as Donald Peters in
The Quiet One (Sidney Meyers, 1948).

"The Problem of Negro Character and Dramatic Incident," by William Couch Jr., in the African American journal *Phylon*, published at Atlanta University (now Clark Atlanta University). *The Quiet One*, Couch writes, "is a sensitive exploration of a Negro child's response to an unfriendly society, and succeeds without either preconceptions or preachment."[19]

Half a century and more later, a spectator's response to the racial aspect of *The Quiet One* may differ from that which prevailed in the early postwar years. The film's cinematic strength appears to lie in its central sequences depicting Donald's family relations and social milieu in Harlem prior to his entering Wiltwyck rather than in the framing scenes representing the crises and resolutions of his treatment at the school. A worn photograph of an intact family—father, mother, grandmother, and Donald at the beach—signifies for Donald his shattering loss, as his father has abandoned the family, while his mother has had a baby with another man and relegated Donald to the care of his grandmother. This crone regards the boy as a "little good for nothing" and a "no account." Agee's voice-over commentary describes Donald's life as characterized by "misunderstanding, rage and pain and fear and hatred," as his grandmother beats him and he cries. The Harlem street scenes that depict Donald's meandering loneliness and his estrangement from loving care are distinguishing elements of the film's cinematography.

A question for the present-day spectator is how much it is possible to endorse de Moraes's view that beyond the filmmakers' aims and perhaps even their awareness, the film can be read as an impassioned cry for social justice. He describes Donald's Harlem world as an "urban cancer" and asserts that "it is not merely love that the unhappy child needs, but justice, equality of treatment, respect, and dignity, in order to live in the community of men without distinction of color or creed." One can come away from the film with this conviction, but does the film itself support this view? Or is it more likely that the "unfriendly society" that the *Phylon* writer describes is a fact of life for the filmmakers, a circumstance of broken families, angry grandmothers, and a bleak environment that the film does not seek to interrogate or ameliorate except to extract Donald from it for psychiatric adjustment on an individual basis, far from home. Perhaps it is telling that there is an unexplained gap—a lacking transition—in the film between Donald's final acts of delinquency on the street and his arrival at the school. "So Donald came to Wiltwyck," Agee's commentary passively notes the change of scene, eliding whatever intermediary factors—cops, courts, or philanthropic cash—have mandated or enabled his residence there.[20]

The Quiet One, like *Shoeshine* before it, gained unusual recognition from the U.S. motion picture establishment. It was nominated for an Oscar in the documentary feature category in 1948 and then scored another nomination the following year for its story and screenplay, credited to Levitt, Loeb, and Meyers, where it competed against fiction features; one of the other four nominees was Rossellini's *Paisà*. Agee's name was not included in the nomination.

In a 2002 interview, Helen Levitt, then nearly ninety years old, recalled the making of the sixteen-minute short film *In the Street*. She had been taking still photographs in a New York neighborhood, she said, and began to think about making a film there. Agee encouraged her, she recounted, "so I borrowed a 16-millimeter camera from a friend, and Jim and I went up to Spanish Harlem. . . . [H]e shot a lot in the street." However, Agee was only available for one day, and Levitt got Loeb to help her complete the film. "A lot of what Jim shot that first day is in the film," Levitt said. "He was an all-around genius—he was able to shoot marvelous stuff, even though he'd never shot anything in his life."[21]

This is a considerably simpler but also more plausible account than Manny Farber's version, in a 1952 *Nation* review, which speaks doubly in its first sentence of Levitt, Loeb, and Agee shooting the film with a "concealed" and "sneak" camera. Farber goes into considerable detail about how the camera operators pulled off "acting like a spy or a private eye," so it is difficult to believe that he was making up the story, that someone had not provided him with the account of the production procedure that he conveys. Still, unless and until one encounters corroborating evidence, it reads like an urban myth—as does, for that matter, Farber's interpretation of the film. "Every Hollywood Hitchcock-type director should study this picture if he wants to see really stealthy, queer-looking, odd-acting, foreboding people," he writes. It was made "in one of the toughest slum areas extant: an uptown neighborhood where the adults look like badly repaired Humpty Dumpties who have lived a thousand years in some subway rest room and where the kids have a wild gypsy charm and evidently spend most of their day savagely spoofing the dress and manners of their elders."[22]

Amateur anthropology and a clever wit: It seems, as with *The Quiet One*, that the passage of decades prompts different and in this case less hyperbolic readings. Looking at the film now, it is almost impossible to credit that the vitality and movement in its mise-en-scène could have been captured by a "concealed," "spy" camera device such as Farber describes. The children are not only "savagely spoofing the dress and manners of their elders" but also wearing many different kinds of costumes as well as masks: The visual evidence overwhelmingly suggests that Levitt and Agee picked Halloween Eve as the day to make their movie, which would explain the children's pranks and playacting as well as much of the "stealthy, queer-looking, odd-acting, foreboding" behavior that the filmmakers recorded.

A Halloween hypothesis also fits in with what appears to be a social theory underlying the film, as expressed in a written prologue. "The streets of the poor quarters of great cities are, above all, a theatre and a battleground," it states. "There, unaware and unnoticed, every human being is a poet, a masker, a warrior, a dancer: and in his innocent activity he projects, against the turmoil of the street, an image of human existence. The attempt in this short film is to capture this image." The tropes of this statement suggest a way of life that is both performative and combative, combining mask and menace, as when costumed children swing containers filled with a powdery substance on a long string, hitting other kids and making several boys cry. Although there appears to be no specific reference linking *In the Street* to neorealism, as was the case with *The Quiet One* and with *Shoeshine*, that duality of tone, the melding of playfulness and threat in daily life among the poor, seems even more compatible in spirit with the ambiance of postwar Italian cinema.[23]

After ending his work as a critic, Agee went on to write screenplays for Hollywood productions. He received a coscreenplay credit—as well as an Academy Award nomination—with director John Huston for *The African Queen* (1951) and was listed as sole screenwriter on *The Night of the Hunter* (1955), although director Charles Laughton completely rewrote the script before production. On these and several other projects, Agee adapted the fiction of other writers, largely set in the past, and his scripts do not appear to lend themselves to linkages with neorealism.[24] Generally speaking, parallel with Agee's change of career and emphasis, discourse on issues of realism in the cinema and on Italian neorealism more specifically waned in the United States during the 1950s—the former as postwar hopes for a new social cinema were quashed, the latter as Italian filmmaking took on a broader, more variegated nonideological coloration.[25]

The year 1960, however, brought an unexpected revival of concern regarding questions of film realism with the publication of one of the era's major efforts to define and characterize the medium of cinema, Siegfried Kracauer's *Theory of Film: The Redemption of Physical Reality*. (Perhaps less widely noted but of more lasting significance was the English-language translation of André Bazin's essay, "The Ontology of the Photographic Image," appearing that same year in *Film Quarterly* magazine.)[26] After a volume of Bazin's essays came out as *What Is Cinema?* in 1967, a brief season ensued of comparison between the two authors' theories of realism, but it was soon eclipsed by the rise of structuralist and poststructuralist theories in which notions of realism, except as objects of critique, played little or no part. Kracauer's reputation fell into eclipse, while Bazin, as a writer of brief suggestive essays rather than grand theoretical tomes, paradoxically gained in stature.[27]

Kracauer's theses had already been battered by a brutal critique from Pauline Kael, appearing originally in 1962 in the British film quarterly *Sight and Sound* and collected in her *I Lost It at the Movies* in 1965. Among her more conciliatory concessions is the thought that "What it comes down to in Kracauer is that film is Lumière's 'nature caught in the act'—or neo-realism: the look of so many good movies during the period he was gestating this book becomes his definition of cinema itself." Kracauer's discussions of *The Quiet One* and *In the Street*—suggestive and useful as they are—indicate the author's ambiguous and contradictory notions of realism that so vexed his critics.[28]

His comments on *In the Street*, for example, center on questions of reportage and "imaginative readings" in the documentary form. He appears to admire the film both for its "reporting job" and its "unconcealed compassion" for its subjects. However, these qualities are treated as theoretical binaries, with an on the one hand/one the other hand approach that ultimately leads him to conclude that the film's "lack of structure" weakens its "emotional intensity." His praise of *The Quiet One* has a similar bifurcated, paradoxical character. Under the heading "stark reality," he suggests that the film's "real life" scenes take on the appearance of dream images. "Women are standing, all but motionless, in house doors, and nondescript characters are seen loitering about," he writes. "Along with the dingy façades, they might as well be products of our imagination, as kindled by the narrative. . . . Perhaps films look most like dreams when they overwhelm us with the crude and unnegotiated presence of natural objects—as if the camera had just now extricated them from the womb of physical existence and as if the umbilical cord between image and actuality had not yet been severed." He links these impressions to "shots comprising 'reality of another dimension,' and passages that render special modes of reality."[29]

"Reality," Kael commented, "like God and History, tends to direct people to wherever they want to go."[30]

Reality or some other principle directed several of Agee's filmmaking collaborators, like Agee himself, toward Hollywood in the years after *The Quiet One* and *In the Street* were released. After directing several educational documentaries in the early 1950s, Meyers received a screen credit as film editor on a 1957 MGM feature, *Edge of the City*, directed by Martin Ritt. Levitt worked in several capacities on independent productions developed by Joseph Strick, a businessman turned filmmaker, and Ben Maddow, a Hollywood screenwriter who, like Meyers, had worked under a pseudonym on *People of the Cumberland*.[31] These four figures came together as collaborators on a 1960 hybrid feature film, *The Savage Eye*, that melded aspects of *The Quiet One* and *In the Street*, combining the motifs of loneliness and lack of love from the former with a visual exploration of ambiguous urban revels touched by violence from the latter. The novelty of the work, from the viewpoint of those earlier films, was its different setting—not New York but Los Angeles.[32]

Strick launched and privately financed the project, supervising several cinematographers, Levitt among them, who shot actuality footage of Los Angeles scenes over several years in the late 1950s. Maddow became involved to craft a story that required adding and interweaving acted scenes. Meyers's skills as an editor melded the material together. The three men shared billing as codirectors, and Levitt was one of three people credited with principal cinematography. One further link to *The Quiet One* was the soundtrack voice of actor Gary Merrill, who had voiced Agee's commentary on the earlier film; Merrill is the dominant audio presence in *The Savage Eye*, with a character heard but not seen and listed as The Poet.

The film's title invites the spectator to consider multiple meanings of *savage* and how a "savage eye" might see—in a naive, unpolished, or rudimentary way or with a fierce, angry, or cruel gaze. Whatever the status of perception, its object is the physical setting and culture of Los Angeles. A woman perhaps in her thirties, Judith (portrayed by actress Barbara Baxley), arrives at Los Angeles airport following a divorce in another city. Alone, she confronts an inhospitable urban environment; in this way she is not unlike an adult version of Donald in the earlier film. She visits a pet cemetery. She drinks in bars. She meets a plainly unsatisfactory man. They attend a burlesque show, a professional wrestling match, the roller derby—settings in which the film-makers persistently portray grotesque-appearing spectators lusting after the display of sex or violence—and a party filled with what appear to be desper-ately unhappy people pretending to be having fun. Judith and the man sleep together—for her, to be sure, abjectly. Amid her growing despair, she attends a Christian revival meeting where a faith healer lays hands on and verbally soothes a succession of distressed supplicants—the only sequence in the film that has synchronized sound and that appears to have been set up and lighted for the camera.[33]

Punctuating these scenes at various moments are shots of car crash victims, dead or injured, being tended by police. Perhaps these scenes offer foretastes of what constitutes delinquent acting out for a lonely divorcée in a modern automobile civilization, for Judith at wit's end climbs into a convertible and crashes it on a Los Angeles freeway, ending up seriously injured in a hospital. As with Donald, she thus receives a form of institutional care (medical rather than psychiatric) and the hope of a brighter future (which seems to be partly signaled by shots of a gathering of flamboyantly cross-dressing men, no less grotesque appearing than the people photographed earlier at wrestling match-es but treated in a rather more lighthearted way).

The raw animus of this merciless vision can be exhilarating. The problem of *The Savage Eye* lies with its voice-over soundtrack. Judith's aloneness at the airport is broken by a male voice (The Poet) that begins a colloquy with her that extends throughout the film. Its source, it seems, is her consciousness. "I'm your angel, your double, your conscience, your dreamer, your god, your ghost," it introduces itself to her; regrettably, such rhetorical excess is its mode. The best that might be said of this voice is that it parodies a Beat Generation poet: "Out of a handful of dust, garbage, and alcohol, God created man."

Amid international praise—including a prize at the Venice Film Festival—*The Savage Eye* was harshly criticized by Jonas Mekas in his *Village Voice* col-umn in terms that comment on the trajectory of realist U.S. filmmaking. Of the filmmakers, Mekas wrote, "Thirty years ago they were socially minded men who wanted to improve the world. By now they have given that idea up. Now they look at the world with cynicism and disgust. Like most of the generation of the 30's, they have understood the changing of man only as an outward manifestation."[34]

An appropriate assessment of *The Savage Eye*'s relationship to *The Quiet One* and *In the Street* might compare it to the transformation of Italian cinema from postwar neorealism to the late 1950s–early 1960s films of Federico Fellini and Michelangelo Antonioni, such as *La dolce vita* (1960) or *L'avventura* (1960).

Agee had called for films that "would not be documentaries but works of pure fiction, played against, and into, and in collaboration with unrehearsed and uninvented reality." Perhaps the answer to his quest was to be found in films for which the postwar definitions of realism and reality no longer applied.

Notes

Thanks to Saverio Giovacchini, Adrienne Harris, and Vojislava Filipcevic for comments and suggestions on earlier drafts and to Jonathan Retartha for research assistance.

1. The Oscar citations for *Shoeshine* and *Bicycle Thieves* are quoted in Robert Osborne, *70 Years of the Oscar: The Official History of the Academy Awards* (1989; New York: Abbeville, 1999), 97, 115. A detailed account of the censorship struggles over *Bicycle Thieves* appears in Leonard J. Leff and Jerold L. Simmons, *The Dame in the Kimono: Hollywood, Censorship, and the Production Code from the 1920s to the 1960s* (New York: Grove Weidenfeld, 1990), 141–61. The offending scenes involved little Bruno peeing against a wall and a brothel.

2. For neorealism and black independent cinema, see, among many writings, Paula J. Massood, "An Aesthetic Appropriate to Conditions: *Killer of Sheep*, (Neo)Realism, and the Documentary Impulse," *Wide Angle* 21.4 (October 1999): 20–41; Chris Norton, "Black Independent Cinema and the Influence of Neo-Realism," *Images* 5, http://www.images-journal.com/issue05/features/black.htm (accessed January 25, 2011). Robert Frank's interest in neorealism is noted in Blaine Allen, "The Making (and Unmaking) of *Pull My Daisy*," *Film History* 2.3 (September–October 1988): 189. Stan Brakhage discusses neorealism's example in an oral interview included on the DVD compilation *By Brakhage: An Anthology* (Criterion Collection, 2003).

3. Osborne, *70 Years*, 96; "All about Oscar," *Encyclopaedia Britannica*, http://www.britannica.com/oscar/article-9397588 (accessed January 25, 2011).

4. Elia Kazan, *A Life* (New York: Knopf, 1988), 627–29.

5. Manny Farber, "Movies Aren't Movies Any More," *Commentary*, 1952, reprinted as "The Gimp," in *Negative Space: Manny Farber on the Movies* (New York, Praeger, 1971), 71–72.

6. André Bazin, "*Bicycle Thieves*," *Esprit*, November 1949, reprinted in *What Is Cinema?*, trans. Hugh Gray (Berkeley: University of California Press, 1971), 2:48.

7. Agee's biography is most fully recounted in Laurence Bergreen, *James Agee: A Life* (New York: Dutton, 1984).

8. On *People of the Cumberland* and Frontier Films, see William Alexander, *Film on the Left: American Documentary Film from 1931 to 1942* (Princeton: Princeton University Press, 1981).

9. Ivan Obolensky published *Agee on Film: Reviews and Comments* in 1958, and Beacon Press issued a paperback edition in 1964. It contains all of Agee's *Nation* reviews, a selection of his writings for *Time*, and several other film essays. It is currently in print in an expanded

volume, James Agee, *James Agee: Film Writing and Selected Journalism*, ed. Michael Sragow (New York: Library of America, 2005).

10. Agee, *James Agee*, 223, 225–26.

11. Ibid., 226, 228–29.

12. Ibid., 275. In his second commentary on *Open City*, Agee acknowledged having read an essay by James T. Farrell that made "clearer to me" that the film was "among other things Communist propaganda." See James T. Farrell, "The Problem of Public Sensibility," *New International* 12.6 (August 1946): 183–88.

13. Agee, *James Agee*, 317, 321.

14. Ibid., 322–23.

15. Ibid., 515–16.

16. Bosley Crowther, review of *The Quiet One*, *New York Times*, February 14, 1949.

17. Vinicius de Moraes, "The Making of a Document: 'The Quiet One,'" *Hollywood Quarterly* 4.4 (Summer 1950): 378.

18. Crowther, review; de Moraes, "Making," 375. De Moraes's view is somewhat supported by the filmmakers themselves. In a 1977 interview, Levitt emphasized that their interest was in "the problems of delinquent kids" and "ideas about treating them." Because the Wiltwyck School was at that time "in a very sensitive stage of community relations about the Negro problem," however, "we picked a story common to whites *and* Negroes." See Bari Lynn Gillard and Victoria Levitt, "*The Quiet One*: A Conversation with Helen Levitt, Janice Loeb, and Bill Levitt," *Film Culture* 63 (1977): 128.

19. De Moraes, "Making," 376; William Couch Jr., "The Problem of Negro Character and Dramatic Incident," *Phylon* 11.2 (1950): 133.

20. De Moraes, "Making," 375. A recent essay that touches briefly on similar questions is Michelle Wallace, "Race, Gender, and Psychoanalysis in Forties Film: *Lost Boundaries*, *Home of the Brave*, and *The Quiet One*," in *Black American Cinema*, ed. Manthia Diawara (New York: Routledge, 1993), 257–71.

21. Michael Coles, "A Conversation with Helen Levitt," *DoubleTake* 28 (Spring 2002): 46. Earlier secondary accounts credit Agee with greater involvement in shooting the film. Jan-Christopher Horak states that Agee spent two days filming; see "Helen Levitt: Seeing with One's Own Eyes," in Jan-Christopher Horak, *Making Images Move: Photographers and Avant-Garde Cinema* (Washington, D.C.: Smithsonian Institution Press, 1997), 142.

22. Manny Farber, "In the Street," *The Nation*, 1952, reprinted in *Negative Space*, 45–46. Farber presumably was aware that Levitt used a right-angle viewfinder in her still photographic work and incorrectly assumed that a similar device was utilized for the film.

23. Recent scholarly commentary on the film shifts emphasis away from realism toward the carnivalesque (Horak, *Making Images Move*, 146, 148) or surrealism (Juan A. Suárez, "Inner City Surrealism: James Agee, Janice Loeb, and Helen Levitt's *In the Street*," in *Pop Modernism: Noise and the Reinvention of the Everyday* [Champaign: University of Illinois Press, 2007], 237–71, 309–14).

24. A companion volume to *Agee on Film: Reviews and Comments* was published as *Agee on Film: Five Film Scripts* in 1960; the two books appeared simultaneously in paperbound editions in 1964.

25. The postwar debates were carried on longer and more avidly in Britain, where a movement toward a social realist cinema took form in the late 1950s.

26. André Bazin, "The Ontology of the Photographic Image," *Film Quarterly* 13.4 (Summer 1960): 4–9; translation by Hugh Gray.

27. Bazin, *What Is Cinema?*

28. Pauline Kael, "Is There a Cure for Film Criticism? or, Some Unhappy Thoughts on Siegfried Kracauer's *Theory of Film: The Redemption of Physical Reality*," *Sight and Sound* 31 (Spring 1962): 56–64, reprinted in *I Lost It at the Movies* (Boston: Atlantic–Little Brown, 1965), 273.

29. Siegfried Kracauer, *Theory of Film: The Redemption of Physical Reality* (New York: Oxford University Press, 1960), 203, 164.

30. Kael, *I Lost It*, 288.

31. As "David Wolff," Maddow was listed on *People of the Cumberland* as assisting in writing the film's voice-over commentary; years later, he claimed that he had written it all but that the filmmakers gave the credit to popular southern novelist Erskine Caldwell for the publicity value of his name.

32. Saverio Giovacchini assesses the relationship of New York filmmakers to Hollywood in "'Hollywood Is a State of Mind': New York Film Culture and the Lure of Los Angeles from 1930 to the Present," in *New York and Los Angeles: Politics, Society, and Culture, a Comparative View*, ed. David Halle (Chicago: University of Chicago Press, 2003), 423–47. He discusses *The Quiet One* and *The Savage Eye* (436–38).

33. A more detailed account of the film appears in Benjamin T. Jackson, "*The Savage Eye*," *Film Quarterly* 13.4 (Summer 1960): 53–57.

34. Jonas Mekas, "On *The Savage Eye*," *Village Voice*, June 23, 1960, reprinted in Jonas Mekas, *Movie Journal: The Rise of the New American Cinema, 1959–1971* (New York: Macmillan, 1972), 16–17.

MARKETING MEANING, BRANDING NEOREALISM

Advertising and Promoting Italian Cinema in Postwar America

NATHANIEL BRENNAN

The New York premiere of Roberto Rossellini's *Roma, città aperta* (rechristened *Open City* for its American release) in the early months of 1946 in many ways signaled a turning point in the critical and popular reception of international cinema in the United States. Foreign films—especially those from Italy—were by no means new to New York's film culture, but *Open City* represented something different: a foreign film that made money. Most foreign-language films were little seen and largely unprofitable, relegated either to small neighborhood theaters catering to ethnic audiences or to art houses patronized primarily by small bands of devoted cinephiles. *Open City*, however, was an unprecedented critical *and* financial success. The film made its American debut at the World Theater, a 300-seat art house theater on Forty-ninth Street. By June 1946, an estimated 150,000 people had seen the film. By December, the film, which by then had opened in Chicago, Washington, D.C., and Los Angeles, among other cities, had grossed "more than $1,600,000."[1] In New York, the film remained at the World for two years before moving into subsequent-run theaters elsewhere in Manhattan and the outer boroughs.

On one hand, *Open City*'s critical and popular success in the United States may be seen as part of a broader shift in early postwar American film culture toward a more sustained engagement with cinematic realism. As numerous commentators pointed out, through its wartime roles in military training and civilian morale boosting, the documentary film had developed in the United States during the war, leading to a greater appreciation for realism. *New York Times* film critic Bosley Crowther, for example, repeatedly argued during and after the war that Hollywood's highly polished escapist fantasies and reliance on artificial sentiment and emotion could no longer serve as a viable model of popular cinematic art in a world so visibly changed by war. *Open City*, with its nonprofessional actors, location shooting, and uncompromising presentation of everyday life in wartime Italy, provided the most obvious antidote to

Hollywood's form of detached un-realism. *Open City* was not just a movie; it was a surrogate experience in celluloid form. As one reviewer for the *Wall Street Journal* put it, "Here in episode after terrifying episode American audiences can see what probably is the closest approximation of what we would have been subjected to if it had happened here."[2]

On the other hand, the importance of cinematic realism and the need to come to terms with the experience of the war cannot entirely account for the film's overwhelming success. The majority of New Yorkers, in all likelihood, were tired of war and were not particularly interested in confronting for themselves the realities of human suffering. A more common scenario, driving thousands of spectators to a small art house theater off Seventh Avenue, may have been the promise of titillation, of depictions of sexuality and violence that would have been unthinkable in mainstream American cinema. This view does not discount the role of critical commentary and the intellectual importance of the film to the nascent development of postwar American film culture, nor did most people see the film simply out of puerile fascination. What compelled people to see *Open City*, the cause célèbre of the New York film scene in 1946, was curiosity. What drove that curiosity was the discursive feedback loop involving word of mouth, the critical response in leading periodicals and newspapers by writers such as Crowther and James Agee, and the promotional strategies engineered by its American distributors, Joseph Burstyn and Arthur Mayer.

This essay examines the last of these discursive formations—the rhetorical strategies of promotion—to investigate the ways in which American audiences were encouraged to respond to and make sense of postwar Italian cinema. Promotion and advertising played a key role in the popularization of Italian cinema in postwar American film culture, but the importance of such strategies has been somewhat lost in the standard histories of the era. Mark Betz has described the most common approach to the production or reception history of art cinema as "a closed circuit of exchange between text, spectator, and director."[3] That is, the contingent political, industrial, and economic factors historians instinctively cite to explain the reception of popular cinema are largely absent from discussions of art or alternative cinematic practices. But as this essay shows, these geopolitical and economic mechanisms—what Betz refers to as the "generative forces in the institutionalization of art cinema"[4]— played a major role in shaping the postwar American response to international cinema in general and Italian neorealism in particular.

"A New Kind of Movie!"
Burstyn and Mayer and the Rhetoric of Postwar Foreign Film Advertising

Burstyn and Mayer were already experienced independent film distributors when they brought *Open City* to American filmgoers. "There are two requirements for pictures," Burstyn told an interviewer in 1952, "first, they've got to be good; second, audiences must be informed about them properly."[5] This statement accurately encapsulated Burstyn's business model: Find a worthy film and rigorously promote it. This task often proved difficult, for importing foreign films brought many problems. Such enterprises typically lost money, and the sometimes-risqué content of films from Europe made independent distributors the frequent targets of state censorship boards. To attract an audience beyond the aesthetes and cinephiles who most often frequented art houses, distributors and exhibitors had to make novel use of advertising and promotion to entice spectators who would not otherwise have noticed foreign-language films. The act of properly informing audiences consisted of a sometimes contradictory blending of titillation and suggestion playing on the foreign film's proclivity for nudity or risqué subject matter as well as (and sometimes alongside) an emphasis on critical accolades and aesthetic quality. Distributors such as Burstyn and Mayer used these techniques to target potential audiences from vastly different backgrounds.

Because foreign films were not often financially remunerative, distributors and exhibitors had very little money with which to promote these films.[6] The promotion of art cinema must be contextualized not just in terms of visual advertising strategies but also in the broader discourses of geopolitics and popular culture into which these films were imbricated. The promotional strategies Burstyn and Mayer utilized for the postwar Italian cinema derived from earlier proven techniques as well as from the two men's experiences during the war. In other words, fully understanding Burstyn and Mayer's promotional strategies for films such as *Open City*, *Paisà* (1946; released in the United States as *Paisan* in 1948), and *Ladri di biciclette* (1948; released in the United States as *The Bicycle Thief* in 1949) requires contextualizing practices of actual advertisement into other discourses to which both men actively contributed.

Burstyn and Mayer had been in business together for nearly a decade before *Open City* became their first real success. In personality, the two could not have been more different. Burstyn was publicly reserved but fiercely dedicated to the films he imported, making a habit of challenging censors over scene eliminations that would have compromised a film's artistic value or left its narrative an incoherent mess.[7] Mayer, conversely, had cultivated the oversized persona of a showman, becoming a fixture of the New York film scene early in the 1930s. As he self-deprecatingly characterized his working relationship with Burstyn some years later, "My contribution was unbounded ignorance and limited capital; his a wide acquaintance with the European market and something approaching genius in acquiring, editing and merchandising its product."[8]

Although Mayer often downplayed his contributions while working with Burstyn, Mayer's input in shaping the promotional strategies for postwar Italian films was crucial, for he had a rich background in promotion that more often than not made use of sex and sensation to bring in patrons. In the early 1930s, for example, Mayer had worked in Paramount's publicity department, where, he later claimed, he helped devise Mae West's "Sex" campaign; by 1933, Mayer had taken over as owner and operator of the Rialto Theater at Forty-second Street and Broadway in New York, a small auditorium that under his direction specialized in low-budget mysteries, thrillers, and horror films. As an independent exhibitor, Mayer often had little money for newspaper advertisements, so he resorted to using "the theatre front and the lobby for my major shilling."[9] These over-the-top visual displays and promotional stunts earned him the nickname "The Merchant of Menace" among New York film critics and entertainment reporters.

It would be easy to dismiss Mayer as nothing more than a flagrant opportunist based on the similar advertisement strategies he devised for both foreign films and horror films, but he, like Burstyn, truly believed in the cultural potential of the art films he imported. For both men, the experiences of World War II helped to bring these commitments to the fore and introduced a note of geopolitical dedication to their promotional strategies for the Italian neorealist films they distributed.

Like many other professionals in the film field, both Burstyn and Mayer lent their expertise to the war effort. Burstyn remained in New York but worked with the Soviet film distributor, Artkino, to ready Soviet documentaries about the war for American consumption, even directing a compilation film, *Our Russian Front* (1942). Mayer was more active, working first for the film industry's War Activities Committee and later as a film consultant to the secretary of war. In his work for the War Department, Mayer turned a more critical eye toward the ways that film could inform and enlighten, particularly in documentaries and a greater commitment to realistic filmmaking practices. "The movie, playboy of the past fifty years, has come of age," he wrote in 1944. "In it we can speak to a world audience which comprehends it, cherishes it and responds to it. With it we can accent the common needs and common faiths of all mankind."[10] Mayer noted enthusiastically that the war had led to a greater utilization of the documentary form in training and education and that audiences now responded more positively to images of real life. Audiences, he suspected, wanted to see popular entertainment films move in the same direction. In this he was encouraged by the tropes of documentary realism that he saw in such wartime American feature films as *Wilson* (1944) and *Dragon Seed* (1944), though he also realized that these practices would have to be maintained well into the postwar era if they were to have any positive effect. Popular movies, Mayer argued, could still show romance and melodrama, but the characters no longer needed to be one-dimensional stereotypes "endowed inexplicably with 1948 model cars and thousand-dollar gowns."[11]

Foreign films such as *Open City*, like documentaries, provided the most obvious counterpoint for Mayer, who enthusiastically promoted them as such. For example, in one speech before the National Board of Review several months after the release of *Open City*, Mayer noted, "Responsible members of the motion-picture industry"—here he meant himself—"are making a greater effort than ever before to import into the United States films made in the other countries of the United Nations." The American audience's failure to heed the call of an international cinema, Mayer warned, would signal to the rest of the world "that we don't care to know our neighbors or understand their problems and aims. We will be saying that we do not seek to evaluate any way of life save our own, or any viewpoint save our own."[12] Mayer, in other words, saw foreign film distribution not just as a lucrative business but also as a key vector in establishing international understanding through the supposed universal language of film. *Open City* and other films that dealt explicitly with the war's aftermath in a frank and uncompromising manner represented to Mayer the first, best option of film art's global potential. These much grander discourses in turn shaped the promotional strategies used for postwar neorealism, although Mayer's promotional efforts would not abandon the ever-present appeal of sex and violence to lure patrons.

The advertising rhetoric of postwar Italian cinema was anchored by two seemingly contradictory poles: One emphasized critical merit and aesthetic qualities, the other relied on verbal suggestions and visual intimations of more sordid cinematic content. Each ad depended on the newspaper or magazine in which it was published as much as it did on the specific character of the theater at which the films were screened. The *New York Times* and *New York Herald Tribune* advertising for *Open City*'s initial run at the World Theater, for example, features a very consistent pattern of promotion that emphasized quality and critical merit. Ads for the film's first months at the World were typically small and located below the fold. Most prominent in the advertisements other than the title of the film were brief quotations of critical

endorsement ("It is more than excellent. Too rare to be missed by anyone!"—
Post). These ads occasionally featured discreet graphics pulled from publicity
stills. These graphics would typically be modest and fairly accurately represent
the characters in the film: the priest, Don Pietro (Aldo Fabrizi), looks to the
heavens for answers, while the rebel, Giorgio (Marcello Pagliero), stoically
clenches a cigarette in his mouth. Marina (Maria Michi), the fallen woman,
is prominently portrayed in her black slip, but she is not overtly sexualized.
Open City was, to put it simply, a serious film, not a sexy one.

A year into *Open City*'s critical success, advertisements in the *Times* and
Herald Tribune had added only notices that emphasized the awards the film
had won and the unprecedented duration of its run at the World. For the
duration of its time at the World Theater, *Open City* was consistently promoted in the *New York Times* and other newspapers to appeal to the kind of
viewer that Burstyn and Mayer imagined might read that particular paper.
This strategy reflected not just the imagined highbrow readership of the *New
York Times* but also the character of the World itself. But again, a highbrow
readership cannot entirely account for the film's overwhelming success and, as
both Burstyn and Mayer tacitly admitted, sex and semantic misprision ultimately turned a profit.

Other advertisements thus played up the film's deviant qualities: lesbianism and sadism, violence and bared flesh. As Burstyn put it, *Open City* did
not really take off until several months after its opening, when the film got an
unintended "assist" from a *New York Times* headline declaring that New York
was not an open city. Burstyn claimed to have understood *open city* only in
the terms presented by the film—"a place where, in a war, you weren't able
to bomb"—but in its new context realized that he could attach the film to
Mayor William O'Dwyer's campaign to rid New York of racketeers, a context
in which *open city* meant "open to gambling and vice."[13] Only at this point,
Burstyn claimed, did he begin to use sex and titillation to promote the film. In
Mayer's recollection, *Open City*'s success resulted from this fundamental misunderstanding. The film, he wrote, "proved an unexpected box-office bonanza
because patrons . . . thought [the title] denoted a wide-open town where vice
and depravity flourished."[14] Other advertising misprinted a quote from *Life*
magazine that originally read, "Its violence and plain sexiness steadily project
a feeling of desperate and dangerous struggle which Hollywood seldom approaches": The much simplified version included in the ad read, "Violence
and Sexiness Hollywood Seldom Approaches!"[15]

The promotional strategy for *Open City* changed over the course of its theatrical run. At the World, advertisements emphasized the film's quality and critical merit, but by 1948, when the film went to second- and third-run theaters,

the rhetoric had resorted to Mayer's old tricks for the Rialto. By the time the film had left the comfortable surroundings of the art house, it had made its way to the grind houses on the city's periphery. Brooklyn's Astor Theater advertised the film in April 1948 solely through sex appeal, reproducing the oft-misquoted *Life* endorsement and utilizing vaguely suggestive images of the female leads. Advertisements during the latter half of *Open City*'s American run also emphasized images of torture and violence, "designed," as Mayer put it, "to tap the sadist trade."[16] The type of advertising used, in other words, was based on distributors' assumptions about the kind of audiences that might encounter it. For foreign films, this strategy led to a diverse audience: Those responding to advertising or critical essays would presumably be members of the upper middle class with some education, but those responding to ads that played up sex and violence were more likely assumed to be the unemployed or transient, most typically men. This diverse imagined audience probably lent art house theaters a certain mystique as well as an air of danger (probably unwarranted). For example, one article on Burstyn in the early 1950s claimed that "The patrons of the unusual accepted the pictures from Cinecittà . . . but there was some trouble with the casual movie fan. When some of them, especially in the afternoon"—that is, the unemployed and listless—"unknowingly stumbled into a movie house featuring an Italian picture, they would cut the chairs in anger."[17] Foreign films, as Burstyn and Mayer promoted them, sometimes straddled the line between the art house and the grind house.

Mayer and Burstyn sought to attract as wide an audience as possible. To do so, they utilized tried-and-true methods culled from years of experience in promoting not just foreign films but lowbrow pabulum as well. These advertisements can tell us a great deal about the ways that films such as *Open City* were marketed and remarketed and how the meaning attached to them changed dramatically.

Other neorealist films released by Burstyn and Mayer took a similar tack. Advertisements for *Paisan*, for example, proclaimed the film "A New Kind of Movie!," further relying explicitly on *Open City*'s success and placing the film within an emerging school of filmmaking—neorealism—that challenged the status quo.[18] Ads for *Bicycle Thieves*, conversely, prominently featured both critical endorsements ("Best Film for 30 Years" in big vertical letters) and a suggestive illustration of a woman's exposed legs that implied that the film had sexual undertones that were in reality completely absent.[19] These advertisements created a discourse around postwar Italian cinema that was, in Karl Schoonover's words, "principled and illicit at once." Moreover, as Schoonover has suggested, this discourse represented the invention of "a new politics of engagement" in American film spectatorship that allowed American viewers to sympathize with the experiences of war and its aftermath while simultaneously disengaging from these images to enjoy the spectacle of violence and exposed bodies.[20] Americans came to expect from Italian cinema not just an attention to the details of everyday life but also more frank depictions of sexuality that could rarely have been found in American mainstream cinema. Local distribution companies, however, were not the only agencies responsible for shaping through promotion and advertising the reception of international art cinema.

From *Cabiria* to De Sica
Unitalia, International Promotion, and the Metahistory of Italian Cinema

Burstyn and Mayer's efforts to promote the new Italian cinema had not gone unnoticed in Italy. In the spring of 1951, the Italian film industry feted Burstyn at a ceremony held at New York's Museum of Modern Art, presenting him with a medal in appreciation of his work for the promotion of Italian films in the United States. "Because of his pioneering work," declared Eitel Monaco through a translator, "the number of people who see our best films is not fifty thousand but five million."[21] Indeed, the Italian film industry owed the success of its films in the United States largely to Burstyn and Mayer and other independent distributors but aspired to expand this market beyond the small field of art house theaters into more lucrative venues. "To enter the circuits of the 'art cinemas' is an honour," wrote one anonymous Italian journalist, damning men such as Burstyn and Mayer with faint praise, "but the cinema which is a costly art must combine box office results with glory."[22] As these anxieties made clear, Burstyn's award contained a certain level of irony in that it tacitly admitted that while neorealism had opened the door to the American market, the neorealist school was simultaneously a source of concern if not an outright hindrance.

Like the other major film industries of Europe in the immediate aftermath of the war, Italy quickly sought to limit Hollywood's advances into the local market. Although Hollywood maintained a large share of the Italian market, the Italian film industry, aided by the Christian Democratic government, had managed by the early 1950s to subsidize film production and limit the number of American films coming into the country. In addition to protecting the domestic market, the Italian government was also interested in promoting its films internationally. The protectionist film laws of the late 1940s had somewhat succeeded in luring foreign capital back into the local economy; at the same time, the Italian market quickly became one of Europe's largest and most profitable.[23] This development gave the Italian film industry more leverage in its dealings with the United States. After a series of negotiations, the Italian film organization Associazione Nazionale Industrie Cinematografiche ed Affini (ANICA) made a deal with the Motion Picture Export Association (MPEA, the international arm of the motion picture producers' association) to limit the number of American films imported into Italy. In exchange for the unblocking of American profits and the loosening of distribution restrictions, American companies would place 12.5 percent of their Italian earnings into Italian Film Export (IFE), an agency for the promotion of Italian films in the United States.[24] The agreement was unprecedented and indicated the value of the Italian market to the American film industry as well as the kind of bargaining power the Italian film industry possessed. As one reporter succinctly put it, "The future of the American film in Italy depends on the future of the Italian film in America."[25]

IFE was not the Italian film industry's first attempt to establish an international public relations office. A year prior to the ANICA-MPEA agreement, ANICA had established an in-house promotional agency, Unitalia Film, described in its literature as the national union for the diffusion of the Italian cinema throughout the world. Throughout the 1950s, Unitalia aggressively promoted Italian cinema whenever and wherever possible, operating as a clearinghouse of information and promotional materials for foreign journalists and organizing weeklong showcases of Italian cinema in major cities around the world. Unitalia's materials and literature were regularly available in five languages—Italian, French, German, English, and Spanish—and by 1955, the organization had established field offices throughout most of Europe as well as in Latin America, Japan, Israel, and Pakistan.[26] IFE operated as Unitalia's American branch.

Although Unitalia and Italian Film Export existed for the same purpose, the two agencies took different approaches to the task of promotion. IFE's familiarity with the American market generally meant that it relied on association with the hip cosmopolitanism of modern Italian culture, placing more emphasis on sex appeal, lifestyle, and technological advancement than it did on art or realism. Prestige was measured not in terms of critical acclaim as much as in terms of name recognition, celebrity endorsement, and the physical endowment of female Italian stars. So, for example, the IFE-produced trailer for Luchino Visconti's *Bellissima* (1951) prominently featured the voice-over endorsement of Bette Davis, who singled out star Anna Magnani for praise in what IFE promotional material described as "a decided switch from the acidulous characters she so often portrays."[27] Other press releases emphasized the attachment of major American stars to international projects—"Kirk Douglas to Co-Star with Silvana Mangano in 'Ulysses'"—or new technological advancements, such as the state-of-the-art dubbing facilities IFE established on West Forty-ninth Street.[28] IFE materials also emphasized the prurience of the themes over the quality of the performance. A press release for *Sensualita* (1952), for example, describes the film as "an explosive drama of primitive passion in the tradition of 'Bitter Rice,' introducing Eleonora Rossi-Drago, Italy's most sultry and provocative new star since the advent of Silvana Mangano."[29] Thus, IFE's promotional strategies emphasized playing up the cosmopolitan chic of modern Italy while retaining only the most basic terms of neorealism's appeal that Burstyn and Mayer had utilized several years before for these films: "Primitive" passions would be exposed, and "sultry" women behaved badly.

In contrast, Unitalia Film maintained a more nuanced approach to promotion that more often eschewed glamour and celebrity culture in favor of artistic aspiration and the endorsement of a more international and less provincial film culture. As a public relations entity, Unitalia prided itself on the courtesies it extended to international journalists, liberally distributing information about current productions as well as the history of Italian cinema. According to one article in *Unitalia Film*, "Daily newspapers and periodicals all over the world [publish] photographs, articles and items of information on the Italian cinema, thus providing our film production with publicity which in no case would it have had if undertaken by [individual] organizations, even the most well equipped production company."[30] In its efforts to distribute as much information as possible, Unitalia produced a wide range of printed materials, including periodicals, newsletters, and commemorative books.

The wealth of literature Unitalia produced served more than a strictly informational function. The successful establishment of any imagined community relies on the mutually accepted terms of a shared past, and Unitalia worked hard to shape an agreeable and useful past for the Italian cinema.[31] This exercise was particularly important as the Italian film industry desperately wanted to distance itself from its prewar and wartime cooperation with the fascist regime. Not surprisingly, then, much of the rhetoric of officially sanctioned history put forth through Unitalia discussed the fascist era only apologetically and dismissively.

Unitalia's historiographic project had three primary goals: the disavowal and denunciation of "fascist" cinema from 1922 to 1943; the establishment of neorealism's attention to human emotion and everyday life as an inherent quality of Italian cinema drawn from centuries-old traditions in Italian art and literature; and finally the identification of an authentic Italian spirit and character represented in and defining of Italian cinema. The promotional effort to convey the Italian past in this light was not limited to editorial asides in *Unitalia Film*; Unitalia released a commemorative volume, *Fifty Years of Italian Cinema*, edited for American release by Herman G. Weinberg in 1954.[32] The book consisted of three essays by prominent Italian critics, each covering a defined era in Italian film history: the early silent to sound period; the fascist middle period; and the current postwar period.

The chronological breakdown of these three essays illustrates the basic historiographic approach to Italian film history after World War II. The first essay, "The Beginnings, 1904–1930," by E. Ferdinando Palmieri, treats the period between 1915 and 1922 as the golden age of Italian cinematic artistry, terminating, almost as a matter of course, with the rise of fascism in 1922. The second essay, "The Transitional Period, 1930–1942," by Ettore M. Margadonna, covers the remainder of the fascist era, characterizing this period as devoid of artistry and full of frivolous excess and distraction. While both essays take a detached and objective tone to their subject, the final essay, "Post-War Period, 1942–1954," by Mario Gromo, is more subjective. Gromo arranges postwar Italian filmmakers into an elaborate hierarchy, with Rossellini and De Sica at the top and everyone else in subcategories below. The cold detachment of the first two essays is striking when compared with the critical jubilation of the third, accurately representing what Steven Ricci has described as a common historiographic approach to Italian film history that almost instinctively seeks a clean separation of postwar neorealism and its afterlives from "that *soulless* and *squalid* past" of fascist contamination.[33]

The apologetic and dismissive rhetoric of everything between 1922 and 1943—the *ventennio*, or "twenty black years"—in Palmieri's and Margadonna's essays is striking. Palmieri, for example, characterizes the slide of the Italian film industry from the golden age of such internationally successful epics as *Cabiria* (1914) to the stagnation of the early fascist period in a series of metaphorical allusions to dusk and decline. Palmieri writes, "World War I ended, and the cinema entered the postwar period. But the war, which had revealed a people, did not inspire any new spiritual themes. . . . The Italian cinema still led the world, but its evening was at hand."[34] Margadonna's essay on the fascist period similarly distances the present from the recent past. In it, he claims, "Although the war ended less than ten years ago, so overwhelming has been the change, so great and terrible the events that separate Italian consciousness of yesterday from the awareness of today, that a full century might have passed. But thanks to that very separation, it is possible to judge the second period of Italian cinema . . . with almost the detachment of future generations." Rather, Margadonna sees the fascist era "as a period of preparation, or better still, of incubation for the new Italian cinema."[35]

This metaphor of incubation rather succinctly captures the overall approach of postwar Italian film historiography. Even though the Italian film industry retained much of the infrastructure from the fascist period and even though many filmmakers who worked under the fascist system continued their careers after the liberation, proper rhetoric distanced free, democratic Italy from any insinuation of its fascist past.[36] It therefore became increasingly necessary to see neorealism existing as a "subterranean artistic tradition," as Richard Griffith put it in his foreword to the American edition of *Fifty Years of Italian Cinema*.[37] That is, it was important to construct a past in which the Italian neorealists labored begrudgingly under the auspices of the fascist regime while secretly harboring the impulse to resist and capture on film Italy as it truly was. Thus, Gromo's essay on contemporary Italian cinema posits the new wave of films as "the 'real' years of Italian cinema"; virtually everything that came before the postwar period was subsequently dismissed as contaminated by fascism and antirealist excess.[38]

Neorealism was, however, simultaneously a source of pride for the Italian film industry and something of a problem. Unitalia's promotional rhetoric encapsulated this dilemma, as frequent reports praised the tradition of neorealism for bringing Italian cinema to the world at large even though by the early 1950s, neorealism already represented an outmoded or obsolete model. Cesare Zavattini began his preface to a collection of essays published by Unitalia on the development of the postwar Italian cinema, "The Italian cinema has been acclaimed the world over. It will not be easy for it to defend itself against praise which threatens to bury it under the definition of neo-realism."[39] Neorealism in and of itself was a noble accomplishment, but to the film industry, with its eyes on the future of Italian cinema, neorealism produced the anxiety that the global market would come to expect *only* neorealist films and reject anything else. This conundrum produced a curiously apologetic view of neorealism. As Pasquale Ojetti wrote in a 1952 piece in *Unitalia Film*, the early postwar

> period should be looked upon as a short and successful period, which doing away with the prewar "mannerism" has indicated a new way of interpreting and representing cinema-wise reality and fantasy. We have used the word "fantasy," because we feel it would be a great mistake to limit the Italian cinema to the recounting of an every-day happening or the picturing of a square or a corner of Italy. This would be too great a limitation and in the long run would lead to considering "artists" only those Directors who follow the path of the first neo-realism. It would also implicitly admit that the evolutionary process of production had stopped.[40]

Furthermore, as Ojetti wrote defensively, "A production program which did not take into consideration public taste and did not bring to the screen 'escape' films . . . would be completely out of touch with reality." "The cinema would be most sterile," he concluded, "if it was to be only somber and thoughtful, picturing exclusively bitterness and sadness and driving the people to skepticism and desperation."[41]

It was important, however, not to give up entirely on the possibilities of future neorealist films. Thus, it was necessary to project an image of a successful present (and future) industry that had one eye still directed toward the past. Unitalia and IFE addressed this approach in practical terms through the organization of weeklong Italian film festivals in major world cities, dubbed Italian Films Week, to present "dozens of varied and very interesting Italian films and documentaries . . . thus creating a new approach both by the critics and those sections concerned with film distribution, and by the public itself."[42] The October 1952 New York Italian Films Week featured the latest from Rossellini and De Sica—*Europa '51* (1952) and *Umberto D.* (1952), respectively—but also more prominently displayed popular (though finely crafted) comedies and romances, among them the French-Italian co-production *Le petit monde de Don Camillo* (The Little World of Don Camillo, 1952) and *Altri tempi* (Times Gone By, 1952), alongside melodramas such as *Anna* (1951) and *Il cappotto* (The Overcoat, 1952).

At the same time that the Italian film industry was attempting to distance itself from the recent past, it attempted to link neorealism to much older traditions that it claimed were inherent to Italian art and national character. To do so, Unitalia's literature consistently maintained a form of national mythology attaching the overarching goals of neorealism—the honest presentation of the world and the human condition—to deeper, more metaphysical conditions than international trade or the economic conditions of the market. A typical example of this rhetoric appears in a 1952 article: "Art, which is deeply ingrained in the nature of the Italians, was founded on the suffering of the people, thus creating works which, hav[ing] no kinship with existing schools or tendencies, spoke the language of the people to whom rhetoric was alien."[43] This statement, then, sidesteps issues of responsibility, indicating that neorealism's appearance was heralded first by the "suffering of the people" and subsequently by the nationally inherent Italian feeling for the arts. This kind of national pride sought to define the Italian brand of cinematic realism as deeply innate to the Italian tradition and as a cinematic form of a different, perhaps more authentic quality than any other competing national cinema. By trading on national essence, the Italians were, in the words of Vanessa Schwartz, "marketing and trading 'nation-ness' as a series of visual [and rhetorical] clichés."[44] In this sense, nation-ness embodied not just films but film history itself. Unitalia's version of Italian film history, in short, constructed an idea of Italian national cinema that was then exported to the rest of the world, where it would be reworked and reinterpreted but would nonetheless maintain much the same basic structure.

Griffith's foreword to the American edition of *Fifty Years of Italian Cinema* inscribes the impact of this broad historiographic project. To Griffith, the book's historical accounts are a series of "revelations." He notes, "We in this country have thought of the great post-war renaissance of the Italian films as a self-generating phenomen [*sic*] without discernible antecedents—a by-product of war and social upheaval rather than of artistic tradition. Similarly, we have been accustomed to think of the desolate middle period of the Italian film as an era of grandiose and empty spectacle . . . ground out by listless hacks." Rather, as Griffith came to see through Unitalia's promotional litera-ture, the roots of neorealism lay dormant through a period of disease and artis-tic inertness, finally emerging through men such as Rossellini and De Sica as a "subterranean artistic tradition" that "Mussolini had bottled up."[45] Griffith, for his part, had internalized the history that Unitalia sought to promote—literally reading Italian film history in the light of neorealism—but had also maintained the illusion that art films, unlike popular cinema, were organic and based not on industrial or economic factors but rather on the artistic impulses and visions of a handful of auteurs.

Notes

1. A. H. Weiler, "By Way of Report," *New York Times*, June 9, 1946, 47; A. H. Weiler, "Assorted Notes about People and Pictures," *New York Times*, December 22, 1946, 49.

2. C.R.S., "Heroes under the Nazis," *Wall Street Journal*, March 6, 1946, 6.

3. Mark Betz, *Beyond the Subtitle: Remapping European Art Cinema* (Minneapolis: University of Minnesota Press, 2009), 9.

4. Ibid., 12.

5. Herbert Mitgang, "Transatlantic 'Miracle' Man," *Park East*, August 1952, 36, Joseph Burstyn Clippings File, New York Public Library for the Performing Arts, New York (here-after NYPL).

6. See Barbara Wilinsky, *Sure Seaters: The Emergence of Art House Cinema* (Minneapolis: University of Minnesota Press, 2001), 120–22.

7. See Laura Wittern-Keller, *Freedom of the Screen: Legal Challenges to State Film Censorship, 1915–1981* (Lexington: University Press of Kentucky, 2008), 135–36.

8. Arthur Mayer, *Merely Colossal: The Story of the Movies from the Long Chase to the Chaise Longue* (New York: Simon and Schuster, 1953), 216.

9. Ibid., 174.

10. Arthur L. Mayer, "Films for Peace," *Theatre Arts*, November 1944, 642.

11. Arthur L. Mayer, "People to People," *Theatre Arts*, June 1946, 362.

12. Ibid.

13. Mitgang, "Transatlantic 'Miracle' Man," 36.

14. Mayer, *Merely Colossal*, 134.

15. "Movie of the Week: *Open City*," *Life*, March 4, 1946, 111; handbill for the Brandt's Apollo Theater, ca. 1947–48, *Open City* Clippings File, NYPL.

16. Mayer, *Merely Colossal*, 233. The degree to which these advertisements played up sex and violence changed from city to city. Nothing that I have seen in the New York press equals the frenzied rhetoric of *Open City*'s ad campaign in Chicago, which prominently featured tag lines proclaiming the film to be, among other things, a "Savage Orgy of Lust!" (Wilinsky, *Sure Seaters*, 126).

17. Mitgang, "Transatlantic 'Miracle' Man," 36.

18. *New York Times*, March 28, 1948, X6.

19. Ibid., December 14, 1949, 45; Wilinsky, *Sure Seaters*, 124.

20. Karl Schoonover, "The Comfort of Carnage: Neorealism and America's World Understanding," in *Convergence Media History*, ed. Janet Staiger and Sabine Hake (New York: Routledge, 2009), 130–31.

21. Mitgang, "Transatlantic 'Miracle' Man," 33.

22. "The Italian Film Week in New York," *Unitalia Film* 3.2 (July 1952): 52.

23. On the postwar reorganization of the Italian film industry, see David Forgacs and Stephen Gundle, *Mass Culture and Italian Society from Fascism to the Cold War* (Bloomington: Indiana University Press, 2007), 125–42; Film Centre, *The Film Industry in Six European Countries* (Paris: UNESCO, 1950), 88–116.

24. Thomas H. Guback, *The International Film Industry: Western Europe and America since 1945* (Bloomington: University of Indiana Press, 1969), 77.

25. Jane Cianfarra, "Italy Seeks Wider Support for Its Films," *New York Times*, April 1, 1951, 101.

26. *The Italian Production, 1954–1955* (Rome: Unitalia Film, 1955).

27. *Italian Film Newsletter* 2.2 (March 30, 1953): 3, Italian Film Export (IFE) Clippings File, NYPL.

28. *Italian Film Newsletter* 2.1 (March 15, 1953): 1, "News from IFE Releasing Corporation," press release, August 26, 1953, both in IFE Clippings File, NYPL.

29. "News from IFE Releasing Corporation."

30. "Unitalia Activity," *Unitalia Film* 3.2 (July 1952): 16.

31. My understanding of this concept comes from Benedict Anderson's seminal work, *Imagined Communities: Reflections on the Origins and Spread of Nationalism* (New York: Verso, 1983).

32. Luigi Malerba and Carmine Siniscalo, eds., *Fifty Years of Italian Cinema*, American ed., ed. Herman G. Weinberg (Rome: Bestetti, Edizioni d'Arte, 1954).

33. Steven Ricci, *Cinema and Fascism: Italian Film and Society, 1922–1943* (Berkeley: University of California Press, 2008), 22.

34. E. Ferdinando Palmieri, "The Beginnings, 1904–1930," in *Fifty Years*, ed. Malerba and Siniscalo, 32.

35. Ettore E. Margadonna, "The Transitional Period, 1930–1942," in ibid., 39, 40.

36. Ennio Di Nolfo, "Intimations of Neorealism in the Fascist *Ventennio*," in *Re-Viewing Fascism: Italian Cinema, 1922–1943*, ed. Jacqueline Reich and Piero Garofalo (Bloomington: Indiana University Press, 2002), 84.

37. Richard Griffith, "Foreword to the American Edition," in *Fifty Years*, ed. Malerba and Siniscalo, 7.

38. Mario Gromo, "Post-War Period, 1942–1954," in ibid., 75.

39. Cesare Zavattini, "Preface," in *Italian Cinema, 1945–1951*, ed. Luigi Malerba (Rome: Bestetti, Edizioni d'Arte, 1951), 4.

40. Pasquale Ojetti, "Activities of the Directors," *Unitalia Film* 3.1 (March 1952): 43.

41. Ibid., 44.

42. "Unitalia Activity," 16.

43. Ibid. 15.

44. Vanessa R. Schwartz, *It's So French! Hollywood, Paris, and the Making of Cosmopolitan Film Culture* (Chicago: University of Chicago Press, 2007), 7.

45. Griffith, "Foreword," 7.

NEOREALISM

Another "Cinéma de Papa" for the French New Wave?

CAROLINE EADES

When the expression that would come to designate a group of bold, young French filmmakers first appeared in the French weekly *L'express*,[1] Italian neorealism already belonged to the history of film. "Neorealism—The New Wave": critics immediately associated the two movements. And indeed, they had much in common in terms of context (an unprecedented political and social crisis), style (natural, realistic, improvised), technology (basic and light), and plot (marginalized characters, dramatic situations) as well as in terms of the fact that they formed a minority within a very prolific mainstream film industry. In addition, neither movement constituted a homogenous group or led to the creation of a school.[2] While their characteristics, dates, and corpus have since been much debated, the role of these two seminal movements in film history remains unquestioned, and their complex relationship has been periodically explored by the critical discourse that both prepared the way for their related genesis and took up where they left off.

The two movements share both a national border and a temporal one, spanning successive decades of midcentury cinematic history. The French New Wave followed immediately[3] on the heels of the Italian neorealist movement, which emerged after World War II and declined in the early 1950s. Efforts to establish firm beginning and ending dates for either movement beyond this initial sequencing are of course futile: Luchino Visconti's *Ossessione* (1943) was dubbed "the first neorealist film" by its editor, Mario Serandrei, while André Bazin and other critics emphasized the thematic and stylistic innovations of Roberto Rossellini's *Roma, città aperta* (Rome, Open City, 1945) and *Paisà* (1946).[4] French New Wave production reached a peak in 1959[5] and received international recognition in 1961 at the Cannes Film Festival with two nominations: *Les 400 coups* (The 400 Blows, 1959) by François Truffaut and *Hiroshima mon amour* (1959) by Alain Resnais. But the emergence of the movement can be traced back to Roger Vadim's *Et Dieu créa la femme* (. . . And God Created Woman, 1956) with Brigitte Bardot and Louis Malle's *Les amants* (The Lovers, 1958)—even earlier if one includes the thirty short films produced between 1951 and 1958[6] by *Cahiers du cinéma*[7] critics as well as a few pioneering feature films: René Wheeler's *Premières armes* (The Winner's Circle, 1948), Roger Leenhardt's *Les dernières vacances* (The Last Vacation, 1948), and Jean Pierre Melville's *Le silence de la mer* (The Silence of the Sea, 1949).

Critics played a similar role in the decline of both movements, which also became the launching pad for new careers for some movement "members." The Christian Democratic and Marxist presses joined forces to criticize the "involutions" of neorealist directors, to quote Guido Aristarco, whereas the New Wave was vilified by critics both from the Right (Michel Audiard and Jacques Lanzman in *Arts*, Jean Aurenche in *Cinéma 60*, Henri Jeanson in *Cinémonde*, *La croix*, and *Le journal du dimanche*) and the Left, with *Positif*'s relentless and systematic attacks against the "irresponsible and reactionary" authors affiliated with *Cahiers du cinéma*.[8] The cohesion of the New Wave was constantly threatened by its diversity: "Everyone remained who he was, with his own ideas, personality, aesthetics."[9] Directors met differing fates as they went their separate ways: Jean-Luc Godard's audience soon dwindled, whereas Eric Rohmer and Claude Chabrol became more and more popular. In 1952, Bazin had sensed that a similar "dissolution" awaited neorealism when he distinguished Alberto "Lattuada's calculating and subtly architectural vision, [Giuseppe] De Santis' baroque excess and romantic eloquence, and Visconti's sophisticated theatrical sense."[10]

The impact of both movements on contemporary and later filmmakers must be qualified: Only "traces" of the neorealist legacy survived in the works of Ermanno Olmi, Bernardo Bertolucci, Marco Bellocchio, Marco Ferreri, Paolo and Vittorio Taviani, and Ettore Scola.[11] In France, the success of the New Wave did not prevent mainstream cinema from flourishing: 1960 was a prosperous year for the old guard of Jean Delannoy, Gilles Grangier, and Henry Verneuil as well as for such younger filmmakers as Alain Cavalier, Pierre Granier-Deferre, Claude Lelouch, Pierre Mocky, and Gérard Oury, who were not associated with the New Wave and who benefited from new laws awarding public subsidies to first-time directors. French critics subsequently have heralded the arrival of a "New New Wave," first in the 1980s with Leos Carax, Jean-Jacques Beineix, and Luc Besson, champions of a new formalist cinema (*le cinéma du look*), then in the late 1990s with a group of filmmakers born during the heyday of the New Wave: Arnaud Despléchin, Olivier Assayas, and Bruno Podalydès. To no avail: it seems that they shared with their famous predecessors only an interest in describing the mores of a younger generation.[12]

As Richard Neupert recalls, "During the late 1950s and early 1960s, the New Wave rejuvenated France's already prestigious cinema and energized the international art cinema as well as film criticism and theory, reminding many contemporary observers of Italian neorealism's impact right after World War II."[13] To grasp the complex influences and heterogeneous network of people and productions involved in both movements, one needs also to examine the critical discourse that prepared and accompanied the emergence of a different brand of films. This "New Film Critique"—"Cinema Nuovo" in postwar Italy and French "analytical" criticism with Jean Mitry, Georges Sadoul, and Bazin—contributed to a significant development of the discussion on literary adaptation, form and content, documentary and fiction, before the radical turn Christian Metz would bring to film theory at the end of the 1960s by drawing on Saussurian linguistics and Russian formalism.[14]

Neorealism's fundamental legacy to *Cahiers du cinéma* critics might have been to look thoroughly into what was "new" and what was a "new reality" not so much for their Italian predecessors as for themselves. Neorealism pointed toward a radical upheaval in terms of contexts and representations, thus becoming more of an ideal, an objective, than a school, which could account for neorealism's unprecedented impact in a postwar world. In contrast, the term *New Wave* emphasized the unrelenting succession of generations, each one striving to gain its autonomy and specificity. It seems therefore logical that New Wave directors would try to break all ties with their elders, "le cinéma de papa," to establish their own social and aesthetic position. In fact, these directors consistently searched for referents and models under the guidance of a few pioneers in film criticism and filmmaking: neorealist cinema, being avant-garde, foreign, and revered by Bazin, easily joined the New Wave genealogy. The young filmmakers also rejected the mottos, slogans, and values of French society—past and present—to become the advocates of their own credo: cinema as an art that had, however, a history and a past and now counted neorealism as an established reference. Similarly, these filmmakers took advantage of the most recent breakthroughs in filmmaking technology while acknowledging their debt to neorealist style and aesthetics. Could we then assume that the influence of neorealism on New Wave directors lies precisely in the realization that it was neither new nor realistic, at least for a younger and restless generation?

The "Family Romance"

As Guy Gauthier observes, "both ('neo,' 'new') 'schools' mortgaged the future, the difference being that neorealist 'artisans' could only dream of the technology that later became available to New Wave directors."[15] Thus, it is more in terms of correspondence than legacy that the anxiety of a generation of Italian filmmakers reemerged in the detached and sober works of their successors as they worked to challenge the codes and representations of a society with an aesthetics of freedom and simplicity.[16] But whereas Bazin saw the objective of the neorealist style as "attain[ing] totality in its simplicity,"[17] the "poverty" advocated by New Wave directors must be understood as the response of young people to an industry—and a society—that, while not short of resources, reserved access to them to its elders.

The young filmmakers of the New Wave wanted to create a new relationship with their audience that would be more direct and free from any control or authority: "We thought that we needed to simplify everything to work freely and make inexpensive films on simple topics, hence this mass of New Wave films which had only one thing in common: saying 'no.' 'No' to figuration, 'no' to dramatization, 'no' to large sets, 'no' to explanatory scenes."[18] The New Wave style, decried by Robert Benayoun as a "mystic of trial and error which extolled the act of sketching and glorified the unfinished," was hailed as such by these young filmmakers.[19] Godard defined it as the posture of the novice: "What I wanted was to take a conventional story and remake, but differently, everything the cinema had done. I also wanted to give the feeling that the techniques of filmmaking had just been discovered or experienced for the first time."[20] The mythology of youth bore its own mythology of origins.

According to Antoine de Baecque, "Between 1959 and 1962, approximately 150 young people made their debut as filmmakers in France. Among them, a small group stood out for offering young viewers the spectacle of young actors performing stories written by young filmmakers. . . . This conjunction, almost too perfect and ephemeral, transformed a particular moment of film history into a mythology of modern times."[21] The sometimes unsettling reactions and attitudes of a generation that had not experienced war and rejected traditional values were immediately presented as a generational conflict; after all, Truffaut, Chabrol, Godard, Rivette, and Roger Vadim were but teenagers in 1945.

The search for the spiritual and aesthetic fathers of a movement characterized by its youthfulness was thus inevitable. The appearance of the New Wave recalled in many ways the conditions under which neorealism had emerged: Italian directors who had started working under the fascist regime

were struggling to confront the political and economic crisis of the immediate postwar period.[22] The situation in the mid-1950s in France, while still
one of questioning, was more on the order of moral and social conflict: De
Baecque notes that "the number of young French people aged from 15 to 29
was higher, almost 8 million, but, because the population was aging, they had
a lesser place in society. . . . For example, it was more difficult to reach positions of responsibility and initiative."[23] The film industry was no exception:
"A protectionist regulation had implemented a rigorous control on access to
the profession. One could become a director only after long and strenuous
training as an assistant. . . . Although France could pride itself on significant
filmmakers such as Jean Cocteau, Robert Bresson, Jacques Tati, the production system gave them very few opportunities to express themselves."[24] Italian
filmmakers who were then in their forties[25] often depicted the crisis of the
adult world through the eyes of younger characters, thus building spectator
empathy toward the passive and innocent victims of *Ladri di biciclette* (Bicycle
Thieves, 1948), *I vitelloni* (1953) and *Umberto D* (1952) rather than fostering
debate over the causes and shared responsibilities in Italy's demise. In contrast,
the new generation of French filmmakers directly engaged in the reassessment
of values, structures, and institutions challenged by World War II, decoloniza-
tion, and the failure of the Fourth Republic.[26]

Young French critics endeavored to build for themselves an ideal genealogy
at a time when Italian neorealism had taken its place alongside other significant
influences, such as the American productions of the 1940s that had inundated
France at the close of the war.[27] But whereas Cesare Zavattini encouraged his
compatriots to articulate their relationship to Hollywood cinema in critical
terms, the "hitchcocko-hawksian" *Cahiers du cinéma* critics had no qualms
about extolling American auteurs: Once these critics turned to filmmaking,
they claimed to follow the Hollywood masters' example by emphasizing the
concept of mise-en-scène as the true form of their personal and unique vision
of the world. One must also recognize the particular French artistic context
in which the New Wave emerged: an avant-garde[28] that included surrealism,
Isidore Isou's "Lettrist" cinema, and situationist Guy Debord's film debuts with
Hurlements en faveur de Sade (Howlings in Favor of de Sade, 1952).[29]

Nonetheless, the 1930s French film movement of poetic realism and its
innovative depiction of the working class (as well as the debate over the representation of reality on the screen to which it gave rise) must be seen as the
most substantial and problematic influence both for neorealist directors—
combined with references to the Italian literary tradition of *verismo* and other
realistic traditions[30]—and for *Cahiers du cinéma* critics. According to Dudley
Andrew, the particular realistic vocation of French cinema has extended "from

Louis Lumière's warm and funny 1895 family portraits to Maurice Pialat's grimmer family exposés of the 1980s. . . . Set this tendency off against the historical vision of Soviet silent cinema or against the breadth of classes and issues that arise in Italian neorealism, and you can understand why it is tempting to take Poetic Realism as the apotheosis of a tradition of the intimate that spans the continuum of French film history."[31] The question facing postwar critics and directors was not so much whether Marcel Carné, Julien Duvivier, or Jean Renoir would be able to reactivate a movement that had been so closely associated with the political and social issues of the 1930s, including the hopes raised by Léon Blum's short-lived socialist government, but whether a new cinema emerging from a radically different context could guarantee the survival of the idiosyncratic features of French realism while competing with powerful rivals in Europe and America.

Across postwar Europe, the representation of reality remained a major topic of artistic experimentation for painters and sculptors—Yves Klein, Arman, Jean Tinguely, and César Baldaccini, who signed the Manifesto of New Realism in 1960, playwrights such as Eugène Ionesco, Samuel Beckett, Arthur Adamov, and *nouveau roman* authors.[32] In this euphoric atmosphere, the legacy of poetic realism appeared both as a model and a foil for the new generation: "In postwar France, the politically motivated dissension these films caused at their premieres evaporated: suddenly everyone missed 'the school of poetic realism' that had brought such glory to the nation."[33] Even abroad, including in Italy, poetic realism had left its mark, but French criticism seemed particularly committed to reading any film with a social subject through poetic realism's filter: for Bazin, the plot of *Ladri di biciclette* is based on "one of these extraordinary events which happen to predestined working class characters à la Gabin";[34] other critics saluted "a potential sentimental sincerity" typical of poetic realism in *Les 400 coups* and "echoes both of Sartre and *Le quai des brumes* [Port of Shadows, 1938] in the crudely direct behaviour they variously attributed to Jean-Paul Belmondo's character in *A bout de souffle* (Breathless, 1960), Michel Poiccard, and to Godard's abrasive style."[35] At the same time, Truffaut was defending the pariahs of poetic realism, Jean Vigo[36] and Jacques Becker, and blaming Carné and Duvivier for setting the thematic and aesthetic foundations of the *cinéma de qualité française*.

Jean Renoir's affiliation with poetic realism and later in his career Hollywood cinema is at the same time attested and problematic: the independence of this true auteur thus made him a favorite of New Wave critics and filmmakers who acknowledged his influence and claimed his legacy in terms of ideas, values, and stylistic choices, just as their neorealist predecessors had done a decade earlier. Truffaut is said to have seen *La règle du jeu* (The Rules

Anna Magnani kissing Jean
Renoir (1952). © Bettmann/
Corbis.

of the Game, 1938) more than ten times;[37] Jean-Luc Godard acknowledged
his debt to Renoir's early films in *Histoire(s) du cinéma*.[38] For Georges Sadoul
and André Bazin alike, the neorealist films of Visconti (who had been Renoir's
assistant) are characterized by a naturalistic style as well as a taste for theatricality, a particular attention to the actors' performances, and a preoccupation
with social distress and marginal characters, all of which are typical of Renoir's
work in *Le crime de Monsieur Lange* (The Crime of Monsieur Lange, 1936)
and *Toni* (1935). Both Visconti, the Italian aristocrat, and Truffaut, the young
Parisian rebel, discovered in Renoir the power of an individual conscience free
to produce his own vision of the world, even at the risk of failing his family
and social origins, to challenge ideological and aesthetic conventions.

Critics of the time therefore played a crucial role in constituting the genealogy of both movements and articulating the influence of neorealism on
the New Wave. The young Turks acknowledged other spiritual fathers, such
as Henri Langlois, the dynamic director of the Cinémathèque Française, and
Maurice Schérer, a professor of German literature who was ten years older
than they and wrote for *Cahiers du cinéma* before turning to filmmaking under the alias of Eric Rohmer. But Georges Sadoul, pioneer of the history of

film in France,[39] deserves a special mention for his "dissident" writings in the communist press[40] in support of neorealist directors and New Wave authors at a time when, like their Italian counterparts, French Marxist critics defended the primacy of social subjects over mise-en-scène and blamed the young directors—"fils à papa"—for their lack of explicit political and social commitment.

The Spiritual Father

Within the artistic genealogy of the New Wave, Bazin can be singled out as the critic who established the most relevant and detailed link between neorealist directors and their young French successors. He proved instrumental in promoting and disseminating the works of the former movement and in fostering the creative projects of the latter. Whether in the pages of *Esprit*[41] or speaking to *ciné-club* audiences, he was a partisan of Rossellini's films as soon as they were released, even before they received any attention in Italian critical circles. He later made a point of justifying the evolution of Rossellini's subsequent work, *Viaggio in Italia* (Voyage to Italy, 1954), against the accusations of the Italian Left in his famous letter to Guido Aristarco, editor in chief of *Cinema nuovo*: "Even if Rossellini had in fact Christian-Democrat leanings (and there is no proof, public or private, so far as I know) this would not be enough to exclude him *a priori* from the possibility of being a neorealist artist. . . . One does have a right to reject the moral or spiritual postulate that is increasingly evident in his work, but even so to reject this would not imply rejection of the aesthetic framework within which this message is manifest."[42] Bazin died in 1959, so he did not witness or report on the consecration of the New Wave in the eloquent and subtle style he had used to demonstrate the neorealists' debt to Georges Rouquier's documentary realism in *Farrebique* (1946) and Orson Welles's aesthetic realism in *Citizen Kane* (1941).

Although common ground exists between Bazin's and Zavattini's definitions of cinema as an exploration of reality, they were working from two quite different concepts. For Zavattini, the goal of postwar cinema was to uncover and dramatize "the reality buried under myths . . . : a tree, an old man, someone eating, sleeping, weeping,"[43] with particular attention to the daily life of ordinary people. Bazin not only adhered to the neorealist agenda, including its depiction of social and economic oppression (since "it [did] not subject reality to any *a priori* point of view . . . to serve the interests of an ideological thesis, a moral idea or a dramatic action"), but also upgraded its role to the level of "a phenomenology: its ultimate objective is to transcend iconic reproduction in order to reveal an invisible reality."[44]

Such essential differences prompted Rohmer to question neorealism's influence on Bazin's theory.[45] For Rohmer, the "objectivity" of cinema according to Bazin consists in providing an experience that supersedes a subjective and thus manipulative vision and allows the watchful viewer to access the deep structures of reality. This particular function of cinema necessarily precedes any condition or style of production: it just happens that some filmmakers (Welles, Renoir, Robert Flaherty, Rossellini) and certain cinematographic codes (depth of field and long takes) are more likely than others to verify the "ontology of the photographic image." Rohmer concludes that neorealism provides an "objective" vision in Bazinian terms but that it does not differ in this regard from other movements and is therefore more an example of than a model for Bazin's argumentation.

Andrew, conversely, underlined the specific role played by neorealism in the elaboration of Bazin's theory after he joined the editorial board of *Esprit*.[46] At *Esprit*, Bazin became familiar with Emmanuel Mounier's Christian phenomenology, a postwar philosophical posture combining the concepts of Maurice Merleau-Ponty and Jean-Paul Sartre with a Christian perspective. For Bazin, neorealist films illustrated the aesthetic dimension of a new "revolutionary humanism"[47] that had been defined by Visconti in his 1943 essay, "Il cinema antropomorfico" and by Rossellini in an interview with François Truffaut and Maurice Schérer: "The point is to come close to human beings, to see them for what they are, with objectivity, without preconceived ideas, without moral debates, at least in the beginning."[48] Such obvious affinities between Bazin's humanism and the "deinstitutionalized Christianity" permeating Vittorio De Sica's, Federico Fellini's, and Rossellini's films—to use Peter Bondanella's expression—could account for the importance of the moral question in the definition of the *politique des auteurs*, which, according to James Monaco, "owed a great debt to Bazinian moral realism"[49] and at the same time lay at the heart of the conflict between the young critics at *Cahiers du cinéma* and their spiritual father as well as their rivals at *Positif*.

Godard's famous formula—"a tracking shot is a moral issue"—illustrated his allegiance to Bazin's convictions and guidance inasmuch as he was referring not to reality itself but to its representation. This difference must be considered a major departure from the neorealist agenda: The Italian movement had been defined by Bazin, among others, as "inseparable from a special conjunction of historical circumstances,"[50] whereas the New Wave filmmakers made a point of refusing any philosophical or political commitment.[51]

But even if they distanced themselves from the metaphysical and moral perspective shared by Bazin and some neorealist directors,[52] the critical work of the New Wave filmmakers was nonetheless deeply influenced by the issues

Directors Jean Renoir and Jean-Luc Godard (1968). © Jacques Burlot/Apis/Sygma/Corbis.

raised by Italian directors regarding realism, characterization, and narrative structure. The *politique des auteurs* was developed as part of their challenge to the traditional opposition between form and content; neorealism demonstrated in vivo, so to speak, that cinema had the ability to induce a political consciousness by subjecting the viewer to the emotional impact of aesthetic and narrative choices. The social function of cinema envisioned in such terms could then justify the definition of cinema as art and ultimately the necessity of writing its history.

The *cinéma d'auteurs*—that of Jean Renoir, Robert Bresson, Jean Cocteau, Jacques Becker, Abel Gance, Max Ophuls, Jacques Tati, and Roger Leenhardt—was the true alternative to mainstream cinema, as Truffaut advocated in his famous article, "A Certain Tendency of French Cinema" published in the January 1954 issue of *Cahiers du cinéma*.[33] He pitted the "auteurs" against the "littérateurs," the professional screenwriters of the "cinéma de papa," also known as the "tradition of French quality": Jean Aurenche, Pierre Bost, Charles Spaak, and Henri Jeanson. Truffaut blamed them for their use of unworthy characters, literary dialogue, studio sets, sophisticated cinematography, and confirmed stars. In truth, young critics at *Cahiers du cinéma* did not reject literature and writing outright; they remained faithful to the practice of argumentative rhetoric in their essays[54] and drew numerous references and citations from their rich literary heritage before turning to screenwriting and eventually filmmaking.

Similarly, although denied by Zavattini,[55] Italian literary heritage—and much of its artistic tradition[56]—remained tangible in postwar cinema, not so much as a source of inspiration but through the idiosyncratic practice of "the *literary* narrative, the *sceneggiatura*, a double columned text oriented towards the film to be shot."[57] In France, as Andrew acknowledges, the question of literary adaptation "crystallized a productive contradiction that ran through French film theory right up to its apotheosis in the writings of André Bazin."[58] The special issue of *Esprit* devoted to the relations between novel and cinema was already considered obsolete in 1951 with its questioning of cinema's ability to express abstraction. The emergence of the *nouveau roman* as well as the young Turks' own critical work at *Cahiers du cinéma* encouraged them to switch from "novelistic cinema" to "literary cinema"[59] as advocated by Bazin in his review of Renoir's *Le fleuve* (The River, 1951). The neorealist model had convinced these young filmmakers that screenwriting could borrow certain techniques from literature (subjective voice, *caméra-stylo*)[60] and still proclaim its specificity by de-dramatizing the narrative and focusing on ordinary characters, "micro-action," "image-fact," and the "actual duration of the event."[61] Most New Wave directors then tried their hands at the adaptation of literary texts per se: Rohmer's first attempts at "impure cinema" with *Bérénice* (1954) and *La sonate à Kreutzer* (The Kreutzer Sonata, 1956) were soon followed by Truffaut's *Jules et Jim* (Jules and Jim, 1961) and Godard's *Le mépris* (Contempt, 1963).

"I Don't Like Young People!"

For Neyrat, "the ultimate objective of the *politique des auteurs* is the invention by Truffaut and his friends at *Cahiers du cinéma* of an ideal relationship between fathers from America and Europe and sons destined to pick up the baton and use the principles of *cinéma d'auteur* in their own films."[62] Neorealist films reassured the French critics that this connection could be achieved in a different temporal, geographical, cultural, and political context. In other terms, it proved that mutatis mutandis, France in the 1950s could produce its own generation of auteurs. If critically acclaimed masterpieces had emerged in a country devastated by political rifts, utter poverty, and moral incertitude after the war, there was hope for a young generation of filmmakers coming into their own in a much more peaceful, stable, and technologically advanced environment.

The situation was nonetheless not idyllic. Under the pressure of rapid economic recovery, social tensions were heightened by an open conflict between generations. "I don't like young people!," Michel Poiccard ironically replies to the woman selling *Cahiers du cinéma* in *A bout de souffle*. We are far from De Sica's compassion in *Umberto D.* or his transgenerational complicity in *Ladri di biciclette*. Rebelling against absent, guilty, or passive fathers is an integral part of the French social landscape in the 1950s as a reaction against what French historian Henry Rousso calls the "Vichy syndrome": The silence maintained by elders about compromises and mistakes made during the war exacerbated young people's mistrust of political institutions and their representatives.[63] Phenomenology and existentialism also played a role in the primacy given to a solitary conscience over the Marxist principle of class consciousness.

The issue of political commitment and collective action thus lies at the center of the conflict between *Cahiers du cinéma* and *Positif*, a journal devoted to film and founded in Lyons in 1952 by Bernard Chardère and a group of Marxist critics at odds with the pro-Stalinist French Communist Party. Following up on a financial, editorial, ideological, and aesthetic rivalry that had lasted for more than half a century, Michel Ciment, the editor in chief of *Positif*, faults the young auteurs for their lack of political *engagement* and their inclination toward provocation, a tactic commonly used by French fascists in the 1930s. He observes that New Wave filmmakers waited until 1966 to openly "stand up to De Gaulle's administration" when Jacques Rivette's film, *La religieuse* (The Nun, 1966), was censored.[64] *Positif* targeted Truffaut in particular because he contributed 528 articles in five years to *Arts*, a journal that welcomed rightist writers, the "hussards" (Jacques Laurent, Roger Nimier, Antoine Blondin), and even former collaborators such as Lucien Rebatet.

But the new generation did not remain altogether silent. Neorealist cinema had endeavored to represent the brutality of war and its consequences; New Wave filmmakers wanted to reflect the deliquescent climate of the 1950s. Some of their films—Paul Carpita's *Le rendez-vous des quais* (The Appointment of the Quays, 1953), Godard's *Le petit soldat* (The Little Soldier, 1960), Jacques Rozier's *Adieu Philippine* (1960), Alain Resnais's *Muriel* (1962), Jacques Demy's *Les parapluies de Cherbourg* (The Umbrellas of Cherbourg, 1963)—include direct allusions to the Algerian War and its consequences: insubordination, torture, and censorship. Resentment toward restrictions on freedom of expression was accentuated by the fact that they were being imposed by a democratic government. Even Truffaut agreed to sign the "Manifesto of the 121," a petition against war and torture initiated by Marguerite Duras and Dionys Mascolo.

In short, the members of the new generation shared a general distrust of any institution, ideology, or convention that would force the values and codes of a group on an individual. This situation was interpreted by some contemporary critics as the return of libertinage, in all senses of the term, whereas leftist commentators analyzed the phenomenon more as a radical questioning of sexuality and women's role in society. As French sociologist Evelyne Sullerot wrote in *France-Observateur* in April 1961, "Miss New Wave still has taboos. They are not sexual taboos, but social taboos [that challenge] the myths of virginity, monogamy, all-beneficent-maternity, and marriage-as-the-unique-solution."[65]

Deep-rooted social conventions, including sexual roles, had already changed in Italy, where women had gained the right to vote after the war. As Lesley Caldwell suggests, "Female identity increasingly assumed a sexualized and eroticized bodily signification in many, especially popular, Italian films of the 1950s. These developments sought both to displace and to accommodate stereotypes inherited from Catholicism and fascism, but also from Communism, and from Italian mores in general."[66] But neorealist films were still permeated with patriarchal conventions and Hollywood clichés: Mary Wood notes that female characters interpreted by Anna Magnani were systematically marginalized by "narratives in which she was a social outsider, and usually killed off at the end."[67] The Italian audience soon deserted "Mamma Roma" and fell for Gina Lollobrigida, Sophia Loren, and the other "sex bombs" of mainstream cinema.

The image of Miss New Wave appears to be more emancipated than neorealist female characters as well as Hollywood "compositions," as Truffaut used to call the likes of Marilyn Monroe. According to Ginette Vincendeau, in the footsteps of Bergman's character in *Sommaren med Monika* (Monika, 1953), Vadim's *Et Dieu créa la femme* turned Brigitte Bardot into an icon of "sexual freedom in a transitional period in France in terms of sexual mores and the legislation regulating sexuality, particularly women's."[68] But neither the (very relative) transformations of a conservative and patriarchal society nor the search for new aesthetics by New Wave directors resulted in a dramatic change of the narrative and visual treatment of female characters. Just as in most neorealist films, "the tragic dimension of the character—the element that elicits empathy on the part of the spectator—is systematically displaced on the male protagonist, the director's (auteur's) alter ego, even when it is a woman who dies, as in *Le petit soldat* or *Tirez sur le pianiste*," notes Geneviève Sellier.[69] The critical discourse is no different in this regard: women rarely appear as narrative subjects in New Wave films. They are also conspicuously absent from the team of contributors to *Cahiers du cinéma* and from writings as critics and directors. Sadoul stands out as the only critic to fully acknowledge the groundbreaking role of Agnès Varda's *La pointe courte* (1955) in French postwar cinema.[70]

A Single Slogan
"Cinema"

There was, however, one particular and explicit commitment shared by *Cahiers du cinéma* and *Positif* critics, as Ciment acknowledges: "If there was a cause they would all stand for, it was not the Algerian war, it was the Cinémathèque."[71] Cinephilia can be considered a typically French phenomenon that arose from the population's fondness for grassroots societies based on the practice of a common hobby or activity: Defined and regulated by the 1901 Loi sur les Associations, these groups served as an alternative to institutionalized entities such as unions and political parties. Cinephilia's collective and subversive dimension benefited both neorealist cinema and the New Wave by providing them with a forum and an audience aside from commercial theaters, official festivals (Cannes and Venice), and the columns of the professional press (*L'Écran français*).[72] The *lieux de la cinéphilie* included *cinéclubs* (the Ciné-Club du Quartier Latin, favored by Rivette and Rohmer; the more traditional Ciné-Club Universitaire; and Bazin's Ciné-Club de Travail et Culture); critical reviews (Godard contributed to *La gazette du cinéma* under the alias Hans Lucas, and Bazin wrote for *La revue du cinéma* before founding *Cahiers du cinéma*); and alternate festivals (the Festival du Film Maudit launched in Biarritz in 1949 by Doniol-Valcroze and Bazin; the 1959 Mar del Plata Festival attended by Langlois, Martin, Aristarco, Zavattini, and Sadoul).

The phenomenon of cinephilia in France can also be understood as a reaction to the ongoing institutionalization of cinema. In both countries, the period between the two world wars had confirmed the importance of film as a means of information, communication, and propaganda and had thus ensured its use by those in power. In Italy, the fascist administration created the General Directorate of Cinema in 1934, the Centro Sperimentale di Cinematografia in 1935, and Cinecittà in 1937. A similar project, contemplated in France under the Popular Front of 1936, was implemented by the Vichy government with the creation of the Comité d'Organisation de l'Industrie Cinématographique in 1939 (which was replaced in 1946 by the Centre National de la Cinématographie) and the Institut des Hautes Études Cinématographiques in 1942.

The structure of the Italian industry differed markedly from its French counterpart, which was highly hierarchical and organized according to a strict division of labor: No one could direct a film without conforming to the regulations established and controlled by producers, confirmed directors, and unionized technicians. This situation contributed to the "impersonal" nature of mainstream French postwar film production and led the younger generation to explore alternate strategies. Thanks to inherited money, Chabrol shot his first films in 1957 and sponsored Rivette's *Paris nous appartient* (Paris Is Ours, 1960) together with Truffaut, who was financially more secure after the success of *Les 400 coups*. New legislation that liberated funds for artistic support helped a few bold producers willing to cofinance unusual projects: Anatole Dauman, Georges de Beauregard, and Pierre Braunberger, who in 1957 produced Godard's first fiction film, *Charlotte et Véronique; ou, Tous les hommes s'appellent Patrick* (All the Boys Are Called Patrick, 1959), and convinced him to work with confirmed cinematographer Raoul Coutard on *A bout de souffle*, thus initiating a lasting and fruitful partnership.

The commercial success of *Les 400 coups* (450,000 tickets sold) and *A bout de souffle* (300,000 tickets sold) also stemmed from the fact that young filmmakers were not strangers to the distribution system. Truffaut had learned how to appeal to critics and festivalgoers from Bazin's efforts to promote neorealist cinema; Godard remembered from his work as a press attaché at Fox how to launch a promotional campaign for *A bout de souffle*.[73] The first ten years of the "trente glorieuses" (the thirty years of French postwar prosperity) and the elaboration of the *politique des auteurs* thus gave a new generation of filmmakers the opportunity to appropriate the dominant strategies of film production and distribution to transcend the system's genres and conventions.

In committing to cinema as their ultimate object, the New Wave was complying with Rossellini's statement to the effect that "whatever will there is to invent a fiction, a film remains the documentary of its own production." In his introduction to Rossellini's collection of writings and interviews, Bergala notes that "this conviction which will be shared by many modern filmmakers, from Rivette ('the method used to shoot a film is always its true subject') to Wim Wenders ('the claustrophobic atmosphere of many films is the result of their conditions of production'), resulted in Godard's idea that in order to change cinema, one first had to change methods and conditions of production."[74] Technology gave these young French filmmakers a chance to implement their aesthetic project.

The advent of light cameras, Nagra sound recorders, and professional 16mm stock allowed New Wave directors to capitalize on the artistic potential offered by the neorealist stylistic use of "documentary" features such as grainy photography, amateur actors, daily actions, and dramatic events as well as archival material and "fragments of raw reality," to use Bazin's expression. Jean Rouch's documentary films, first seen by *Cahiers du cinéma* critics at the Biarritz Festival du Film Maudit in 1949, also had a significant influence on New Wave directors for his appropriation of surrealist and neorealist influences[75] and his use of light technology, improvisation, and postsynching.[76]

Similarly, location shooting in Parisian apartments and districts—Pigalle, Saint-Germain-des-Prés, the Champs-Elysées, among others—can be interpreted as an effect of the neorealist legacy combined with the new resources provided by technological innovation and the necessity to challenge the *cinéma de papa*. But whereas neorealist directors had described the difficulties of constructing Italian unity out of a juxtaposition of diverse regional cultures, languages, and populations—peasants from the Po Valley, Sicilian fishermen, Roman workers—New Wave filmmakers struggled to invest the capital city with its double face: the *lieu de pouvoir* of the French Jacobinist system where all political and administrative decisions are made and sent out to the rest of the metropole and the colonies as well as the *lieu de résistance* to centralized power, with its streets, cafés, and movie theaters populated by students, intellectuals, and artists as portrayed by Jean Rouch in *Chronique d'un été (Paris 1960)* (Chronicle of a Summer, 1961).

In spite of the accusations formulated by *Positif* critics, young New Wave directors adopted an explicit political stance when claiming the neorealist aesthetic legacy in a context that favored conspicuous mass consumption. Bazin was the first to pinpoint the multifaceted dimension of the neorealist model for *Cahiers du cinéma* critics when it came time for them to elaborate their own aesthetics. Annette Insdorf points out that "French critics/filmmakers made virtues of necessities similar to those of their Italian mentors and turned theory into a practice relevant to their own ideological, technical and artistic conditions of production."[77] Whereas the novelty that characterized postwar Italian cinema can be seen as a prescriptive argument designed to cut ties with an embarrassing past, French New Wave critics and directors seem to have been deeply involved in a search for spiritual, moral, and artistic fathers: What could appear as the privilege of a generation allowed to establish its own genealogy became the spectacular and foreboding message of young people asserting their agency and their right to build a new society.

"Rapidity. Art. Novelty. Cinematograph. Originality. Impertinence. Seriousness. Tragedy. Renovation. Ubu-Roi. Fantasy. Ferocity. Affection. Universality. Tenderness": This is how Godard described Truffaut's style in a review of *Les 400 coups*,[78] prompting Antoine de Baecque's definition of the New Wave as "the first movement in cinema since its beginnings to stylize the contemporary world in the present tense, in the immediacy of time."[79] The new role given to cinema by the New Wave had its roots in neorealism, a movement that, according to Harry Harootunian, marked the moment when "cinema itself constituted the privileged mode of cultural expressivity in this postwar historical moment and was, in fact, indistinguishable from the history of those years it had made its task to represent."[80] In this regard, both "new" styles of Italian realism and French filmmaking contributed to a significant turn by revealing the historical function of cinema beyond the objections formulated by critics on both the right and the left. It took two generations of filmmakers to address the ideological, economic, social, moral, and aesthetic consequences of World War II in terms that would be specific to cinema, thus verifying the ability of film as an art form to shape social consciousness and reflect latent historical conditions through the "inner logic of its content," as Fredric Jameson proposed,[81] or "slips of History," to use Marc Ferro's expression.[82] The Italian neorealist generation innovated by presenting images of the streets; the French New Wave took these images to the streets before May 1968 activists subsequently claimed and invested both.

Notes

I am grateful to Lauretta Clough for her generous and expert help in reading and revising this text.

1. Françoise Giroud, cofounder of *L'express* in 1953 with Jean-Jacques Servan-Schreiber, decided to publish the results of a survey of opinions and trends among young French people. The article appeared on October 3, 1957, with the title "The New Wave Is Here!," and the expression was subsequently used to designate the new generation at large before being applied to young filmmakers by Pierre Billard in *Cinéma 58*, February 1958.

2. See Michel Marie, *The French New Wave: An Artistic School*, trans. Richard Neupert (Malden, Mass.: Blackwell, 2002).

3. Unless one agrees with André Bazin that "five years in cinema are equivalent to one generation in literature" ("La terra trema," *Esprit*, December 1948, reprinted in *Qu'est-ce que le cinéma?* [Paris: Cerf, 2002], 291; translated into English by Hugh Gray as *What Is Cinema?* [Berkeley: University of California Press, 1971], 2:44).

4. See Peter Bondanella, *The Cinema of Federico Fellini* (Princeton: Princeton University Press, 1992), 45.

5. For Marie (*French New Wave*) and other critics, 1959 marks the "official" debut of the New Wave with the nomination of *Les 400 coups* and *Hiroshima mon amour* at the Cannes Film Festival and the production of Rohmer's *Le signe du lion*, Rivette's *Paris nous appartient*, and Chabrol's *A double tour*.

6. See Cyril Neyrat, *François Truffaut* (Paris: Cahiers du Cinéma, 2007), 16: "In 1954, with Rivette and Rohmer's support, Truffaut shot his first short film, *Une visite*, in the apartment of Jacques Doniol-Valcroze, who was then the editor in chief of the *Cahiers du cinéma*. Unhappy with the result, he refused to show the film to anyone."

7. The famous journal was founded in 1951 by Bazin, Jacques Doniol-Valcroze, Léonide Kriegel, and Joseph Marie Lo Duca.

8. See Thierry Frémaux, "L'aventure cinéphilique de Positif (1952–1989)," *Vingtième siècle: Revue d'histoire* 23 (1989): 21–34.

9. Roberto Rossellini, interview by Fereydoun Hoveyda and Eric Rohmer, *Cahiers du cinéma* 145 (July 1963): 3.

10. Bazin, *What Is Cinema?*, 2:66–67.

11. Vincent Pinel, *Genres et mouvements au cinéma* (Paris: Larousse, 2000), 130. Jean-André Fieschi addressed the issue of a possible "new neorealism" in "Neo-neo-realism: Bandits d'Orgosto," *Cahiers du cinéma*, March 1963, 271–75.

12. See "The New Wave at 50: Riding the Wave," *Sight and Sound* 19 (May 2009): 26; René Prédal, *Le cinéma français contemporain* (Paris: Cerf, 1984); René Prédal, *Le cinéma français depuis 1945* (Paris: Nathan, 1991); René Prédal, *Le cinéma d'auteur: Une vieille lune?* (Paris: Cerf, 2001).

13. Richard Neupert, *A History of the French New Wave Cinema* (Madison: University of Wisconsin Press, 2002), xv.

14. Christian Metz, *Langage et cinéma* (Paris: Larousse, 1971).

15. Guy Gauthier, "Nés de la vague," *CinémAction* 104 (Fall 2002): 40.

16. For Pinel (*Genres et mouvements*, 132), the neorealist influence on Cinema Novo, Free Cinema, and Eastern European "dissidents" (Milos Forman, Ivan Passer, Sergei Paradjanov, Otar Iosseliani) came from a political, moral, and aesthetic concern for social questions, whereas the New Wave spirit was based on a claim for freedom: "freedom of expression against dominant ideologies, (still relative) freedom of mores evading the scissors of censorship, formal freedom challenging the 'transparency' of commercial cinema."

17. André Bazin, "In Defense of Rossellini: A Letter to Guido Aristarco, Editor-in-Chief of Cinema Nuovo," reprinted in *What Is Cinema?*, 2:101.

18. *Le nouvel observateur*, interview by Louis Marcorelles, October 1961, quoted by Antoine de Baecque in *La Nouvelle Vague: Portrait d'une jeunesse* (Paris: Flammarion, 1998), 142.

19. Robert Benayou, "Le roi est nu," *Positif* 46 (June 1962): 1.

20. Tom Milne and Jean Narboni, eds., *Godard on Godard* (New York: Viking, 1972), 73.

21. de Baecque, *Nouvelle Vague*, 17.

22. For a more detailed discussion of Italian film criticism and production during the fascist regime and its impact on neorealism, see Peter Bondanella, *Italian Cinema: From Neorealism to the Present* (New York: Continuum, 1990); Millicent Marcus, *Italian Film in the Light of Neorealism* (Princeton: Princeton University Press, 1986); Vito Zagarrio, *Cinema, intellettuali, fascismo* (Venice: Marsilio, 2002).

23. de Baecque, *Nouvelle Vague*, 43. See also Richard Jobs, *Riding the New Wave: Youth and the Rejuvenation of France after the Second World War* (Stanford: Stanford University Press, 2007).

24. de Baecque, *Nouvelle Vague*, 43

25. Zavattini and De Sica were born in 1902, Visconti and Rossellini in 1906, Lattuada in 1913, De Santis in 1917, and Fellini in 1920.

26. De Gaulle responded to the crisis on the political front by instituting the Constitution of 1958 and on the cultural front with the creation of two agencies for the benefit of young people: the Ministry of Culture, headed by André Malraux, and the Haut Commissariat à la Jeunesse et aux Sports. The institutional response did not succeed, however, in preventing the uprising of a large part of the younger generation in May 1968.

27. "The second half of 1946 witnessed an American invasion: Paris hosted premieres of *Citizen Kane*, *Double Indemnity*, *Murder My Sweet*, *The Maltese Falcon*, *Phantom Lady*, *How Green Was My Valley*, *The Little Foxes*, *The Westerner*, *The Magnificent Ambersons*, and many other films" (David Bordwell, *Making Meaning: Inference and Rhetoric in the Interpretation of Cinema* [Cambridge: Harvard University Press, 1989], 45).

28. See also Tom Conley, *Les Mistons and Undercurrents of French New Wave Cinema (The Geske Lectures)* (Lincoln: University of Nebraska Press, 2003); Naomi Greene, *The French New Wave: A New Look* (London: Wallflower, 2007).

29. For François Albera (*L'avant-garde au cinéma* [Paris: Colin, 2005], 138), "there is no doubt that if urban drifting in *Traité de bave et d'éternité* [by Isidore Isou (1952)] may have influenced Michel Poiccard's desperate wandering in *A bout de souffle*, the Situationist approach greatly impacted Jean-Luc Godard's so-called 'sociological' period . . . as well as his 'activist' days in 1968."

30. On Italian realism since the early 1940s, see Jean A. Gili, *Le cinéma italien* (Paris: Martinière, 1996); Jean A. Gili, *L'Italie de Mussolini et son cinéma* (Paris: Veyrier, 1985).

31. Dudley Andrew, *Mists of Regret: Culture and Sensibility in Classic French Film* (Princeton: Princeton University Press, 1995), 196.

32. The 1950s were the heyday of the *nouveau roman*, with the publication of *Un barrage contre le Pacifique* (Marguerite Duras, 1950), *Les Gommes* (Robbe-Grillet, 1953), and *L'emploi du temps* (Michel Butor, 1956). Nathalie Sarraute pioneered the movement with *Tropismes* (1939) and *Portrait d'un inconnu* (1948). See Dorota Ostrowska, *Reading the French New Wave: Critics, Writers, and Art in France* (London: Wallflower, 2001); Claude Murcia, *Nouveau roman, nouveau cinéma* (Paris: Nathan, 1998); Robert Stam, *François Truffaut and Friends: Modernism, Sexuality, and Film Adaptation* (New Brunswick: Rutgers University Press, 2006).

33. Andrew, *Mists of Regret*, 14.

34. André Bazin, "*Bicycle Thief*," *Esprit*, November 1949, reprinted in *What Is Cinema?*, 2:49.

35. Andrew, *Mists of Regret*, 338.

36. See "The Fever of Jean Vigo," in François Truffaut, *The Films of My Life* (New York: Harcourt, 1978).

37. Truffaut named his production company Les Films du Carrosse after Jean Renoir's film, *Le carrosse d'or* (1952).

38. Philippe Roger, "Le dernier cinéma muet? La place du cinéma des années 20 dans les histoire(s)," *CinémAction* 109 (2003): 200.

39. Sadoul's major work is the monumental *Histoire générale du cinéma*, 6 vols. (Paris: Denoël, 1946–54).

40. See Georges Sadoul, "A propos de quelques films récents," reprinted in *Écrits: 1. Chroniques du cinéma français, 1939–1967* (Paris: Union Générale, 1979), 14.

41. André Bazin, "An Aesthetic of Reality: Cinematic Realism and the Italian School of the Liberation," in *What Is Cinema?*, 2:31–40.

42. Bazin, "In Defense of Rossellini," 96.

43. Cesare Zavattini, *Sequences from a Cinematic Life*, trans. William Weaver (Englewood Cliffs, N.J.: Prentice-Hall, 1970), 27.

44. André Bazin, "De Sica metteur en scène," in *What Is Cinema?*, 2:64–65.

45. Eric Rohmer, "La Somme d'André Bazin," *Cahiers du cinéma* 91 (January 1959): 36–45.

46. Dudley Andrew, *André Bazin*, foreword by François Truffaut (New York: Oxford University Press, 1978), 118–19.

47. André Bazin, "An Aesthetic of Reality: Cinematic Realism and the Italian School of the Liberation," in *What Is Cinema?*, 2:21.

48. Luchino Visconti, "Il cinema antropomorfico," *Cinema* 173–74 (September–October 1943): 108; Roberto Rossellini, "Entretien avec Maurice Schérer et François Truffaut," *Cahiers du cinéma* 37 (July 1954): 59.

49. James Monaco, *The New Wave: Truffaut, Godard, Chabrol, Rohmer* (Cambridge: Oxford University Press, 1977), 8.

50. Bazin, *"Bicycle Thief,"* 47.

51. May 1968 events, however, turned Godard into a "militant in the field of anti-imperialistic information" (François Nemer, *Godard [Le cinéma]* [Paris: Gallimard, 2006], 20). He then cofounded a group of film activists, the Dziga Vertov group.

52. References to religion are not totally absent from New Wave cinema. But I agree with Bordwell (*Making Meaning*, 46) that Truffaut's accusation of blasphemy against "cinéma de papa" is another one of his provocations *à la Surréaliste*. Rivette is in fact the only New Wave filmmaker to have claimed a modern vision of religion, deeply influenced by Rossellini's *Viaggio in Italia*. The ideological, social, and historical dimensions of his version of *La religieuse* (The Nun, 1966) and his films on Joan of Arc (*Jeanne la Pucelle* I and II [Jeanne the Virgin, I and II, 1994]) owe more to the neorealist influence than to Robert Bresson's mystical approach in *Journal d'un curé de campagne* (Diary of a Country Priest, 1951) and *Procès de Jeanne d'Arc* (The Trial of Joan of Arc, 1962), for example.

53. François Truffaut, "A Certain Tendency of French Cinema," *Cahiers du cinéma*, January 1954, in *Movies and Methods*, ed. Bill Nichols (Berkeley: University of California Press, 1976), 1:224–35.

54. See T. Jefferson Kline, *Screening the Text: Intertextuality in the New Wave French Cinema* (Baltimore: Johns Hopkins University Press, 1992), 4. According to Kline, the method used by New Wave critics consisted in throwing "a literary cast to film criticism" and "recasting the metaliterary concerns of the 1960s into metacinematic ones."

55. See P. Adams Sitney, *Vital Crises in Italian Cinema: Iconography, Stylistics, Politics* (Austin: University of Texas Press, 1995), 88–89.

56. "Schapiro recognized, as no Italian critic of the time seems to have done, the degree to which the Italian cinema, at least exemplified by *Roma, città aperta*, reflects and recasts the iconographic tradition of Renaissance art" (ibid., 33). Bazin had previously linked neo-realism to "Italian traditions such as the fairy tale, commedia dell'arte and the technique of the fresco" ("An Aesthetic of Reality: Cinematic Realism and the Italian School of the Liberation," in *What Is Cinema?*, 2:40).

57. On the prolific teams of neorealist screenwriters and directors (Vittorio De Sica/ Cesare Zavattini, Luchino Visconti/Suso Cecchi d'Amico, Rossellini/Sergio Amidei and Fellini), see Bondanella, *Italian Cinema*, 31–40.

58. Andrew, *Mists of Regret*, 199.

59. The "group of the Left Bank" can be considered more innovative in this regard: the tandems Alain Resnais formed with Marguerite Duras (*Hiroshima mon amour*) and Alain Robbe-Grillet (*L'année dernière à Marienbad*) can be considered as a compromise between the traditional model and the Italian example. Resnais did not interfere with the writing process, but his screenwriters' collaboration stopped the moment he started directing the film. See Jeanne-Marie Clerc, *Littérature et cinéma* (Paris: Nathan, 1993), 61–63.

60. For Rohmer, "Cinema reaches for novelistic perfection as a curve toward its asymptote" (Eric Rohmer, *Le goût de la beauté* [Paris: Flammarion, 1989], 151–52).

61. Bazin, "De Sica metteur en scène," 65.

62. Neyrat, *François Truffaut*, 16.

63. Henry Rousso, *Le syndrome de Vichy, 1944–198-* (Paris: Seuil, 1987). The ambiguities of the postwar period in France were also examined by Marcel Ophuls and André Harris in their documentary film, *Le chagrin et la pitié* (1969), where they challenged the "legend of the Résistance" that Bazin contrasted to the "slow process of the Italian Liberation" ("Le réalisme cinématographique et l'école italienne de la libération," in *What Is Cinema?*, 2:19–20).

64. Michel Ciment, "Positif et la Nouvelle Vague," *CinémAction* 104 (November 2002): 87.

65. Evelyne Sullerot, "Mademoiselle Nouvelle Vague," *France Observateur* 338 (April 1961), quoted in de Baecque, *Nouvelle Vague*, 127.

66. Lesley Caldwell, "What about Women? Italian Films and Their Concerns," in *Heroines without Heroes: Female Identities in Post-War European Cinemas, 1945–1952*, ed. Ulrike Sieglohr (London: Cassell, 2000), 145.

67. Mary P. Wood, "Woman of Rome: Anna Magnani," in ibid., 157–58.

68. Ginette Vincendeau, *Stars and Stardom in French Cinema* (London: Continuum, 2000), 86–87, 97.

69. Geneviève Sellier, *Masculine Singular: French New Wave Cinema*, trans. Kristin Ross (Durham, N.C.: Duke University Press, 2008), 10. See also Stam, *François Truffaut and Friends*.

70. Georges Sadoul, "Le coeur révélateur d'Agnès Varda, *Cléo de 5 à 7* d'Agnès Varda," *Lettres françaises* 922 (April 12 1962), reprinted in *Écrits*, 269: "We failed to understand in 1956 that *La pointe courte* was the beginning of a new era, the New Wave (even more than Vadim's *Et Dieu créa la femme* or Astruc's *Les mauvaises rencontres*). Filmed with a very small budget, totally independent, without stars (but with the talented yet still unknown Silvia Monfort), *La pointe courte* anticipated French films of the 1960s in terms of both method and style."

71. de Baecque, *Nouvelle Vague*, 29.

72. Rohmer, *Goût*, 13–15.

73. "The distributor selected four of the best theaters in Paris; three different posters were extensively distributed. A novel and a record were released at the same time. And Godard gave away a large number of production photographs" (Nemer, *Godard*, 31).

74. Alain Bergala, "Roberto Rossellini ou l'invention du cinéma moderne," in Roberto Rossellini, *Le cinéma révélé* (Paris: Flammarion, 2008), 26.

75. In his two reviews of *Moi, un noir* (1958), published in *Cahiers du cinéma* 90 (March 1959): 50–52 and 91 (April 1959): 19–22, Godard, a former student of ethnology, explored the influence of neorealism—and more specifically *Roma, città aperta*—on Rouch's work.

76. Peter Wollen, *Paris Hollywood: Writings on Film* (London: Verso, 2002), 93, 244.

77. Annette Insdorf, *François Truffaut* (Cambridge: Cambridge University Press, 1978), 24.

78. *Cahiers du cinéma* 92 (February 1959): 51–52.

79. de Baecque, *Nouvelle Vague*, 15

80. Harry Harootunian, "Detour to the East: Noel Burch and the Task of Japanese Film: History, Signs, and Difference," introduction to Noel Burch, *To the Distant Observer: Form and Meaning in the Japanese Cinema* (1979; Ann Arbor: University of Michigan Center for Japanese Studies, 2004).

81. Fredric Jameson, "Metacommentary," *PMLA* 86.1 (January 1971): 9–18, reprinted in *The Ideologies of Theory: Essays 1971–1986: The Syntax of History* (Minneapolis: University of Minnesota Press, 1988), 2:14.

82. Marc Ferro, *Cinema and History*, trans. Naomi Greene (Detroit: Wayne State University Press, 1988).

"WITH AN INCREDIBLE REALISM THAT BEATS THE BEST OF THE EUROPEAN CINEMAS"

The Making of *Barrio Gris* and the Reception of Italian Neorealism in Argentina, 1947–1955

PAULA HALPERIN

The silhouette of a mounted policeman rapidly crosses the screen. Surrounded by smoldering piles of garbage, a man is desperately climbing a street lamp. He is escaping in a dark night; a dense fog rises from the asphalt. He is dressed as a *compadrito*, a hoodlum from 1930s Buenos Aires. An orchestra starts a tango. The credits announce that Cinematográfica V and Mario Soffici are presenting the film *Barrio gris*. The scene that follows, which is repeated at the end of the film, shows a contrasting image: a bright and sunny neighborhood full of children wearing neat school uniforms and walking to the local public school, accompanied by their mothers; in the distance one sees more children at play.

These two scenes from this 1954 Argentine film speak to the complex process of transformation that Argentine society and its cultural products underwent during the 1950s. The first thirty seconds of the film engage the viewer with familiar tropes of the local film production popular since the emergence of the talkies in 1933—that is, suburban and border spaces embodied by the *guapo* (the thug) running from a brutal and out-of-control police. The second scene is set in temporal, geographical, and social opposition to the first. It shows the previously dark and dirty space now transformed into an open and brilliant landscape. It is still a suburban neighborhood, but this one is more connected to Buenos Aires, as the viewer has a glimpse of a modern highway in the distance. It also situates the spectator in contemporary times, showing happy children, the result of the process of social modernization experienced by Argentine society during Juan Domingo Perón's first administration (1946–52), which promoted the slogan, "The only privileged in this new Argentina are the children."

Barrio Gris (1954): The happy
childhood of the Peronist years.

The juxtaposition of these two scenes in Mario Soffici's *Barrio gris* illuminates an era of significant change in the film industry in Argentina. These
contrasting sequences allow us to grasp the complex process of modernization
endured by Argentine society after the emergence of the Peronist regime; they
also show the transition of a film industry based on genres and the studio system to a new one, more oriented to auteur features, independent producers,
and social and political films.

Further, these scenes highlight what would become a key element during
the 1960s in the field of cultural production: the queries about the relationship of art and politics and the meaning of "national" language in the work
of art. The brief portrayal of a vibrant, noisy childhood at the beginning, together with the images of poor children depicted throughout the film, reveal
a relationship to Roberto Rossellini's *Roma, città aperta* (Rome, Open City,
1945) and to many of the child-centered films produced by Italian neorealists.
These and many other elements present in *Barrio gris* would convince many
in the Argentine press that a dialogue existed between the film and the Italian
movement, creating a public discussion about filmmaking, aesthetics, and the
language of Argentine national cinema.

The vast debate generated by Soffici's film foreshadowed the questions that
would become urgent during the next two decades in the field of cultural production. The film engaged intellectuals and critics in a debate about realism
and film style, the possible connections with the Italian movement, and the
meaning of making truly "national" productions that spoke to the social and
cultural changes of the Peronist decade. However, the link between the film
and the contemporary political situation in Argentina escaped most of the
critics. Emphasizing the association of *Barrio gris* with Italian neorealism and
its technical and formal innovations more than its ideological and political
implications, the press and the specialized critics, most of whom opposed the
regime, avoided openly talking about the relationship and the obvious connections between the film and the changing Argentine society.[1]

Barrio Gris and the Argentine Studio System

It was October 1954, and Mario Soffici had just released his thirty-third movie. He would make more than forty films over his career, including three in 1954. The Italian-born director was one of the masters of Argentine cinema. "White telephones," historical dramas, light comedies, and romantic musicals all were part of his vast repertoire. Prominent in the industry, Soffici had made his films with the support of the major Argentine studios, especially Argentina Sono Film.[2] He had also founded a distribution company with successful directors Daniel Tinayre, Luis César Amadori, Lucas Demare, and Hugo del Carril. Cinematográfica V, which had helped in the making of *Barrio gris*, was an attempt to create alternative, independent channels of film distribution.[3]

Soffici was very pleased with *Barrio gris*. Adapted from Argentine writer Joaquin Gomes Bas's 1952 romance novel by the same title, the film tells a harsh story of Federico, a troublesome little boy who comes of age during the 1930s in a poor suburban "gray" neighborhood at the outskirts of Buenos Aires—a mix of shantytown and lower-middle-class residences. All the tropes that characterize the *arrabal*[4] narratives are part of this story. *Barrio gris* displays the clichés with which the popular classes were so familiar: the dear and suffering mother; the sister who wishes for a better and fancier life; Rosita, the ardent older girl who visits Federico's dreams; the melting pot of Italian, Spanish, and Polish immigrants living together in the same neighborhood; the *galán* (gentleman); the violent and arbitrary police; the corrupted politicians. Physical spaces that compose the barrio also have their place in the narrative: the movie theater, the dangerous streets, the dirty stream running through the neighborhood, the market, the boxing ring, and the factory, where men ruin their health for paltry wages.

Beyond the stylistic and thematic similarities that *Barrio gris* shares with neorealism, Soffici's film was evidence of a complex moment of transition and modernization in Argentine cinema. By the mid-1950s, the studio system that had monopolized film production for two decades was dying. Its most popular genres were slowly but surely withering along with it. During the studio era, the film industry had promoted classical films à la Hollywood, with its formulas and genres. Argentine films were mostly consumed by the popular classes, who enjoyed the generic films and the melodramas produced by the studios.[5] Yet a tradition of realism had also been part of the Argentine cinema since the emergence of the talkies—for example, in the early 1930s work by director Agustín "El Negro" Ferreira, who had traveled with his camera across Buenos Aires, recording its diverse peoples and varied neighborhoods.[6] Studio

Barrio Gris (1954): The poor suburban barrio where Federico grew up.

craftsmen such as directors Daniel Tinayre, Lucas Demare, and Luis José Moglia Barth incorporated into their stories the everyday life of the slums, poor neighborhoods, and rural places of greater Buenos Aires. Soffici was a former apprentice of Ferreira and had used an expressionist realism to tell stories of "regular" people who spoke truth to power and fought injustice. Most of Soffici's films had been located in rural landscapes that endured the process of modernization, and their plots referred to the characters' choices in the face of modernizing change.[7] During the 1930s and 1940s, Argentine studios also integrated Hollywood genres with previous realist traditions, especially those imported from the popular theater and the radio soap operas.[8]

This Argentine studio system had been remarkably successful. Since its creation in 1933, the production of national films had increased considerably (with the exception of the period during World War II when celluloid was scarce), reaching its height in 1950 with fifty-eight releases during the year. When the system started declining in 1952 because of its inefficiency and excessive competition from Hollywood, thirty-five films were made. Five years later, only sixteen movies were released.[9]

In the late 1940s, however, no one would have predicted this crisis. In tune with the wave of realism that became popular after World War II, the studios promoted the making of social dramas with a touch of romance, such as Amadori's *Dios se lo pague* (God Reward You, 1948), loved by the public and praised by Vittorio De Sica.[10] In that vein, Hugo del Carril's *Las aguas bajan turbias* (River of Blood, 1952), León Klimovsky's *Suburbio* (Suburbs, 1951), Tinayre's *Deshonra* (Dishonor, 1952), Carlos Borcosque's *Pobres habrá siempre* (There Will Always Be Poor People, 1954), and Demare's *Mercado de abasto* (Supplying Market, 1954) and *Guacho* (The Bastard, 1954) were some of the big productions that combined love relations with social issues, making the people and the places where they circulated more visible: the humble neighborhood, the market, the workplace, the street, the cabaret.

Peronism and Argentine Cinema

By the time these films were released, Perón's second administration (1952–55) had consolidated the profound transformation started during his first presidency. His reforms resembled many of those implemented by the populist regimes that emerged in Latin America from the 1930s on. Similar to Lázaro Cardenas in Mexico (1934–40) and Getúlio Vargas in Brazil (1930–45 and 1951–54), Perón launched a massive program of social reforms that included progressive legislation on social rights, a significant redistribution of wealth in favor of the popular classes, aid to national industries, and the building of federal systems of public health and education. The state assumed a leading political and economic role, improving the living conditions of the working classes and creating a new notion of citizenship that would include these social strata as a fundamental national component, in stark contrast not only to the previous decade but also to the entire history of modern Argentina. At the same time, the regime's authoritarian populist style alienated the middle class and intellectuals from political life, creating a fracture in Argentine society that would persist for decades. In his public utterances, Perón took pains to express his populist support of the popular classes. As he said in 1954, Argentina had just two political groups, "the people" and "the antipeople."[11]

Until recently, the historiography that delved into the relationship between the Peronist regime and the film industry canonized the notion that the authoritarian state had absolute control over film production, rewarding supporters and punishing opponents, in the vein of the Nazi and fascist regimes.[12] More recent analyses of the connection between Perón's populist administrations and the film industry reveal a more nuanced picture. Through legislation and regulation, the state—more precisely, Alejandro Apold, undersecretary of the Subsecretaría de Informaciones y Prensa de la Nación (Federal Secretariat of Information and Press) attempted to influence an industry carefully organized around the big studios' interests. Both Argentina Sono Film and Lumiton were favored through financial support. Furthermore, the state went above and beyond stimulating the production of national films in a market monopolized by U.S. productions through a system of soft loans given by the state bank, the Banco Industrial, to different film producers. The state also "protected" national productions by implementing the compulsory exhibition of Argentine features, a common demand of directors and producers in Latin America after World War II. Finally, the regime meted out personal favors to directors and actors, thereby guaranteeing authorities limited control of the content of films to avoid provoking resentment, jealousy, and political opposition.[13]

As Clara Kriger has shown, censorship was not absolute. The state "would make suggestions" regarding scenes that were considered potentially critical.[14] Afraid of not receiving financial support from the state, directors and producers also often exercised self-censorship, excluding possible criticism of the regime. A paradoxical situation emerged because of the government's desire to avoid alienating the most popular filmmakers: While the field of cultural production had no space for open opposition to the government, the government also could not implement a cultural policy that had total control over the production of films or cultural artifacts in general. As historian Oscar Terán has recently suggested, some space existed for artistic creation outside the regime's ideological preferences.[15]

In this way, the most powerful members of the film industry took advantage of their relative independence under the Peronist administrations, offering in exchange a timid public support of the regime.[16] Although censorship persisted during those years, creators of fiction films did not experience extreme control; the state was more interested in intervening in the production of institutional documentaries that were to emphasize the good new times, the effectiveness of social reforms, and the happiness of the popular classes.

Much of the film industry went along with the program. The pinnacle of this collaboration between the state and the private sector was the Festival Internacional de Cine de Mar del Plata (Mar del Plata International Film Festival), organized by the government in 1954.[17] This event constituted both an attempt to show the strength of the "national" film industry at a moment when the regime was experiencing a legitimation crisis and an effort to display features of "cosmopolitism" by a regime accused of being uncultivated and provincial by the middle classes and intellectuals.

Barrio Gris and Its Reception

In tune with this political context, the gritty part of *Barrio gris* occurs almost entirely during a pre-Peronist moment. Both Soffici and the original novel located most of their plot in the infamous 1930s, when the state criminalized the poor and the working classes and guaranteed no social or political rights. Viewers of the film (as well as readers of the book) could feel the past unfolding before their eyes, a past close and familiar to many people.

Soffici found Gomes Bas's prestige and the success of his book appealing enough to film. The director believed that the story spoke a truly national language, differing from most of the other literary adaptations that were en vogue, which were based on European classics (Gustave Flaubert, Alexandre

Dumas, Stendhal).[18] Even though it was not the first time he or other directors adapted Argentine literature,[19] *Barrio gris* had a large impact on the media because the novel was both "national" and very successful.

Soffici and Gomes Bas, who served as screenwriter, also chose not to write the script with any particular star in mind. For the first time, the director looked for the performers after the story had been written. This approach represented a big blow to the star system. Before *Barrio gris*, Soffici recalled, scripts were always created for the stars. During preproduction and shooting of the film, the press was amazed, commenting, criticizing, and interviewing almost everyone involved. Accounts stressed the feature's engagement with national issues and its distinctive use of nonprofessional actors. A national contest to find performers for the major roles caused great excitement. Soffici commented to the sophisticated film magazine *Gente de cine* that he could not find the right actors; otherwise, he would never have turned to nonprofessionals.[20] The "unknown" young woman chosen to play the provocative and sexual Rosita was from Sarandí, the same suburban barrio where the story takes place. "Coincidence?" a journalist wondered. "There was even a bus driver playing a key character."[21]

Many journalists and critics thought *Barrio gris* was some kind of vernacular neorealism, as it incorporated new young prospects.[22] Soffici "was in love" with Italian neorealism, they argued, as the film style influenced filmmakers around the world. They saw an Italian-Argentine director who wanted to create a sense of reality—in the vein of De Sica in *Ladri di biciclette* (Bicycle Thieves, 1948)—using nonprofessional actors.[23] Others, however, refused to associate the production with any "foreign" tradition. Despite the clear predominance of amateurs that led to the film's identification with the Italian movement, these critics stressed the appearance of major Argentine stars in a few secondary roles.[24]

The journal *Sintonía* did not buy this argument and wrote that Soffici was "imposing" an innovation, as the industry was not used to nonprofessional actors in primary roles.[25] A few months later, a journalist from the same fanzine pointedly congratulated Demare for choosing popular star Tita Merello, one of "the most versatile actresses of our industry," for the central role in his 1955 social drama, *Mercado de abasto*. That decision was "the first smart move. There was no space for improvisation."[26] *Mundo radial* and *Radiofilm* defended *Barrio gris*, claiming that Soffici had not in fact tuned the subject to Italian neorealism. Instead, they argued, he had told the story in "*our* language," in "*our* way," and had developed a theme that was the quintessence of Argentina yet was not something that happened only in "*our* country." "The film narrates our problems and our hopes," *Radiofilm* wrote.[27]

Neorealism in Argentina

As Mariano Mestman points out in his essay in this volume, Argentine and Latin American filmmakers and critics of the 1960s were deeply conversant with Italian neorealism. The production and reception of *Barrio gris*, however, show how this conversation had already started in the 1950s. The extent and meaning of the polemic about Soffici's film and its association with Italian neorealism are inextricably connected to the ways in which the movement was seen and interpreted by Argentine critics in the late 1940s and early 1950s. Both the screenings of neorealist films and the intensity of their critical reception had been at best intermittent. Immediately before the release of *Open City* in Buenos Aires in November 1947, fanzines emphasized Rossellini's passion for nonprofessional actors and improvisation; little was said about any ideological or political orientation.[28] After a few thousand patrons had seen the movie, mostly in art house theaters, *Open City* was praised "as a signal of renewal in the world cinema" in terms of production and technical innovation.[29] Anna Magnani was called "ugly, fat, and a great actress, even though not a star. . . . [S]he has the appearance of the people who suffer," making her appropriate for that film.[30] Rossellini's subsequent movies and De Sica's work also had very controversial receptions because of their "improvisation."

The overtly anti-Peronist fanzine *El hogar* periodically published articles on neorealism from the late 1940s to the mid-1950s, with particular focus on the personalities and aesthetic choices of these acclaimed directors.[31] Journalists primarily targeted "the method" proposed by the trailblazers: nonprofessional actors and "open contempt for the studio system."[32] An article quoted Rossellini's statements to Roger Regent in Paris: "I'll be crazy, but I still refuse to know how I'll finish my movie the day I start it. A strict plot, a fancy studio, all that preplanning of lights and sets is for me the most hateful thing that can happen. . . . How do I work? But do people know how *they* work?"[33] An indignant Argentine journalist also established the difference between the Parisian Institut des Hautes Études Cinématographiques (Institute for Advanced Cinematographic Studies), with all its technical sophistication, and Rossellini: "Many young filmmakers would say, 'Let's make movies à la Rossellini' and would try to cheat the producers with those charming and anarchic theories. . . . [T]hat would never work here."[34] In a moral tale about the irresponsibility of using amateurs in films, a journalist from *El hogar* dramatically narrated the misfortunes of Lamberto Maggiorani after the shooting of *Ladri di biciclette*. Rejected by his old friends in the poor neighborhood where he had lived because of his ephemeral fame, Maggiorani had ended up broke, jobless, and neglected by the star system.[35] De Sica, too, went through difficult times. To make *Miracolo a Milano* (Miracle in Milan, 1951), he had to work as an actor in Léonide Moguy's *Domani è troppo tardi* (Tomorrow Is Too Late, 1950) because producers did not want to invest in his movies, which were not financially successful.[36] Many of these critiques resembled the comments on Soffici's film published by mainstream fanzines and newspapers. For a significant part of the Argentine press, the Italians had created a style that critiqued the studio system and the normative ways of making films within the film industry.

A more specialized group of critics and cinephiles approached neorealism differently, promoting and praising Italian films. In that vein, the magazine *Gente de cine* founded an art house theater in 1947 and periodically organized neorealist film series. In 1950, the theater showed Rossellini's *Amore* (Ways of Love, 1948) and *Paisà* (Paisan, 1946) and called them truly neorealist. Each issue of the magazine included at least two columns dedicated to neorealism, in which critics incisively analyzed this film style and the debates surrounding its development in Italy and Europe. They showed little interest, however, in examining the similarities between the Italian movement and the contemporary Argentine film, even though filmmakers in both countries wanted to transform their national film scenes in the pursuit of a national language able to tackle and represent the oncoming modernization process.

It is difficult to grasp Italian neorealism's meaning for critics, directors, and audiences in postwar Argentina and its eclectic reception in the first decade of its existence. During this first phase, most of the reviews in the mainstream media emphasized neorealism's novelty and the stark differences between the style of the classical films made by the studios and the neorealist way of approaching a topic. In particular, critics highlighted the use of non-professional actors as a distinctive trait of neorealism and a definite change in cinema style. They said little about ideological changes or political statements made by the Italian filmmakers. Neorealism was first and foremost a style, a denomination that the Argentine press chose to emphasize technical skills over ideological values.

Barrio Gris, Neorealism, and Argentine Modernization

By passionately discussing possible similarities between *Barrio gris* and the Italian movement, the critics and the press showed the implications in the film's possible connection to neorealism. The buzz around the film reflected less a difference of opinion in terms of film style than the expression of a

widespread sense of uncertainty regarding Argentine cinema. The studio system clearly was decaying, along with Argentine cinema's glamour, financial
prosperity, and clout in Latin America. The media thus interpreted this film as
an open criticism of the studio system and its classical mode of representation.

But this debate also showed critics' and intellectuals' difficulty in accepting that the Peronist decade had produced changes in Argentine society as
well as in the field of cultural production, leading to a modernization of film
language. *Barrio gris* combined elements that both emulated and broke with
classical narrative forms. Like *Open City* by "el maestro Rossellini," as some
in the Argentine press called him, Soffici's film was "full of old ingredients":
melodrama as a main narrative resource, continuity editing, medium-long and
medium shots, and psychological motivations as the causes of actions.[37] At the
same time, *Barrio gris* cast nonprofessional actors in central roles, had a script
that was modified several times while shooting, and triggered a debate about
the meaning of the national as part of the artistic production.

The dispute regarding the neorealist character of *Barrio gris* did not specifically concern the Italians and their movies. Rather, it concerned the emergence of indigenous cinemas and the pursuit of a new film grammar that
could speak the language of the nation and/or the people. *Barrio gris* expressed
Argentina's sense of social modernization as a consequence of the transformations made by the populist regime in the mid-1940s. The film's opening
scenes show us first a young Federico surrounded by fog and darkness and
running from the police; immediately thereafter, we see an older Federico
walking through his barrio, which now has been transformed into a modern,
shiny, and clean part of town full of happy children in bright uniforms. It is
the 1950s, when social reforms have been enacted, when the neighborhood is
supposedly no longer gray, when the previously displaced and forgotten have
a chance to attain a better life. Federico is the teller of the story; his voice-over
is like a tango without a melody, full of sad and dry notes. A marked contrast
exists between the sadness of his voice and the children's shouts of joy. Past
and present meet in this scene, which is repeated at the end. He whispers, "It
does not exist any longer" while walking as a ghost through his former barrio,
which has ceased to be a lost suburban area but has become an integral part
of the capital city, linked to it by modern highways and public transportation.
The camera then leads us back to his childhood, when the neighborhood was
poor, foggy, and ugly and so was everyday life.

Popular classes' experiences were featured in other Argentine films, and
other films also had reality as their principle. *Barrio gris*, however, carried
an awareness of modernity, as it featured the same picturesque characters,

melodrama, and classical narratives but with an appreciation of the present; it visually demonstrated the Peronist discourse of historical rupture, the active intervention of the state in everyday life, the slogan of a new Argentina leaving behind the familiar past. The story of Federico's life, the neighbors, and the place in which he lived is also a narrative of loss that ironically gives space to the future, to a more modern society. The film shows that societies pay a price for modernization. When Federico emphasizes in the opening as well as at the end of the film that the barrio no longer exists and that "progress, in an effort to equalize things and men, eliminated its picturesque suburban appearance," he is saying good-bye to the traditional community made by European immigrants and natives. And that society was reproduced in the stereotypes that nurtured Buenos Aires folklore as well as the melodramas of the radio soap operas of the 1920s and 1930s and the classical films of the 1930s and 1940s that had made the studios rich and powerful.[38] That change explains Federico's profound melancholy, telling a story of something inevitably erased by the progress and the bright, shining future in the modern 1950s.

The feeling that the viewers were seeing a "real" portrayal of 1950s Argentine society, reinforced by the emphasis on childhood and the use of nonprofessional actors, ultimately led critics and journalists to label the film neorealist. But how much did the film truly relate to the Italian movement? This association between neorealism and *Barrio gris* responded to a significant change in ways to perceive and represent the "real" in Argentina. More than just the bleak depiction of the 1930s created such controversy. That picture had already been shown. The articulation of the old and the new, the past and the present, made the film an issue of public discussion and allowed the association with the Italian movement, which was also based on the dialectic between present and past.

At the same time, the label of neorealism helped the press to avoid the particular historical circumstances addressed in *Barrio gris*, especially those related directly to the Peronist regime. In the 1940s and 1950s, Italian neorealism was perceived more as a technical transformation than an ideological and political statement, as the movement would be read in Latin America during the next decade.

By questioning whether a relationship existed between *Barrio gris* and neorealism, the media articulated the Argentine quest for the construction of a national cinema in a time of profound transition. The most pressing issue that critics and journalists raised concerned whether Argentine cinema needed the influence of a foreign film tradition to make realist movies. "Why neorealism?" they proclaimed. "We have a strong realist tradition here!"[39]

Kriger has argued that del Carril's *Las aguas bajan turbias* abandoned any psychological scrutiny of the characters and their individual—and thus useless—rebellions à la Soffici, focusing more on collective fight and social change.[40] Del Carril, however, constructed a narrative rooted in the Argentine cinema from the silent period to the mid-1940s that located social dramas in the rural world. Soffici instead built a more modern narrative as he juxtaposed the 1930s world, inhabited by melodrama, to the contemporary one populated by the promises of the new times.

This intertwining of modernization and tradition was one of the legacies of the Peronist years. Audiences confirmed their place in this new Argentina that featured a radical transformation of the social structure to empower the working classes for the first time but retained traditional values (represented in *Barrio gris* by the pure love of Federico's mother and Zulema), vindicated the work ethic (represented by Federico's brother), condemned lust (Rosita), and punished crime.

The picturesque depiction of the barrio and its characters and a happy ending that fulfilled the promises of a collective upward mobility elicited a positive response from the public. Soffici's film was Argentina's fourth-most-successful at the box office during November and December 1954, topped only by *The Robe* (Henry Koster, 1953), Luigi Comencini's *Pane, amore, e fantasia* (Bread, Love, and Dreams, 1953), and *The Prisoner of Zenda* (Richard Thorpe, 1952). Almost 135,000 people saw *Barrio gris* in the first six weeks after its release, an impressive number for a national feature.[41] Viewers recognized themselves and the places they inhabited in this archetypical suburban town depicted by Soffici: Here were the neighborhood with its market and the characters that lived in it; here were the streets made of clay; here were the old movie theater and the boxing ring where the children eagerly waited to see bouts. There was the stream—dirty, dangerous, and exciting for Federico as a teen; there was the cabaret where an already grown-up Federico drank, smoked, played cards, and had sex. This vernacular *Odyssey* was attractive for the audiences, as it displayed the unprivileged tragedy of their lives, seen so many times in plays, listened to in tango songs and radio soap operas.

Some of the press had trouble with scenes that were not part of the novel and showed a positive image of the government in a film by a director who was not openly a Peronist but who had been favored by the regime. An explicit critique of a film with these characteristics was, however, problematic. Magazines and fanzines did not dare openly to reject the film for its obvious connections with the regime and for the historical narrative it presented. The press consequently did not mention the added scenes, labeled the movie "lame and simplistic," and stopped talking about it.[42]

Conclusion

By 1955, *Gente de cine* wrote the obituary for neorealism, arguing that "commercialization" and a lack of ideas had led the movement to its decadence.[43] A new and more political perspective on the Italian movement would be born the following year, when a young Fernando Birri founded the Instituto de Cinematografía de la Universidad Nacional del Litoral (Film Institute of the National University of Santa Fé) and wrote a series of articles about De Sica in the fanzine *El hogar*. In his columns, the father-to-be of the Argentine political cinema discussed technical, artistic, ideological, and political elements of neorealism, giving expression to his own experience as a student of the Centro Sperimentale di Cinematografia in Rome from 1950 to 1953. Immediately thereafter, the Instituto would make the collective thirty-three-minute documentary *Tire dié* (Throw Me a Dime, 1960), considered Argentina's first neorealist film. From that moment on, neorealism would take a different path in Argentina than it had in Italy. The radicalization of politics and culture led to a divergent reading of what the movement was and what its ideological and historical mission meant.

Beginning in the 1960s, producers and filmmakers embraced neorealism and the lessons they believed it taught about the relationship between art and politics. That new position toward the Italian movement had much to do with the emergence of both a vanguard and avant-garde cinema in Argentina and Latin America. The Argentine press would now establish an unmediated connection between neorealism and what they perceived as a real social and political Argentine film production, leaving the lesson of *Barrio gris* behind and not including it in the genealogy of the New Latin American Cinema.

Yet by contrasting Federico's childhood with the childhood of a new time, Soffici was not only introducing social change as a critical element in reading Argentine reality but also referencing the canonical Italian neorealist films. The children of *Open City* take to the devastated and occupied streets of Rome promising to build a new story/history from the ruins of fascism. The children who open and close Soffici's film are also telling another story. They are not connected with anyone or anything that Federico has been telling the spectator about. They are pure diegetic disruption. When Federico says at the beginning and the end that "nothing is left," he means his words literally. These young boys and girls are there to build a modern Argentina full of happiness and opportunities for all. They are part of a future that is already happening. In that sense, the Peronist regime is placed as a tabula rasa in terms of the historical account. In this narrative, Argentine history starts again in 1946.

And Soffici thought that he stood on safer ground than Rossellini did. The Argentine director could not know that a dictatorship would take over in 1955, touching off a period of political violence that would last three decades. He also did not suspect that his happy children playing in swings and slides were the young adults from suburban places such as Sarandí who would become part of the radical unions and the guerrilla movements of the late 1960s and early 1970s. They would fight against a series of authoritarian governments and for a socialist *patria*. Some of them would probably *desaparecer* in the dungeons of the worst dictatorship (1976–84) in all of Argentine history. The New Argentine Cinema (Nuevo Cine Argentino) of the 1990s would tell that story. Those films, too, were called *neorealisti*.

Notes

The slogan in the essay title was part of the October 1954 advertisement campaign for *Barrio gris*. I appreciate the insightful comments of Saverio Giovacchini, Robert Sklar, Mariano Mestman, Omar Acha, Ingalisa Schrobsdorff, and Leandro Benmergui. I especially thank Andrés Insaurralde, Fabián Sancho, and Andrés Levinson from the Museo del Cine Pablo Ducrós Hicken in Buenos Aires. I could not have written this essay without their help.

1. The historiography on the relationship between the press and the two first Peronist administrations is sparse. See Carlos Ulanovski, *Paren las rotativas: Una historia de los grandes diarios, revistas y periodistas argentinos* (Buenos Aires: Espasa Calpe, 1997); Alicia Poderti, *De Güemes a Perón: Revistas culturales y periodismo en la Argentina* (Buenos Aires: Nueva Generación, 2005).

2. Argentina Sono Film and Lumiton were the country's first studios, founded by 1933. Others followed, including more than thirteen studios by 1955. See Claudio España, *Cine argentino: Industria y clasicismo, 1933–1956* (Buenos Aires: Fondo Nacional de las Artes, 2001), 220–21.

3. Cinematográfica V was founded in 1952 by Amadori to distribute the films made by five of the most successful Argentine directors at that time. All except Demare released at least one film promoted by the company. It folded in the mid-1950s.

4. *Arrabal* translates as "slum" or "poor quarter," but it means more than that. This literature describes the life and culture of the popular classes in the marginal areas of Buenos Aires, mostly inhabited by immigrants from the end of the nineteenth century to the 1930s. This literature prominently engages marginality and prostitution as well as the culture of the tango.

5. Matthew B. Karush, "The Melodramatic Nation: Integration and Polarization in the Argentine Cinema of the 1930s," *Hispanic American Historical Review* 87.2 (1995): 293–326.

6. Ferreira's acclaimed *Puente Alsina* (Alsina Bridge, 1935) draws on both realism and melodrama and tells the story of the building of a bridge that connects Buenos Aires with its suburban area while narrating the romantic liaison of a dark-skinned worker with the daughter of a businessman. On Ferreira, see John King, *Magical Reels: A History of Cinema in Latin America* (London: Verso, 1990). The Lumiton studio in particular exploited the realist format and delighted popular audiences.

7. Elina M. Tranchini, "El cine argentino y el imaginario de un cine criollista," in *El cine argentino y su aporte a la identidad nacional* (Buenos Aires: FAIGA, 1999), 101–69.

8. Ibid.

9. España, *Cine argentino*, 22–121.

10. *El hogar*, March 3, 1950.

11. Oscar Terán, *Historia de las ideas en la Argentina: Diez lecciones iniciales, 1810–1980* (Buenos Aires: Siglo XXI, 2008), 256–79.

12. Domingo Di Nubila, *Historia del cine argentino* (Buenos Aires: Cruz de Malta, 1959–60); José Agustín Mahieu, *Breve historia del cine argentino* (Buenos Aires: EUDEBA, 1966); Alberto Ciria, *Política y cultura popular: La argentina Peronista, 1946–1955* (Buenos Aires: Ediciones de la Flor, 1983); España, *Cine argentino*.

13. Clara Kriger, *Cine y Peronismo: El estado en escena* (Buenos Aires: Siglo XXI, 2008).

14. Ibid., 103.

15. Terán, *Historia*, 256–79.

16. Of course, some members of the film industry openly and enthusiastically supported the Peronist regime. Directors such as Amadori and Hugo del Carril were forced into exile or blacklisted after the 1955 anti-Perón coup because of their absolute identification with Peronism. Most directors, actors, and producers, even those who had showed some degree of support to the regime, did not have a problem (Di Nubila, *Historia*, 67).

17. Kriger, *Cine y Peronismo*, 80–81.

18. Soffici was believed to have gone through a "foreign-ish" phase when he adapted Robert Louis Stevenson (*El extraño caso del hombre y la bestia* [The Strange Case of Dr. Jekyll and Mr. Hyde, 1951]) and Henrik Ibsen (*La dama del mar* [The Lady of the Sea, 1954]). Interview with Daniel Oppenheimer, "Cine argentino: El camino hacia una cultura nacional," *Revista Siete Días*, August 1973.

19. Soffici's successful *Prisioneros de la tierra* (Prisoners of the Land, 1939) was based on three short stories by Horacio Quiroga; del Carril's *Las aguas bajan turbias* was based on Alfredo Varela's novel.

20. *Gente de cine*, August 1954.

21. *Notícias gráficas*, July 19, 1954.

22. *Antena*, November 1954.

23. *Radiolandia*, October 1954.

24. "Promesas y realidades," *Antena*, June 1954.

25. *Sintonía*, June 1954.

26. Ibid., November 1954.

27. *Radiofilm*, June 1954. See also *Mundo radial*, August 1954.

28. *Set*, May–June 1947.

29. Ibid., September–October 1947.

30. Ibid.

31. *El hogar*, June 1951.

32. Ibid., May 5, 1949.

33. Ibid.

34. Ibid.

35. Ibid., April 21, 1950.

36. Ibid., February 10, 1953.

37. Tag Gallagher, *The Adventures of Roberto Rossellini* (New York: Da Capo, 1998), 184.

38. España, *Cine argentino*, 22–121.

39. *Set*, December 1954.

40. Kriger, *Cine y Peronismo*, 169–85.

41. *El heraldo*, December 28, 1954.

42. *Gente de cine*, November–December 1954.

43. Ibid., January–March 1955.

LIVING IN PEACE AFTER THE MASSACRE

Neorealism, Colonialism, and Race

SAVERIO GIOVACCHINI

In a lecture he gave in the late 1980s at Purdue University, neorealist director and communist intellectual Giuseppe De Santis argued that neorealism had no fathers but only "a great mother, the Resistance."[1] Thirty years earlier, in 1951, the director had suggested that neorealist cinema reflected the Resistance as the "new phase of our Risorgimento."[2] In many neorealist films, the representation of the Resistance pivoted as much on the figure of the ordinary Italian as anti-Mussolini fighter as on the absence of his antithesis, the ordinary Italian as fascist. At their center was often the iconic Italian Resistance fighter or the famished rural or urban proletarian who has been victimized by fascism. Partisans and poor abounded in De Santis's *Caccia tragica* (The Tragic Hunt, 1945), Carlo Lizzani's *Achtung! Banditi!* (Attention! Bandits!, 1951), and Roberto Rossellini's *Roma, città aperta* (Rome, Open City, 1945) and *Paisà* (1946).[3] Fascism was depicted as a regime supported only by a bloodthirsty, socially defined minority that had oppressed the Italian *popolo*. Both fascism and antifascism, however, shared a positive notion of the *popolo*. Thus, Anna Maria Torriglia correctly points out that *Open City* reset the "national popular project" by replacing the fascist notion of the *popolo italiano*—centering on a bloody mystique of violence, subjection to Il Duce, and nationalistic destiny—with a more progressive and antifascist vision of the people typified especially by Pina (Anna Magnani), the proletarian heroine of the film, "as the source of regeneration for Italian democracy."[4]

The people, whom De Santis called "ragged, suffering humanity" and "the humbled and the wounded," were the victims rather than the supporters of the fascist homicidal fantasies. And *neorealismo* now wanted to represent them. In neorealist cinema, De Santis wrote, "the streets of Italy filled with the partisans, the veterans, the homeless, the unemployed, the workers struggling for their future."[5] De Santis's long list of the victims of fascism who are now to receive space on the screen is telling. It is both a statement of the visual goals of the director's cinema as well as an ideological and historical interpretation of fascism and of recent Italian history. The inventory enumerates some of the staple characters of neorealist films: the people who took arms against fascism (the partisans) as well as those who had at some point taken arms to uphold its goals (the veterans). The partisan, the famished Italian, and the war veteran are placed on the same continuum of nonparticipation with the regime, all members of the new citizenry, the *popolo*, ushered in by the Resistance.

The cohabitation of all these people in De Santis's catalog signified a general victimization of Italians and was obtained via a cavalier attitude toward their past. In his acute essay on *Paisà*, American critic Robert Warshow noted that Rossellini's pervasive notion of defeat obscured all differences between an Italian fascist and an Italian partisan: Both, in fact, had suffered, "a view that has a special attraction for a defeated fascist nation, and Rossellini cannot restrain himself from taking a special advantage of it." Thus, Warshow continues, from this point of view, *Paisà* "can be plausibly interpreted as representing the fantasies of the eternally defeated as he tries anxiously to read his fate in the countenance of a new master."[6]

This difficult past, however, existed and often involved the acting out of Italian racial ideologies and their fateful and bloody enactments. Even before the passage of the Racial Laws of 1938–39, Italian armies had conquered Ethiopia and sung songs about the "*faccetta nera* [little black face]" waiting for "the new law and the new king" the Italians were going to give her.[7] Furthermore, historians now argue that racism was not even confined to the *ventennio*, nor was it as marginal to Italian culture as we have long thought. Just as Italian attempts to create an empire in Africa began in the nineteenth century, racial hierarchies and Italian racism predated fascism.[8]

Yet this aspect of Italian history is only recently being integrated into the Italian national narrative. Angelo del Boca has written for decades of "the (conscious or unconscious) deletion of colonial crimes and the missing debate on Italian imperialist expansion," but Italian academe and Italian public discourse have done little to address this issue.[9] Italians are *brava gente* (nice people), untouched by fascism's racist dicta and curiously uninvolved in its criminal actions. Italian amnesia vis-à-vis Italian behavior during the war and its colonialist prologue has been, as Nicola Labanca has argued, the result of a "triple silence."[10] Not only were Italian politicians uninterested in delving into the bloody pages of recent Italian military history, but Italian intellectuals—in particular, professional historians—have showed no better memory.[11] Next to the silences of the statesmen and the historians, ordinary people have provided the third, thunderous, silence—that of public opinion.

This third silence arguably implicates cinema. Most people learn history not from history books but from other forms of public and private articulation of memories of past events. Among these articulations, cinema plays a prominent role.[12] As studies on the mythology of the *italiano brava gente* multiply,[13] scholars also research cinema's role in the creation of this mythology. Millicent Marcus has recently called our attention to the "reticence" with which Italian cinema addressed Italian anti-Semitism and the Italian role in the Shoah.[14] For example, she notes, in *Open City*, Rossellini's camera stayed far from the Roman ghetto, "the most wretched and least open area of the city."[15]

Marcus's volume is pathbreaking and gives a complete account of the treatment of anti-Semitism in Italian cinema, including neorealism. The erasure of the Jew is only one of the elements of what Marcus calls the "behindness" of Italian film in regard to race and racism.[16] Possibly endorsing the budding *brava gente* mythology, postwar Italian cinema also papered over Italy's role in the Western history of racism. Not surprisingly, Italian mainstream cinema offered a revisionist view of the Italian defeat in World War II where heroism abounded and racism had disappeared. In the 1950s, directors such as Duilio Coletti, Francesco De Robertis, and the former cameraman of the Italian African corps, Antonio Leonviola, hit domestic box office gold by telling hyperbolic war stories about Italian troops in Africa. But how about the progressive neorealist project? How did neorealism see race in Italy's past and present? Did it forget or retouch this long and bloody past to imagine a present and future lily-white Italy? This essay begins investigating these questions by examining the early career of one unlikely protagonist of the neorealist movement, African American actor John Kitzmiller.

Born in Battle Creek, Michigan, in 1915 and trained as an engineer, Kitzmiller was deployed in the Italian campaign in the engineering corps of the all-African American Ninety-second Infantry (Buffalo) Division. Redeployed at the end of the war, he was discovered on the American base of Tombolo, near Livorno, by director Luigi Zampa and producer Carlo Ponti.[17] Kitzmiller was not the first person of color to appear in Italian cinema but was the first to achieve a certain degree of stardom in it. At the time of his death in Rome in 1965, Kitzmiller had appeared in almost fifty feature films directed by some of the most important European filmmakers and had won the award for best male actor at the 1957 Cannes Film Festival.

He was also the most important black actor to consistently work in neorealist films. Of course he was not the only one. The son of an Italian woman and an African American GI adopted by Italian actor Dante Maggio, Angelo Maggio played a racially mixed street urchin in a couple of minor films, *Angelo tra la folla* (Angelo in the Crowd, 1950) and *Il mulatto* (Angelo, 1950). In the Neapolitan episode of *Paisà*, Rossellini had employed musician Dots Johnson as Joe, a black MP wandering about the ruins of the city. Written by Alfred Hayes, a Hollywood-trained screenwriter who had come to Italy as a soldier in the Fifth Army, the episode is rightly famous: drunk, Joe is preyed upon by a street urchin, Pascà (Alfonso Bovino), who takes Joe around and finally, when he is asleep, steals his shoes and harmonica. The eight-minute episode is intense, poignant, and insightful. Rossellini and Hayes attached an adult black male to a child—a narrative direction fashioned by Hollywood films (the most famous and recent example at the time being the pairing of Shirley Temple and Bill "Bojangles" Robinson).[18] More originally, Rossellini shows his awareness of the place of race in Italian cultural history; more interestingly, he imagines the reactions this notion may elicit among people of color. Pascà takes the inebriated Joe to a puppet show in which a white knight, a "paladino," is fighting a "giant moor," screaming that he is not afraid because "I am white and you are black." When the paladin humiliates the moor, Joe understands what is at stake: He jumps on the stage and attacks the white marionette.

Paisà was a crucial film, but Dots Johnson soon went back to the United States, and Rossellini did not revisit the topic in his neorealist films. Kitzmiller stayed behind and became relatively prosperous by largely cornering the market for black roles in the Italian cinema of the immediate postwar era. In 1951, the African American magazine *Ebony* noted that the actor was "still without fame in America" but was "the negro actor who enjoys the most steady and consistent employment in the movies. . . . [H]is face is as familiar to moviegoers [in Italy] as Gregory Peck in this country."[19]

Kitzmiller's first important film for Italian cinema, *Vivere in pace* (To Live in Peace, 1947), was hailed by many as another film marking the intellectual and aesthetic renaissance of Italian cinema after the fascist dusk. In New York City, where it was released in November 1947, the film replaced *Open City* at the World Theater, where Rossellini's film had run for ninety-one weeks.[20] In truth, the film, directed by Luigi Zampa from a script by Zampa, Suso Cecchi D'Amico, Aldo Fabrizi, and Pietro Tellini, points to the blurred confines of neorealism.[21] *Vivere in pace* obviously employed soundstages, broad comedy, and a capable crew of professional actors to tell its story. In addition, *Vivere in pace* grafted social themes onto a strong comedic flair. Fabrizi, who had just starred as the martyred Catholic priest in Rossellini's *Open City*, played Zio Tigna, the embattled patriarch who is trying to keep his family safe in the midst of the war; Kitzmiller portrayed Joe, a black GI who, along with a white companion, Ronald (played by one of *Paisà*'s American actors, Gar Moore), is saved and hidden by a family of Italian farmers. The story ends in tragedy when the Germans, withdrawing from Italy, shoot Tigna in retaliation for the help the village provided the American GIs.

Vivere in pace was a critical and popular success: It garnered the Italian film industry's awards for best original script and best supporting actress (Ave Ninchi, playing Tigna's wife, Corinna), and in December 1947, Zampa's movie snagged the New York Film Critics' award for best foreign film. The script "excels in the minute description of the characters," and the directing is "neat and dry," wrote Luigi Rondi in *Il tempo*.[22] "Very good Italian film," noted Italian film magazine *Cine bazar*.[23] "The revivified Italian film industry which has sent us such powerful postwar films as *Shoeshine* and *Open City* has now sent another one along that takes a place of distinction among the fine motion pictures of our times," Bosley Crowther echoed in the *New York Times*.[24] "An affectionate and colorful picture of little people . . . a clear record of real people living in a real world," commented Otis Guernsey Jr. in the *New York Herald Tribune*.[25] James Agee deemed it the "wisest and most humane movie of its time," "even more remarkable" than Rossellini's *Open City* and De Sica's *Shoeshine*.[26] In his review, Crowther described Moore and Kitzmiller as "remarkably forthright" in embodying, respectively, the "American journalist and the Negro."[27]

Like Crowther, the film seemed confident that being a "Negro" could constitute a profession or a state of being. The narrative economy of *Vivere in pace* confidently enacted a separation of roles between white and black Americans: Ronald is in charge of blandly romancing Mirella Monti (Silvia), while Joe is left alone to shoulder the comedic moments. He sings like a rooster on top of the chicken pen, drinks copiously, plays the trumpet (extremely well), and even reveals his presence to the Germans, precipitating the killing of Zio Tigna in the film's tear-jerking finale.

Italian critics were not bothered by the representation of Kitzmiller. *Bianco e nero*, the flagship film magazine published by the Centro Nazionale di Cinematografia, praised Kitzmiller's performance as possessing "an animalesque innocence [*un animalesco candore*]."[28] Some American critics took issue with Kitzmiller's character. The *Hollywood Reporter* remarked that the "American Negro soldier is regrettably caricatured."[29] The *New York Daily News* asserted that "the handling of the Negro is the sort of thing that you would never see in an American picture."[30] Nevertheless, some of the most prestigious white American progressive film critics shared the Italian admiration for the film and the character. Echoing Crowther, Agee remarked that Kitzmiller's role was "the only pure presentation of a man of his race that I have seen in a movie."[31]

Quality of the film aside, *Vivere in pace* worked as a compendium of some of the racist stereotypes at large in Italian culture and more broadly in the West. Moreover, the film hints at the Italian colonial past as a benevolent enterprise. Black people are seen both as sexually threatening (Corinna coyly whispers in Tigna's ear about what *i negri* have done to women in a nearby village) and asexual, as it is clear that Joe, unlike Ronald, has no desire to romance any of the women. Upon seeing Joe, two young children innocently ask their father, "How do Negroes know whether they have dirty feet?" Uncle Tigna comments that Joe is not really black but "just a little tanned."[32] In truth, Joe's actions amount to primitive behaviors determined by simple desires: He loves wine and, of course, cannot hold it. When inebriated, he dances and plays the trumpet. Yet the coloring of the black character also assumes local nuances. Via Kitzmiller's character, Zampa creates an image of the *popolo* from which blackness is automatically excluded. As opposed to Ronald, who entertains the idea of settling down with an Italian woman,[33] *Vivere in pace* takes pains to make clear that Joe does not consider this option.

Vivere in pace, in fact, uses Kitzmiller to evoke and simultaneously exorcise Italian colonialism, performing what cultural anthropologist Michel-Rolph Trouillot has called a "formula of silence."[34] Through the character of Kitzmiller and his relationship with Granpa (Ernesto Amirante), a veteran of the 1911 Libyan campaign, the film both erases the crimes of Italian colonialism and trivializes it as an essentially benign process performed by *italiani brava gente* who meant no harm to the natives. The jovial, benevolent Granpa repeatedly asks Joe to play the trumpet and whether he is an *ascaro* (a member of the colonial troops that served the Italian colonial governments in Libya and later Africa Orientale Italiana). The former soldier of the colonial army refers to both the conquest of Ethiopia and that of Libya and asks Joe if he has met the *Negus* and whether he has seen the war at Sciara Sciat.[35]

This film's cultural work in 1947 Italy is more relevant than may at first be apparent. In the aftermath of World War II, Ethiopians and Libyans—and next to them many Serbian and Greek victims of Italian occupation—were demanding that Italy be condemned for decades of genocidal colonialist wars.[36] The performances of Kitzmiller and Ernesto Amirante must be understood in this context. The joviality of the grandfather's character and his persistence in identifying Joe as a former colonial servant of the Italian empire subsumes the history of Italian colonialism—including the genocide following the defeat at Sciara Sciat—under the mythology of the *italiani brava gente*. (Granpa is certainly *brava gente* even though he is both a racist and an imperialist.)[37]

If Kitzmiller was dissatisfied with the role he played in *Vivere in pace*, his following film must have been an even worse disappointment. *Tombolo, paradiso nero* (1947), the film in which Kitzmiller was cast immediately after *Vivere in pace*, played on the fears engendered in the Atlantic community by the news that African American GIs were dating local women in the areas close to American bases.

The presence of soldiers and the lure of American goods had caused makeshift settlements to spring up in the piney woods between Pisa and Livorno, the Tombolo of the title. The area soon acquired a bad reputation, especially for the interracial affairs between American soldiers and Italian *segnorine*. In 1964, one of the key directors of photography of neorealism, Aldo Tonti, who shot *Senza pietà* (Without Pity, 1948) in Tombolo, remembered it as "a nest of debased people" and metaphorically relocated the forest outside of Italy and directly to Africa: "You would have thought that you were in Congo."[38] For John Schillace, the author of *The Tragic Forest: Tales of the Forest of Tombolo* (1951), the piney woods were a "mysterious forest" peopled by GIs and deserters, girlfriends and prostitutes, whites and Negroes. One of the GIs, named Lincoln, was a notorious African American giant who, supposedly driven to insanity by the death of his two little sons, had killed his Italian companion and was known to roam the woods dressed only in a blanket ("running through the forest naked with that bloody blanket, which many fanciful retellings of the story had changed into leopard skin").[39]

Schillace's sordid tale of Lincoln had its roots in the *Corriere della sera*, where one of the scriptwriters for *Tombolo*, Indro Montanelli, a former officer of the Italian colonial troops in Africa and future dean of Italian pundits, also wrote about Lincoln in 1947. He was "the Negro who goes about shouting in the woods . . . a giant, more than two meters tall, with huge shoulders and with bloodshot eyes with a leopard skin thrown on his naked chest."[40]

In Giorgio Ferroni's *Tombolo*, Kitzmiller plays Jack, a corrupt U.S. Army sergeant who covets Anna (Adriana Benetti), the pawn of a small-time black marketer, Alfredo (Dante Maggio). Her father is the righteous Andrea (Aldo Fabrizi), a former MP in the Italian African Corps who now works as custodian of a warehouse. Easily duped, Andrea lets the gangsters rob the storehouse and then is charged with the robbery. To convince Alfredo to pay his bail, Anna agrees "to go with the Negro," who consents to allow Alfredo to plunder the military depot in return for two hours with her. Notified of the pact, Renzo (Luigi Tosi), Anna's white lover, tries to rescue his girl from the black brute by getting him drunk. As the police and the MPs are alerted to the heist, Andrea dies at the hands of the corrupt Alfredo after pursuing him into a minefield. His sacrifice will buy his—and Anna's—redemption.

An interesting and underexamined film, *Tombolo*, like *Vivere in pace*, connects the political rehabilitation of the Italian colonial troops with the visual debasement of blackness. Once again, Kitzmiller is excluded from the *popolo*. His lust for Anna is as evident as the woman's repulsion toward him. Even as she considers going with Jack to save her father from the gallows, Anna is horrified at the thought that her father may later find out that "I have gone with a Negro, that I have always gone with them."

The script by Montanelli, Glauco Pellegrini, and Rodolfo Sonego transfers onto Jack the same stereotypes as *Vivere in pace* but turns the comedy into tragedy. Like Joe, Jack speaks pidgin Italian, which was meant to elicit a comic response from the audience.[41] Like Joe, Jack drinks but cannot hold his liquor. Like Joe, Jack is again coupled with a former member of the Italian African colonial force, Andrea, who is as saintly as the black man is devilish. If the "little black faces" in Ethiopia were as uncivilized as this brute, Italy obviously had good reasons to be there. The film depicts blackness as both threatening and alluring. When Andrea visits the encampments of the black troops deep in the piney woods, Ferroni's traveling shot reveals seminaked women eating and drinking in the company of black men. Some of the women are bathing mixed-race children as the women's dark-skinned lovers rest nearby. The soundtrack blares threateningly discordant jazz, and we are supposed to contemplate the scene through Andrea's horrified eyes. Yet another perspective is possible in this superficially moralistic film. If one considers this scene against the backdrop of 1945 Italy, where the average daily caloric intake was barely over one thousand per person, these debased Italian women do not seem to be doing so badly.[42] On the contrary, and quite curiously, they seem to be inhabiting the future, where Italian society—fueled by the Marshall Plan—will begin to make available to its citizens liquor, food, African American music, and more relaxed sexual mores in the vicinity of a Mediterranean beach.

Indeed, the scandal of Tombolo might have been largely in the eyes of (white male) beholders such as Andrea or the male *Washington Post* reporter who in May 1947 described Tombolo as the "Tahiti of Italy . . . where scores of American deserters, many of them Negroes, live . . . with Italian girls."[43] Like Ferroni's camera, in fact, local men suspected that these women might be having fun. Their reaction to this interracial fraternization could in fact easily become much more visceral and violent than Andrea's. On the night of August 3, 1947, young men from Livorno attacked several black GIs and the *segnorine* accompanying them. While the soldiers took shelter in the military barracks, twenty-three women were publicly undressed and forcefully hoisted on a merry-go-round in the middle of Livorno's central square.[44]

When the film was exported to the United States, even the *New York Times*'s Crowther could not help noting the "patently biased attitude toward the American Negro soldier in uniform."[45] The righteous Andrea's visits to the makeshift village are constructed as a descent into hell soundtracked by the shrill notes of jazz and peopled by scantily dressed Italian women and African American GIs loitering, drinking, and fornicating. Italian film critics were not, however, appalled: The film was well directed by Ferroni, well interpreted by Fabrizi, and could be called "the triumph of duty" for its idealistic portrayal of the former carabiniere.[46] "The film effortlessly fits in with the neorealist genre of Italian cinema," declared *L'operatore*.[47] The Italian magazine *Film* described the story as set in the midst of "a ferocious congregation of negroes" and "a crew of degraded women" as well as in line with the new Italian cinema, providing an "in-depth character study and a passionate interpretation of souls."[48]

How Kitzmiller saw his participation in these movies must largely be surmised. In a late-1940s interview with journalist Aldo Santini, Kitzmiller appeared much less optimistic than he had been in his conversation with *Ebony*. Kitzmiller spoke harshly of the United States and asserted that many of the black soldiers in the Fifth Army were not sure that the "victorious end of the war [was] going to bring the end of racial discrimination, and they'd rather desert than be pariahs in New York, St. Louis, or Memphis." Moreover, he realized that "sooner or later there won't be any more roles for Negroes in the Italian cinema."[49]

The third neorealist film in which he acted, *Senza pietà* (Without Pity, 1948), may have seemed a good opportunity for redemption. The director, Alberto Lattuada, who also made the celebrated *Il bandito* (The Bandit, 1946), had intellectual clout. The film fit well with the neorealist sensibility by having a topical subject, exterior shots, and nonprofessional actors. Its subject matter and its locale were the same as *Tombolo*, and Lattuada and his scriptwriters, Tullio Pinelli and Federico Fellini, who did uncredited work on the film, built on but reversed preexisting screen personae and narrative lines. Once again, the story takes place in the Tombolo piney woods. Like the previous movie, *Senza pietà* centers on Kitzmiller's obsession with white women. Kitzmiller speaks the same mangled Italian as in his two earlier films. Even his character's name, Jerry, harks back to his past roles as Joe and Jack. Like the preceding film, *Senza pietà* is a tragedy. Angela (Carla del Poggio), the *segnorina* Jerry adores, dies at the hands of Pierluigi (haunting nonprofessional actor Pierre Claudé), a sexually ambiguous Italian gangster who runs Livorno's black market. Heartbroken, Angela's lifeless body next to him, Jerry drives a truck off a cliff.

Tombolo and *Senza pietà* differ substantially, however. Lattuada, Fellini, and Pinelli give the character of Jerry a new substance and density, not just as a consequence of the number of lines Kitzmiller delivers. This time around, Jerry wants to save Angela from the life of a *segnorina*. Because of his

The eternal trumpet player: John Kitzmiller in *Luci del varietà* (1950).

righteousness, Jerry becomes Pierluigi's target. To save Angela, Jerry agrees to help Pierluigi rob a military depot. Angela also differs from Anna. She is not repelled by Jerry: On the contrary, she genuinely likes him. The film makes purposefully clear the nature and depth of her affection for him. Marcella (Giulietta Masina), another *segnorina*, comments that Angela does not love Jerry but rather is fond of him. That their relationship is nonsexual is confirmed not so much by the images (Jerry never kisses her) or by Angela's words ("he is not my fiancé [*non è il mio fidanzato*]," she protests) as by Jerry's words: He tells Angela, "I know. You not love Jerry. I love you. You know this. I am like brother. I not leave you no more. You will see: Jerry strong companion [Io conosco che tu non ami Jerry. Ti voglio bene. Tu conosci questo. Sono come fratello. Non ti lascio più. . . . You will see: Jerry è forte compagno]."

The film had intellectual standing and was part of the Italian contingent at the 1948 Venice Film Festival. Sixty years later, Lattuada still thought that the film had deserved to win a prize at the festival, but Luigi Chiarini, a "former Fascist, former racist, former intellectual, objected."[50] Chiarini may have not been the only one to object, because critics gave the film a lukewarm reception. In the *Corriere della sera*, Stefano Lanocita called the film unoriginal ("*l'ennesima storia della gente di Tombolo* [the nth story about the people of Tombolo]").[51] The organ of the Italian Communist Party called it a disappointment (*delusione*).[52] On the other side of the Atlantic, the *Daily Worker* concurred: The film "yields no significance, only sentimentality and melodramatic action."[53] The *New York Times* wrote that the film "lacked decision," while the *New York Herald Tribune* called it a "lifeless characterization."[54]

The film indeed seems tentative in many different ways. Given its hopeless gloom, it is unclear whether *Senza pietà* constructs the possibility of interracial relations as a goal to be attained or as a permanent source of drama. Furthermore, sharing a focus on Italian issues typical of the new Italian cinema, *Senza pietà* also borrows from film noir and the American gangster film.

Stefania Parigi sees it as a hybrid between "the narrative frames and rhythms of the [Hollywood] noir" and "the will to document typical of neorealism."[55] In their seminal *Panorama du film noir américain, 1941–1953*, Raymond Borde and Étienne Chaumeton describe the film as an Italian homage to the American genre of the film noir ("echoes the noir series"), not unlike Giuseppe de Santis's *Riso amaro* (Bitter Rice, 1951).[56] Lattuada himself called it "really an American film for the way it was shot, its rhythm, its editing, and other formal solutions [*proprio un film Americano per come è girato, per il ritmo, per la cadenza del montaggio, per le altre soluzioni formali*]").[57]

The film invoked the tradition of neorealism by using nonprofessional actors, recognizably "real" locations, natural lighting, and a predominance of medium and long shots. Neorealism, however, had made clear its intent to speak about contemporary and contingent Italian issues. Instead, *Senza pietà* seemed to be speaking about the human condition. Lattuada almost admitted as much in a perfunctory prologue to the film: "The story takes place in Italy but could occur anywhere in the world [*La storia si svolge in Italia ma potrebbe svolgersi in qualunque parte del mondo*]").

Critics used this geographical vagueness to relocate the racism to which the film referred outside of Italy. "Regardless of the use of realist settings, the film does not speak to contemporary Italy but to prewar France or 1930s America," wrote communist Callisto Cosulich in 1948.[58] Christian Democrat Gian Luigi Rondi concurred. The Italian racism the film referenced had been "positively removed into the memories of the past. [Lattuada's] characters today appear remote: they are not big enough to be part of history and they are too remote to be chronicle."[59]

This curious spatial confusion eventually prevents the film from addressing the real topic underlying the Tombolo story: Italians' reactions to interracial fraternization, and indirectly the role of racism in Italian culture and history. In fact, rather than addressing Italian racism, the film indicts Americans. The film's only active racists are the American MPs who beat and harass Jerry and the other African American troops. The African American magazine *Our World* noted that the film "has jumped the gun on Hollywood." It depicted the possibility of a relationship between a white woman and a black man and was critical of the United States.[60] The Italian gangsters, while criminals, are not particularly racist, and Angela, while not attracted to Jerry, is a benevolent presence for him. Wounded by the war and caught in the problematical position of *segnorina*, Angela is actually the personification of the good-hearted victim of circumstances: she is an *italiana brava gente*.

Ultimately, the film fits rather than reverses the racial markings characterizing the cultural practices of Italian cinema. Jerry is an incomplete and far from threatening character. More consistently than Dots Johnson in the second episode of Rossellini's *Paisà*, Kitzmiller is the object rather than the subject of the story. European and American critics noted the character's "doglike devotion to things and loved ones [*canina devozione alle cose e alle creature care*]" and "animal-like candor [*animalesco candore*]" and described him as "a kindly spirit destroyed by circumstances beyond his control."[61] In fact, Lattuada and his scriptwriters devised a strategy that was to become typical of Hollywood films: The black male character received a positive, central role but did so at the cost of his desexualization.[62] His relation to Angela is childish. At the beginning of the film, he lies wounded at Angela's feet, and she calms him by talking to him like a pet, telling him, "Be good, be good [*Stai buono, su, stai buono*]." He is obviously Angela's junior partner, a fact that was quite relevant—and reassuring—in the strongly patriarchal postwar Italian society. More important, the liaison is clearly, in Stefania Parigi's words, "love without Eros,"[63] a relationship in which there is to be no touching, no kissing, and most important, no offspring to pollute the lily-white *popolo*. If anything, the duo wants to leave and live in a faraway place like brother and sister.

Temporarily at least, *Senza pietà* made a star of Kitzmiller. The film premiered at Venice, and Kitzmiller, "the only Negro in Italian cinema," hobnobbed with Anna Magnani and publicly joked that he had come to the Lido to "get tanned."[64] By the beginning of the 1950s, however, the renovating thrust of Italian neorealism was wearing off, and Kitzmiller's career responded accordingly. His role in *Luci del varietà* (Variety Lights, 1950), the first movie codirected by Fellini (with Lattuada), from Fellini's script, avoids most neorealist trappings and uses the story of Checco, a vaudeville hero bypassed by time, to chronicle the changes taking place in Italy in the first decade after the war. Like other Fellini films, most obviously *La dolce vita* (1960), modernity was both a source of spectacle and deeply worrisome.[65] In *Luci del varietà*, Kitzmiller's character, a happy-go-lucky trumpeter whom Checco meets one night in Rome, offers blackness as an example of what James Snead calls "metaphysical stasis" insofar as "the black is seen as eternal, unchanging, unchangeable."[66] He is utopian simplification in the midst of the traumas of modernization.[67]

Before he died in 1965 at the age of fifty-one, Kitzmiller's career took him outside of Italy, to the Yugoslavian sets of *Dolina miru* (The Valley of Peace, 1956), for which he won the 1957 best actor prize at Cannes, and to the James Bond macho überracism of *Dr. No* (1962). By then, his role in Italian cinema had been relatively forgotten. Talking to Goffredo Fofi, director Luigi Zampa remembered the actor as extremely sad, almost suicidal: "He died very badly.

Like a brother: John Kitzmiller
in *Senza pietà* (1948).

He died an alcoholic. He drank too much because he had so many disappoint-
ments: everybody was forgetting him."[68]

Kitzmiller's participation in neorealist movies, however, marked this moment in Italian cinema in ways that can only now be fully considered. The
emergence of the first star of color in Italian cinema cannot but be seen as
one more change brought about by neorealist cinema. It occurred at the end
of World War II, the "war without mercy" that had placed race and racism
at the center of the West's public discourse. Thus, the memory of racial hierarchies and of Italian colonial wars in Ethiopia, Libya, and Eritrea, even
when removed from the history books,[69] remained partially evoked on Italian
screens by Kitzmiller's persona, only to be once again exorcised by the benign
sweetness of Granpa and Andrea or by narrative lines that dehumanized his
characters and implicitly justified the civilizing mission of those wars.

Guido Aristarco was flabbergasted at the treatment of blacks in American
cinema, shouting, "Black man you should not die!"[70] In an essay for the communist magazine *Cinema nuovo*, Rudi Berger argued that the "racial problem"
was gone from Italian cinema because it was just part of the "artificial parentheses imposed [on Italy] by the fascist alliance with Nazism." Looking at "the
films of Italian realism," a group that obviously included *Senza pietà*, *Vivere
in pace*, and *Tombolo*, Berger suggested that blacks were presented "without
prejudice—just like the whites."[71] These critics were being complacent. While
articulated differently than in Hollywood movies, racial codes operated in
Italian cinema, and Italian neorealism was no exception. Kitzmiller's presence
was contained, and his screen roles, while historically important and trailblaz-
ing, were demeaning. Regardless of Aristarco's orations, Italian filmmakers'
most strenuous opposition to Hollywood cinema ultimately boiled down to
politics and trade, not race. The debate concerned the division of roles and
profits within Western film culture and the film industry rather than the relationship between "the west and the rest of us," to borrow the title of Nigerian
historian Chinweizu's pathbreaking book.[72]

When we consider the global history of neorealism, especially in postcolonial Africa, Asia, and Latin America, we should consider how loaded this style was with good intentions as well as their ultimate, albeit unwitting, betrayal. Some postcolonial filmmakers did not trust Hollywood but also had little good to say about European cinema, including neorealism. Ousmane Sembène, for example, on many occasions rejected the assimilation of his cinema (from the camera movements to his work with actors to the stories he liked to tell) to neorealism.[73] Even *Borom Sarret*, Sembène's splendid 1963 film, reveals, in the words of Nwachukwu Frank Ukadike, a "uniqueness that is non western, non European, and non conventional, signalling a different mode of representation and introducing indigenous aesthetics."[74] Ukadike notes that "African filmmakers and neorealists share the view that film is a political tool." But the former had to revise the latter's "cultural codes and political ideology" to make them "relevant" to Africa.[75]

As Mariano Mestman's essay in this volume demonstrates, the transfer of neorealism onto the contexts of African avant-gardes or of the Brazilian Cinema Novo was not easy. By the late 1960s, the Third Cinema theorized by Argentines Fernando Solanas and Octavio Getino situated the cinema of the developing world between Hollywood's first cinema and the second cinema of the avant-gardes still contained within the dominant system.[76] The inability, highlighted by Kitzmiller's career, to see Italian racism and the Italian colonial past may have contributed to the difficulty of the transfer and to the necessity of immediate and radical creolization. Talking to Françoise Pfaff, Sembène identified the good filmmaker with a person "of learning and common sense who is the historian, the raconteur, the living memory and the conscience of his people. The filmmaker must live within his society and say what goes wrong within his society."[77] Much of what the great African director said easily applies to the goals of many of the filmmakers who adhered to the ethical sensibility of neorealism. But judging by the delay with which Italian films registered the taints of Italy's past and by Italian cinema's complicity with the permanence of racial hierarchies and of racist ideologies, this ethical sensibility was incomplete.

Notes

Thanks to Ingalisa Schrobsdorff and Robert Sklar for their comments on this essay.

1. Giuseppe De Santis, untitled notes for lecture at Purdue University, October 7, 1989, De Santis Archive, Scuola Nazionale di Cinematografia, Rome; now published as "La genesi di *Riso amaro*," in Antonio Vitti, *Peppe De Santis secondo se stesso* (Rome: Metauro, 2006), 37–58.

2. Giuseppe De Santis, "È in crisi il *neorealismo*?" *Filmcritica* 1.4 (March 1951): 109–12.

3. However, Rossellini showed no German Resistance fighter in the third installment of his war triptych, *Germania anno zero* (Germany, Year Zero, 1947), where Germans, even those who spent the Nazi years abroad, are struggling with their own material and moral decay.

4. Anna Maria Torriglia, *Broken Time, Fragmented Space: A Cultural Map for Postwar Italy* (Toronto: University of Toronto Press, 2002), 12–13, 183 no. 76.

5. Ibid., 110.

6. Robert Warshow, "Paisan" (1948), in *The Immediate Experience*, intro. Lionel Trilling (New York: Atheneum, 1970), 229.

7. Giorgio Fabre has recently underlined how "Mussolini and Fascism, in their own way, at the level of racism attempted to compete with Nazism" (*Mussolini razzista* [Milan: Garzanti, 2005], 9).

8. In the Italian case, Angelo del Boca has long underscored the role of Italian colonialism in shaping Italian conscience, and a recent collection edited by Alberto Burgio has shown how racial hierarchies, heterophobia, and a racial imaginary have been central to Italian culture since the Enlightenment. See Angelo del Boca, *L'Africa nella coscienza degli Italiani* (Milan: Mondadori, 2002); Alberto Burgio, *Nel nome della razza: Il razzismo nella storia d'Italia, 1870–1945* (Bologna: Mulino, 2000).

9. Del Boca, *Africa*, xi. See also Angelo del Boca, "Il mancato dibattito sul colonialismo," in *Africa*, 111–28.

10. Nicola Labanca, "Colonial Rule, Colonial Repression, and War Crimes in the Italian Colonies," *Journal of Modern Italian Studies* 9.3 (2004): 308–9.

11. See the exception of Giorgio Rochat, *Il colonialismo italiano* (Turin: Loescher, 1973); Giorgio Rochat, *Le guerre italiane, 1935–1943: Dall'impero d'Etiopia alla disfatta* (Turin: Einaudi, 2005); Angelo Del Boca, *I gas di Mussolini: Il fascismo e la guerra d'Etiopia* (Rome: Riuniti, 1996). See also Nicola Labanca, "La tardiva decolonizzazione degli studi storici coloniali italiani," in *Oltremare* (Bologna: Mulino, 2002), 440–48.

12. On the way film and other sorts of public history communicate, see Sergio Bertelli, *Corsari del tempo* (Florence: Ponte alle Grazie, 1994); Robert Brent Toplin, *Reel History* (Lawrence: University Press of Kansas, 2002); Roy Rosenzweig and David Thelen, *The Presence of the Past* (New York: Columbia University Press, 1998).

13. On Italian cinema and the *italiano brava gente*, see Saverio Giovacchini, "Soccer with the Dead: *Mediterraneo* and the Myth of *Italiani Brava Gente*," in *Repicturing the Second World War*, ed. Michael Paris (London: Palgrave Macmillan, 2008), 55–69. The creation of the myth of the *italiano brava gente* has attracted the attention of an increasing number of historians. See Angelo del Boca, *Italiani brave gente?* (Vicenza: Neri Pozza, 2005); Filippo Focardi, *La guerra della memoria* (Bari: Laterza, 2005); Filippo Focardi, "La memoria della guerra e il mito del 'bravo italiano,'" *Italia Contemporanea* 220–21 (September–December 2000): 393–99. On Italian racism and anti-Semitism and the *brava gente* myth, see also David Bidussa, *Il mito del bravo italiano* (Milan: Saggiatore, 1994).

14. Millicent Marcus, *Italian Film in the Shadow of Auschwitz* (Toronto: University of Toronto Press, 2007), 14.

15. Niccolò Zamponi, "Fascism in Italian Historiography, 1986–1993: A Fading National Identity," *Journal of Contemporary History* 29.4 (October 1994): 565 n. 22, cited in Marcus, *Italian Film in the Shadow*, 18.

16. Marcus, *Italian Film in the Shadow*, 28.

17. See slightly different versions of the same story in *Battle Creek Examiner*, June 3, 1960, 2; *Ebony*, November 1951, 75, *Lux* publicity package for *Senza pietà* Clipping File, Margaret Herrick Library of the Academy of Motion Pictures Arts and Science, Beverly Hills, California.

18. See Alfred Hayes, "Author's Note on Birth of *Paisà*," *New York Times*, March 7, 1948, X5. See also the analysis of the film by Leonardo De Franceschi, "Fra teatro e storia, la doppia scena del reale: *Il secondo episodio*," in *Paisà: Analisi del film*, ed. Stefania Parigi (Rome: Marsilio, 2005), 57–63.

19. *Ebony*, November 1951, 71–73.

20. Otis Guernsey Jr. in *New York Herald Tribune*, November 25, 1947, *To Live in Peace* Clipping File, Billy Rose Collection, New York Public Library for the Performing Arts, New York.

21. The debate about neorealism and its meaning exceeds the limits of this essay. On the debate about what constitutes neorealism, see Peter Bondanella, *Italian Cinema from Neorealism to the Present* (1983; New York: Continuum, 2004), 31–47. See also Millicent Marcus, *Italian Film in the Light of Neorealism* (Princeton: Princeton University Press, 1986), 33–127; Tag Gallagher, *The Adventures of Roberto Rossellini* (New York: Da Capo, 1997); Christopher Wagstaff, *Italian Neorealist Cinema* (Toronto: University of Toronto Press, 2007), 7–35. In Italian, see Alberto Farassino, ed., *Neorealismo: Cinema Italiano, 1945–1949* (Turin: EDT, 1989); Lino Micciché, ed., *Il neorealismo cinematografico italiano* (Milan: Marsilio, 1999); Gian Piero Brunetta, *Storia del cinema italiano*, 2nd ed., vol. 3, *Dal neorealismo al miracolo economico* (Rome: Riuniti, 1993).

22. *Il tempo*, March 20, 1947.

23. *Cine bazar*, March 25, 1947, 12.

24. *New York Times*, November 25, 1947, 37.

25. Otis Guernsey Jr. in *New York Herald Tribune*, November 25, 1947, *To Live in Peace* Clipping File, Rose Collection.

26. *Nation*, December 13, 1947, reprinted in James Agee, *Agee on Film* (New York: McDowell, Obolensky, 1960), 285.

27. *New York Times*, November 25, 1947, 37.

28. *Bianco e nero* 2.10 (1948): 73.

29. *Hollywood Reporter*, November 13, 1947.

30. *New York Daily News*, May 14, 1948.

31. Agee, *Agee on Film*, 285.

32. Current Italian prime minister Silvio Berlusconi has echoed this comment apropos of U.S. president Barack Obama. See "Berlusconi: Obama Is Young, Handsome, Tan," *New York Post*, November 6, 2008.

33. Zampa's previous film, *Un americano in vacanza* (A Yank in Rome, 1946), was about a white GI falling for and marrying an Italian schoolteacher.

34. Michel-Rolph Trouillot, *Silencing the Past* (New York: Beacon, 1995), 96. See also Emmanuelle Saada, "L'empire," in *Dictionnaire critique de la république*, ed. Vincent Duclert and Christophe Prochasson (Paris: Flammarion, 2002), 481.

35. In late October 1911, Italian colonial troops were attacked at Sciara Sciat, on the outskirts of Tripoli. Italian troops responded by executing three thousand of the city's thirty thousand inhabitants and deporting several thousand to work in concentration camps in southern Italy. See Labanca, *Oltremare*, 115.

36. Marco Battini, *Peccati di memoria: La mancata Norimberga italiana* (Bari: Laterza 2003), 95. See also Filippo Focardi and Lutz Klinkhammer, "The Question of Fascist Italy's War Crimes: The Construction of a Self-Acquitting Myth," *Journal of Modern Italian Studies* 9.3 (2004): 330–48; Filippo Focardi, "I mancati processi ai criminali di guerra italiani," in *Giudicare e punire: I processi per crimini di guerra tra diritto e politica*, ed. Luca Baldissare and Paolo Pezzino (Naples: L'Ancora del Mediterraneo, 2005), 185–214. On Italian crimes in the Balkans, see Enzo Collotti, "Sulla politica di repressione italiana nei Balcani," in *La memoria del Nazismo nell'Europa di oggi*, ed. Leonardo Paggi (Florence: La Nuova Italia, 1997), 182–208. See also Pamela Ballinger, "Exhumed Histories: Trieste and the Politics of Exclusive Victimhood," *Journal of Southern Europe and the Balkans* 6.2 (2004): 145–59; Gianni Oliva, *Foibe: Le stragi negate degli italiani della Venezia Giulia e dell'Istria* (Milan: Mondadori, 2002). On the African campaigns and the Italian crimes, see del Boca, *Africa*; Gianni Oliva, *"Si ammazza troppo poco": I crimini di guerra italiani, 1940–1943* (Milan: Mondadori, 2006); Rochat, *Colonialismo*; Rochat, *Guerre italiane*. See also del Boca, *Gas*; Labanca, "Tardiva"; Labanca, "Colonial Rule, Colonial Repression," 308–9; Lidia Santarelli, "Muted Violence: Italian War Crimes in Occupied Greece," *Journal of Modern Italian Studies* 9.3 (2004): 280–99.

37. Labanca suggests that *genocide* is the appropriate term to describe the Italian colonialists' reaction to Sciara Sciat (*Oltremare*, 422–23).

38. Aldo Tonti, *Odore di cinema* (Florence: Vallecchi, 1964), 119.

39. John A. Schillace, *The Tragic Forest: Tales of the Forest of Tombolo* (New York: Exposition, 1951), 34.

40. Indro Montanelli, "C'è un negro pazzo che urla nella pineta," *Corriere della sera*, March 30, 1947, 3.

41. Francesco Grassi, "John Kitzmiller Is a Riot When He Says 'Where Go? Over Boat,'" *Hollywood* 125 (1947): 42–43; translation by author.

42. See Tony Judt, *Postwar* (London: Penguin, 2005), 21.

43. George Bria, "Tin Cans, Tombolo, and Reconstruction," *Washington Post*, May 25, 1947, B2.

44. Aldo Santini, *Tombolo* (Milan: Rizzoli, 1990), 68.

45. *New York Times*, December 31, 1950, *Tombolo* Clipping File, Rose Collection.

46. *Corriere della sera*, October 26, 1947, 2.

47. "Intermezzo," *L'operatore*, November 21–22, 1947.

48. *Film*, October 18, 1947, 3.

49. *Il telegrafo*, May 15, 1949, 2.

50. Pasquale Iaccio, *Cinema e storia: Percorsi immagini testimonianze* (Naples: Liguori, 2000), 288–94.

51. *Corriere della sera*, October 3, 1948, 2.

52. *L'unità*, August 31, 1948, 2.

53. *Daily Worker*, March 16, 1950, *Senza pietà* Clipping File, Schomburg Collection, New York Public Library.

54. *New York Times*, March 16, 1950; *New York Herald Tribune*, March 16, 1950.

55. Stefania Parigi, "Senza pietà," in *Alberto Lattuada: Il cinema e i film*, ed. Adriano Aprà (Rome: Marsilio, 2009), 153.

56. Raymond Borde and Étienne Chaumeton, *A Panorama of American Film Noir, 1941–1953*, trans. Paul Hammond (San Francisco: City Lights, 2002), 125.

57. Iaccio, *Cinema e storia*, 288–94.

58. Callisto Cosulich, ed., *Verso il neorealismo: Un critico italiano degli anni quaranta* (Rome: Bulzoni, 1982), 42.

59. *Il tempo*, August 30, 1948.

60. *Our World*, May 1950, 37.

61. *Corriere della sera*, October 3, 1948, 2; *Bianco e nero* 9.19 (December 1948): 72–73; *New York Herald Tribune*, March 16, 1950, *Without Pity* Clipping File, Rose Collection. For *Corriere della sera*'s critic, Arturo Lanocita, Jerry "does not own anything, but wants to be *owned* by somebody, for example by a white woman [*egli non possiede nulla, ma vuole appartenere a qualcuno: per esempio a una ragazza bianca*]" (emphasis added).

62. In his classic study, Donald Bogle describes the early characters of Sidney Poitier, the Afro-Caribbean actor whose rise to stardom chronologically parallels Kitzmiller's career, as "almost sexless and sterile" (*Toms, Coons, Mulattoes, Mammies, and Bucks*, 4th ed. [New York: Continuum: 2002], 176).

63. Parigi, "Senza pietà," 154.

64. *L'unità*, August 31, 1948, 2, September 4, 1948, 3.

65. On *La dolce vita*, see Stephen Gundle, "La dolce vita," in *Movies as History*, ed. David W. Ellwood (Trowbridge: Redwood, 2000), 132–40.

66. James Snead, *White Screens, Black Images* (New York: Routledge, 1994), 3.

67. See Jost Hermand, "Artificial Atavism: German Expressionism and Blacks," in *Blacks and German Culture*, ed. Jost Hermand and Reinhold Grimm (Madison: University of Wisconsin Press, 1986), 68–72.

68. Franca Faldini and Goffredo Fofi, *L'avventurosa storia del cinema italiano raccontata dai suoi protagonisti, 1935–1959* (Milan: Feltrinelli, 1979), 124.

69. Del Boca, *Africa*.

70. "Uomo nero non devi morire!," *Cinema nuovo* 2.11 (May 15, 1953): 1.

71. Rudi Berger, "Italia: Vivere in pace," *Cinema nuovo* 2.11 (May 15, 1953): 312.

72. Chinweizu, *The West and the Rest of Us: White Predators, Black Slavers, and the African Elite* (New York: Random House, 1975).

73. Françoise Pfaff, "The Uniqueness of Ousmane Sembène's Cinema," in *Ousmane Sembène: Dialogues with Critics and Writers*, ed. Samba Gadjigo, Ralph H. Faulkingham, Thomas Cassirer, and Reinhard Sander (Amherst: University of Massachusetts Press, 1993), 19.

74. Nwachukwu Frank Ukadike, "The Creation of an African Film Aesthetic/Language for Representing African Realities," in *A Call to Action: The Films of Ousmane Sembène*, ed. Sheila Petty (Westport, Conn.: Greenwood, 1996), 105–17.

75. Ibid., 109.

76. Fernando Solanas and Octavio Getino, "Towards a Third Cinema," *Afterimage* 3 (Summer 1971): 16–35; http://documentaryisneverneutral.com/words/camasgun.html (accessed January 26, 2011).

77. Pfaff, "Uniqueness," 15.

PART 3

FROM ITALIAN NEOREALISM TO NEW LATIN AMERICAN CINEMA

Ruptures and Continuities during the 1960s

MARIANO MESTMAN

A poor country, Italy was reborn with its miserable and visionary people. Italy, a synthesis of Occident and Orient, liberated its Third World in the Renaissance eruption, a new reality, a cinematographic neorealism.
 –GLAUBER ROCHA (Brazil)

Ever since the beginning of the Revolution, our artistic foundation lay essentially in Italian neorealism, . . . but when we came to assess it as an aesthetic, we did not feel so positive about it, for we had seen all its potential limitations. We were, in fact, looking for something else. However, we were coming from neorealism and, much as we might have tried to deny it, the fact stuck.
 –TOMÁS GUTIÉRREZ ALEA (Cuba)

This essay revisits the influence exerted by Italian postwar neorealist films on the so-called New Latin American Cinema (NLAC) of the 1960s. The connections between the two phenomena are as obvious and as visible as they are complex, and they have given rise to theoretical and/or historiographic discussions and disputes.[1] When we discard the superficial outlook that described a direct transmission of languages/aesthetics from one cinematic movement to the other, the neorealist "influence" on the NLAC can be seen to be mediated by an intricate, complex network of cultural and political processes that developed throughout the years between the immediate postwar period and the 1960s.[2]

It is difficult to speak of a common identity related to the NLAC of the 1960s and 1970s since it encompasses a highly varied group of Latin American filmmakers and films. When we acknowledge this limitation, however, we can still find enough common elements to suggest that toward the end of the decade, a regional movement arose with a more or less definite beginning and end.[3]

A significant amount of research has been carried out on the filmmakers and the national film industries included in the NLAC. Scholars have addressed its origins, its protagonists, its accompanying film clubs and publications, its connections to the film industry and to state policies in each country, the manifestos that promoted it, and so forth. For the purpose of a discussion on the neorealist influence, there are several major trends among the "external" bonds between neorealism and the NLAC.

First, after World War II, many Latin American filmmakers were trained in European teaching centers. Italy and France harbored and schooled about a hundred directors, some of whom studied at the Italian Centro Sperimentale di Cinematografia in Rome. There, these filmmakers met outstanding colleagues, acquired a new film culture, and established collaborations that would ultimately stand them in good stead. Second, First World critics and publications aided the budding Latin American cinema by publishing articles about the films, interviews with directors and groups, and documents and manifestos. Third, some prominent European groups and filmmakers played a significant role in promoting Latin American films. They helped with some aspects of the production by contributing equipment and/or funding, fostered distribution in mainstream or alternative circuits, organized debates in their countries of origin, and attended Latin American film festivals. Finally, the 1960s saw the advent of a space in European festivals where Latin American filmmakers earned recognition.

Studies of the NLAC covering the period from the postwar through the 1960s have included at least two major ideas that aid in providing a full understanding of the significant neorealist influence on the NLAC. A new film culture preceded the rise of the new cinemas. This characteristic was not exclusive to the renovation that took place in Latin America in the 1960s. During the 1950s and early 1960s, future filmmakers first trained as spectators of what was new in the world's cinema by attending film club exhibitions and by reading specialized journals. Under these circumstances, neorealist ethics and aesthetics stood out in several countries from both a quantitative and qualitative point of view, entering into a dialogue with the processes of cultural modernization and the imaginaries of social commitment in the region.

Second, two different generations of filmmakers were crucial to the NLAC: in the immediate postwar period, the neorealist generation worked almost at the same time as the Italian phenomenon; the subsequent generation was the true expression of the 1960s and shared a larger and politically different horizon.

Paulo Antonio Paranaguá has taken up these two notions in *Tradición y modernidad en el cine de América Latina* (2003), in which he deals with the issue of Latin American films in a sharp, polemic fashion.[4] He argues against what he calls the "canonical version" of history, the "golden tale" of the NLAC, which collapses the contribution made by neorealism onto the Cuban short film *El mégano* (1955), made by Julio García Espinosa and Tomás Gutiérrez Alea, and Nelson Pereira dos Santos of Brazil and Fernando Birri of Argentina. Paranaguá states that "such a venerable trinity assumes a chemically pure, obviously militant, kind of neorealism, able to lead to the renovation that took place in the 1960s," and connects this dominant viewpoint to the implicit assumption that history begins with the films of the 1960s.[5]

Paranaguá further researches the continuities and processes of transition and transformation; rather than fostering a perspective that privileges rupture, this process leads Paranaguá to declare that the neorealist impact on Latin America was not restricted to the intellectuals or to the cultural Left. He acknowledges the "undoubtedly defining" influence of the Italian movement but points out that Latin American films of the period do not depend merely on an external influence.[6] In this sense, he identifies a neorealist influence—mediated by and coexisting and interacting with other inspirations—within a wide range of films made in Latin America immediately after World War II.

Even though the idea of an influence exercised over a wide range of national cinemas, a vast space, and an extended period of time refers to various neorealist Latin America offshoots explored and analyzed by Paranaguá, the films and directors he considers differ little from those to which other authors refer with regard to the presence of neorealism in Latin America.[7] In any case, Paranaguá chose examples to draw attention to the extensive neorealist influence in Latin America. This kind of influence seems to go beyond the classic instances, branching out in sundry directions and then reappearing in an articulation with other external and internal influences as Latin American neorealism, a genre "as hybrid as its Italian counterpart."[8]

When we speak about the two generations of filmmakers of the NLAC and when we acknowledge neorealism's pervasive influence, we are referring to NLAC's inner renovation, which became noticeable in the aesthetic and political expressions of the 1960s. For some filmmakers, this renovation meant a complete and explicit rupture with the neorealist influence. Probably the most radical or at least the best-known instance of this position was provided by Brazilian director Glauber Rocha.

Brazilian documentarian Geraldo Sarno's 1994 essay, *Glauber Rocha e o cinema Latino-Americano*, provides a compelling exploration of Rocha's views on aesthetics and politics, starting from a query about the reasons for Rocha's relentless anti-neorealism in the early 1970s. Sarno wonders what could have driven Rocha, who had acknowledged neorealism's influence in the 1950s and saluted its exemplary lesson for young Latin Americans,[9] to regard the film movement as "a sclerotic alienation" and "the colonizer's language" by 1971.[10] Sarno wonders, "How, why, and at what point of the 1960s did Glauber change his mind about neorealism?"[11]

Sarno broaches the issue through an account of the neorealist influence in the 1950s and focuses on three texts that might show Rocha's theoretical and practical agenda as well as his revolutionary practice in the 1960s: "Aesthetics of Hunger," presented at the 1965 Third World and World Community Conference held during the meeting of the Columbianum, which took place in Genoa, Italy, and was entirely dedicated to Brazilian Cinema Novo; "Revolution Is an Aesthetic" (1967), in which the director proposed an epic and didactic aesthetics; and "Aesthetics of Dreams," the 1971 essay presented at Columbia University in New York City.

Sarno believes that unlike the ending of "Aesthetic of Hunger," in which Rocha rejected any kind of connection with the colonizer's art, "Revolution Is an Aesthetic" shows that the director had begun to perceive the possibility of relating to the colonizing culture, finding support in his own films as well as in the revolutionary winds that were sweeping through Latin America. This new stance implied that he had overcome "the impotence and inferiority complex typical of the colonized," leading to his proposal of an epic and didactic aesthetics. After Rocha made his point, Sarno argues, the director introduced a new and major debate: the place occupied by culture within the revolution, an issue aligned with the main theme of "Aesthetics of Dreams." Still, in the early 1970s, Rocha, starting a less affirmative or prescriptive stage, returned to the more radical standpoint of "Aesthetics of Hunger," declaring that "the only way out lies in the rupture with colonizing rationalisms." From then on, he refused to talk "in whatever kind of aesthetic language," for "full-fledged experience cannot be subject to philosophical notions." At the same time, he pointed to a new path: "The encounter between revolutionaries who have shaken off bourgeois reason and the most significant structures of popular culture will constitute the first configuration of a new revolutionary sign."[12]

In spite of Rocha's radical rupture and of other filmmakers' less dramatic though equally profound detachments from neorealism, however, historical neorealism did not completely disappear, perhaps because even when it was "overcome," it remained as an important residue in some films, manifestos, and debates. In addition to the connections already discussed, attempts to account for this lingering permanence have drawn attention to shared factors between the devastated postwar Italy and the circumstances of the subordinate Latin American social classes during the 1960s, a situation denounced by those sociologists, among others, who identified with the theory of dependence.

The hope of historical neorealism and its postwar ethics—perhaps malleable in the long run but fully founded on the ideology of the Resistance—was viewed as compatible with the responsibility to be assumed by Latin American filmmakers and intellectuals during the 1950s and 1960s. They pondered the slogans of "Sartrean commitment" and "Gramscian organicity" and the guerrilla choice.

During the transition from industrial cinema to auteur cinema in Latin America, documentary films took center stage. The documentarians were also strengthened by their dialogue with European filmmakers such as John Grierson, Joris Ivens, Chris Marker, and other *documentalistas viajeros* (itinerant documentarians), to use María Luisa Ortega's words.[13] This transatlantic bond not only was visible in their films but also worked as an external support for the NLAC. Examples include Grierson's solidarity with Fernando Birri's documentary *Tire dié* (Throw Me a Dime, 1960) and the Bolivian testimonial fiction by Jorge Ruiz, *Vuelve Sebastiana* (1953), at the third International Festival of Documentary Cinema of the Servicio Oficial de Difusión Radiotelevisión y Espectáculos in Uruguay in 1958. In addition, some critics interpret Ivens's presence at the 1969 opening of the Cinemateca del Tercer Mundo (Third World Film Library) in Uruguay and at the Viña del Mar Festival in Chile as a sort of "transfer of the torch" from the revolutionary Dutch filmmaker to Cuban director Santiago Alvarez.[14]

In those days, documentaries were regarded as the Latin American cinema's own genre and greenhouse because the region's newcomers to filmmaking initially tried their hands at documentaries and because the documentary film was perceived as a need in view of the dismal social reality of Latin America.

The bond between neorealism and documentaries is well known. The notion of a predominant social mission separated the documentary from fiction and show business. But as Bill Nichols points out in *Representing Reality*, thanks to the neorealist movement in postwar Italy, documentary realism found an ally for its ethical call in the field of fiction "as a form of responsible, if not committed, historical representation."[15] This connection can be traced backward. In her genealogy of the word *neorealism*, Stefania Parigi states that beginning in the mid-1930s, Italians applied the term to various aesthetic experiences—for example, to Grierson's documentaries.[16] Alberto Cavalcanti would suggest that Grierson use the same word for his documentary work— the same Cavalcanti who in the 1950s would explore the untrodden paths of humanistic realism in Brazil. Moreover, are neorealism and the British documentary school not the two basic points of reference of the Documentary School of Santa Fe established by Fernando Birri in 1956 as well as a landmark for the NLAC in the 1960s?

In this sense, the documentary—and by extension the testimonial dimension of fictional cinema in Latin America—facilitated the persistence of neorealistic historical influences over the period. Likewise, the documentary enabled neorealism to achieve presence even in the initial drive of the most organized, visible period of the NLAC, when it became a regional movement in the second half of the 1960s.

Some individual filmmakers or groups could be seen as representative of renovation (both in the aesthetic and the political field) in the main countries of the region. All of these entities converged within the space and time outlined by some initial festivals/exhibitions, including Viña del Mar (Chile, 1967 and 1969), Mérida (the First Exhibition of Documentary Cinema at Mérida, Venezuela, 1968), Marcha (Uruguay, 1967–68), and the Third World Film Library (Uruguay, 1969) as well as in the 1974 creation of the Committee of Latin American Filmmakers in the context of the widespread repression that devastated the Southern Cone.

In those years, a more or less common imaginary about politics and the cinema took shape in this environment. This process was pervaded by some sort of cinematic Latin Americanism that was sometimes articulated with Third-Worldism. The March 1967 Viña del Mar Festival brought together the NLAC's two generations. While many young filmmakers brought their first works to the festival, the pivotal figures running the event were filmmakers of the neorealist generation, such as Chilean director Aldo Francia, who had chaired the festival since 1963; Alfredo Guevara of the Cuban Institute of Cinematographic Art and Industry (Instituto Cubano de Arte e Industria Cinematográficos), which was closely related to the Italian experience;[17] and Argentine filmmaker Fernando Birri, who came with his conational Edgardo Pallero, who had already become a distributor.

Some of Viña's awards and honorable mentions acknowledged the main trends of the regional movement, most of which had already cast aside neorealism; other honors went to filmmakers who were building up a selective tradition in search of their own identity and were looking back on the neorealist heritage. Recognition of this search accounts for the honorable mention awarded to the Documentary School of Santa Fe for its influence on the development of Argentine and Brazilian cinema. The honorable mention granted to the program of the Brazilian direct cinema shared the same spirit.

Toward the mid-1960s, the Brazilian movement joined the renovation process. The new Brazilian cinema received early international recognition (1961–62) and achieved maturity within a couple of years. Although the rise of Cinema Novo reflected the merging of diverse influences, the distinct importance of neorealism was patent. By the mid-1960s, Rocha, a member of the new generation, had taken over the leadership of the movement from neorealist generation pioneer Nelson Pereira dos Santos, but since the late 1950s, Pereira dos Santos had strongly fostered renovation through his films and by producing Roberto Santos's *O grande momento* (The Great Moment, 1958) as well as "with great aesthetic and ideological coherence supportive of neorealism and of the Brazilian Communist Party."[18] In 1965, he was still called "the key figure" of Brazilian Cinema Novo in publications such as the Latin American edition of Guido Aristarco's Italian film journal, *Cinema nuovo*.[19]

The documentary-fiction connection became established in the 1960s and arrived at Viña in 1967 through *The Brazilian Condition*, a project produced by Thomas Farkas that delved into Brazil's popular culture. It originally included some Argentines from the Documentary School of Santa Fe, who travelled to São Paulo with Fernando Birri by invitation of the director of the Cinemateca Brasileira, Paulo Emilio Salles Gomes. Thus, Edgardo Pallero and Manuel Horacio Giménez became actively involved as producer and director, respectively, in the first series of films known as Caravana Farkas, which included four black-and-white documentaries shot between 1964 and 1965.[20] Sarno, who took an active part in the two stages of the project (1964–65 and 1969–70), compared *Viramundo* (1965) and *Viva cariri!* (1969), his two films in the series. He related the former film to neorealism (camera cinema, "in which the director builds up his discourse from only one point of view"), while the latter impressed him as having the potential to use, for the first time, an epic language brought over from direct cinema (image cinema). "It took four years—the time that elapsed between the making of the two films—for the self of the director to shift from the camera to the image," Sarno said.[21]

These were precisely the years when neorealism, which was still a part of the constituent drive of Viña in 1967, made its final exit from the regional movement, lingering in a residual manner in only a handful of particular cases. Neorealism no longer served as anything like the point of reference it had previously been.

What path did Italian neorealism's influence take during those years?

It might be best to start at the end. Although the determination of a date always implies falling into the traps set by conventionalism and oversimplification, the 1974 Mostra Internazionale del Nuovo Cinema in Pesaro, Italy, included two retrospective screenings, one of Italian neorealism (together with a conference), and the other of Chilean cinema under the Salvador Allende administration (1970–73).

On the one hand, Pesaro offered the opportunity for a comprehensive examination of nearly fifty films and a space for the exploration, revision, and critical reexamination of a fundamental moment in Italian cinema. The direct or indirect influence of neorealism on Italian filmmakers and intellectuals still proved tangible, as Italian film scholar and director of the Pesaro Festival Lino Micciché declared in his keynote address. The screenings and debates focused on an ambitious, comprehensive study of neorealism as a historical phenomenon. Whether one agrees or not with *Cinema nuovo*'s harsh treatment of the convention ("it sounded like a summary disposal of the neorealist experience"),[22] the event at least pointed to a change. Unlike previous conventions, such as those held in Perugia (1949) and in Parma (1953), in which neorealism had been discussed while still under the effects of heated postwar political and ideological controversies, Pesaro turned neorealism into an object of historical analysis.[23] On the other hand, along parallel lines at Pesaro was the retrospective exhibition of the latest collective experiences of the NLAC, which had developed during the last revolutionary political movement in Latin America of the era, Chile's path toward socialism. The failure of the Chilean movement also marked the end of the long decade of the 1960s.[24]

As the logical conclusion of a process that had burst onto the scene during 1968, 1974 brought together a series of highlights in which the most significant trends of the world's political cinema could be seen in their prime. Before the Pesaro convention, Caracas, Venezuela, had hosted the First Encounter of Latin American Filmmakers, whose Regional Committee rose to denounce the Chilean coup. The political and cultural dialogue among Third World filmmakers that became apparent at the December 1973 Conference of Argel remained alive in May 1974 in Buenos Aires as demonstrated by the precarious yet intense attempt to form a Third World Cinema Committee.[25] In early June, Quebec, Canada, saw the advent of the year's most politically significant event: the Rencontres Internationales pour un Nouveau Cinema (International Meetings for a New Cinema), organized by André Páquet and Montreal's Committee for Active Cinema and attended by more than two hundred participants from twenty-five countries. This gathering sought to connect the diverse collectives forming the world's militant cinema. However, the process was already beginning to lose strength.

At the NLAC's final stage, alternative cinemas kept a significant and considerable distance from the neorealist influence of the 1950s and early 1960s. At this time, relations were established between the Italian post-neorealist political cinema[26] and the political Latin American cinema that was gathered in the NLAC. On either side of the Atlantic, these relations acknowledged neorealism as a valid precedent, as a fundamental historical stage, but it was a stage from which these filmmakers had moved on. In the Latin American case, the issue was that the second generation of the 1960s, especially those who late in the decade shared a political imaginary that stood closer to Third World radicalization than to postwar humanism, felt closer to Gillo Pontecorvo's *La battaglia di Algeri* (Battle of Algiers, 1966) than to classic Italian neorealists. The differences between countries and filmmakers were complex and important, but the regional movement engine agreed with the revolutionary political imaginary that *Battle of Algiers* represented.

The annual Pesaro retrospectives in the late 1960s and early 1970s played an important role in relations between Italy and Latin America.[27] Uruguayan Walter Achúgar and Argentine Edgardo Pallero, in association with the state broadcasting company Radiotelevisione Italiana, promoted the coproduction of NLAC films (for example, the Italo-Bolivian *El coraje del pueblo* [The Courage of the People, 1971], directed by Jorge Sanjinés). In addition, the films shot by the Argentine group Cine Liberación were processed at a small Italian production company, Ager, operated by Valentino Orsini, Giuliani G. De Negri, and brothers Paolo and Vittorio Taviani, and later by Renzo Rossellini's small production company, San Diego Cinematografica.[28] At the 1968 international opening of *La hora de los hornos* (The Hour of the Furnaces) in Pesaro, Fernando Birri called attention to the fact that the film's strong European reception demonstrated the European Left's cultural and political concern for Latin America and its cinema. In coming years, this concern would become apparent through the influence exerted on an international level by this film as well as by the theorizations of Third Cinema, which became a point of reference for some European political filmmakers.

The same was true of other Latin American films and movements. Europeans were not merely interested in militant, direct action Latin American cinema; rather, this concern had a wider scope. In 1966, Marco Bellocchio published an article about the Brazilian Cinema Novo in *Cahiers du cinéma* in which he argued that "as a movement, neorealism experienced a revolution that has already exhausted its crucial, vital momentum, whereas the new Brazilian cinema is more important insofar as it can stir a revolution."[29]

Among Latin American festivals, Mérida 1968 and more especially Viña del Mar 1969 represent a big leap in the direction of the rupture with neorealist influence, a leap prompted both by the political radicalization at the end of the decade and by the aesthetic explosion shown in the participating films.[30]

Although they did not often develop into debates, some programs echoed the Italian discussions of the 1950s about realism and the overcoming of neorealism. The differences were significant. The discussion in Mérida,[31] for example, was restricted to documentaries or at most the documentary dimension. At this event, the irruption of "the political" as the rule according to which films were to be classified subordinated linguistic and aesthetic issues to the "urgency" of intervention, as was clearly stated in the jury criteria.[32]

In this framework, the necessary relation between the documentary and Latin America depended on presentation of evidence of destitution,[33] but the Mérida discussions made problematic the type of documentary that was suitable for the ongoing situation. The prevailing idea was to move on from a testimonial on destitution to a more arousing stage that emphasized accusation and used various cinematic resources to reveal the causes of the situation through a more comprehensive analysis. This viewpoint echoed the thoughts of the award-winning directors and agreed perfectly with the films chosen by the jury: Santiago Alvarez's *Now* (1965), Jorge Sanjinés's *Revolución* (Revolution, 1963), and the first part of *La hora de los hornos*.

The proposal to move on to the next stage had been clearly stated by Jorge Sanjinés (Ukamau group) in one of the festival's forums. Despite the diversity of the documentaries exhibited at Mérida, the issue stood at the center of the discussions of the most active participants at the festival, to the extent that it brought tension regarding emerging trends such as direct cinema, which encountered militant critical objections at the same time that its makers reconsidered it. Just as Sarno reflected on the transition in his work, perhaps intending to increase the value of direct cinema in the new political arena, Sergio Muñiz, for example, distinguished between the direct technique as used by the French, the Canadians, and the Americans and the ways in which it was used by the Brazilians (which really meant Latin American filmmakers). Muñiz's reasoning included the idea of abandoning the plain registering of reality to achieve a fuller grasp of conflicts and contradictions.[34] In Mérida, Muñiz said that reality should be not only documented but also explained. Direct cinema was to become a filmed piece of research into the predicaments of underdeveloped societies to achieve fuller political awareness. To know is to transform.

This view represented a step forward along the road of a cinema committed to reality and involving the comprehension of its more complex, less visible features and eventually their transformation. Tomás Gutiérrez Alea, a Cuban filmmaker who came from the neorealist generation but would be one of the protagonists of the renovation of the 1960s, linked Cuban filmmakers' distancing process from neorealism with the search for other means of expression and the need to adopt an "analytical attitude" toward reality where "the meaning of external facts became less obvious, less apparent, and more profound."[35]

The separation between the regional movement and neorealism became final at the 1969 festival in Viña del Mar. Notwithstanding the distance, the criticism, and even the attacks leveled at the "limitations" of the Italian film style, the views of Glauber Rocha and Tomás Gutiérrez Alea cited in the epigraphs point to the fact that at least during the period explored here, neorealism, the reborn irruption with which Italy freed its Third World, had an undeniable influence on the NLAC, even for those who wanted to lead it toward new horizons.

Notes

Translated from the Spanish by Marta Merajver.

1. Neorealism has been under constant revision in criticism and historiography alike. See Stefania Parigi, "Le carte d'identità del neorealismo," in *Nuovo cinema*, ed. Bruno Torri (Venice: Marsilio, 2005), 80–102. See also Zagarrio, this volume.

2. Lino Micciché posited that neorealism stood for a cultural and political response to a given historical moment, that it was an "ethics of aesthetics" that would give the possibility of bringing together, in one single movement, the aesthetic and ideological diversity of Rossellini, De Sica, Visconti, and De Santis, turning these directors into models for the chief style variations (*Il neorealismo cinematografico italiano* [Venice: Marsilio, 1975]). In this sense, it is difficult to define one specific Italian neorealist style that arrived in Latin America during these years. Perhaps one could argue that the films and conceptualizations of Vittorio De Sica and Cesare Zavattini were the most popular as "neorealist identity" outside of Italy.

3. Julianne Burton, Zuzana Pick, Ana López, Alberto Elena, Michael Martin, Michael Chanan, Robert Stam, and Paulo Antonio Paranaguá, among others, have dwelled on the continental project of this phase.

4. Paulo Antonio Paranaguá, *Tradición y modernidad en el cine de América Latina* (Madrid: FCE, 2003), 170–99. See also Paulo Antonio Paranaguá, *Le cinéma en Amérique Latine: Le miroir éclaté: Historiographie et comparatisme* (Paris: Harmattan, 2000), 36–42.

5. Paranaguá, *Cinéma*, 18, 36–42. That assumption erases all previous works, at best recognizing a few isolated forerunners.

6. Paranaguá, *Tradición*, 170–74.

7. According to Paranaguá, *Tradición*, 170–99, Pereira dos Santos and Birri, the collective short-length film *El mégano*, and, to a greater or a lesser degree, such early Cuban films as *Historias de la revolución* (History of the Revolution, 1960), directed by Tomás Gutiérrez Alea; *El joven rebelde* (The Young Rebel, 1961), directed by Julio García Espinosa, with Zavattini's participation in the script; *Cuba baila* (Cuba Dances, 1960), also by García Espinosa; and the Venezuelan *La escalinata* (The Perron, 1950), directed by César Enríquez, were all part of Latin American neorealism in the 1950s. Paranaguá also considers the Brazilian film *O grande momento* (The Great Moment, 1958), directed by Roberto Santos, "a paradigm of Latin American neorealism" (183) and sees director Alex Viany ("between

neorealism and socialist realism") and other films and directors of the 1960s as expressions of "the late neorealism" or as coexisting with explorations of other paths (170–99). For another interpretation of this process, see Jorge Ruffinelli, "Un camino hacia la verdad," *El ojo que piensa* 1 (September 2002), http://www.elojoquepiensa.net/ (accessed March 28, 2011).

8. It became integrated with the "thick mesh of influences and trends at work in the 1950s, the maze of modernity," operating on "the twists and turns that transformed genre cinema into author's cinema" (Paranaguá, *Tradición*, 200–217). Paranaguá examines Leopoldo Torre Nilsson and Luis Buñuel to delve into the transition from the old film studios to the new cinema, paying special attention to two social films by these directors: *El secuestrador* (The Kidnapper, 1958) by Torre Nilsson, and Buñuel's *Los olvidados* (The Forgotten Ones, 1950). Paranaguá notes that while Bunuel's relation to neorealism is conflictive, in *El secuestrador* Torre Nilsson's cinema is convergent with neorealism. Along these lines, Paranaguá declares that "both [directors] agree with its ethics rather than with its aesthetics" and that these two films (as well as *Largo viaje* [A Long Journey, 1967], by Chilean director Patricio Kaulen) might show certain aspects typical of "Hispanic realism, a literary and fine arts tradition that comes back to life every now and then" (*Tradición*, 195).

9. Geraldo Sarno, *Glauber Rocha e o cinema Latino-Americano* (Rio de Janeiro: CIEC-UFRJ–Rio Filme, 1994), 13. Sarno refers to a 1958 article in which Rocha discusses a film by Mexican director Benito Alazraki, *Raíces* (Roots, 1953) to highlight a project for a cinematic language of Latin America, which Rocha views as "a synthesis of two antagonistic tendencies that end up in vital stages of the development of universal cinematic thought: the dry antiformalism of neorealism and Eisenstein's ultra-expressionism [*ultra-expressão eisensteiniana*]" (13). Thus, neorealism, as Sarno notes, appears in this context "side by side with Eisenstein's epic cinema (making up a *duality/unity*, a *synthesis/clash*), like one of two opposite poles that are needed to develop a cinematic language of national expression" (13).

10. Quoted in Sarno, *Glauber Rocha*, 14. In an "Open letter to Alfredo Guevara" (May 1971), Rocha linked the sector of the Brazilian Left that opposed Cinema Novo to a defense of "dirty tricks and sclerotic neorealism, populism, and other alienations caused by cultural colonization." And in "Project for a film to be shot in Cuba. Political considerations" (March 9, 1972), Rocha pointed to neorealism as "the colonizer's language."

11. Perhaps Sarno's view emphasizes and dwelled longer on Zavattini's presence in the region. Moreover, he tracks the first "points of rupture" experienced by the neorealist influence to Sanjinés's *Revolución* (1963) and his Eisenstein-inspired epics as well as to the Brazilian films that followed Rocha's *Barravento* (The Turning Wind, 1961).

12. Sarno, *Glauber Rocha*, 64–66. For a further understanding of Rocha's career in this period, see Ismail Xavier, *Allegories of Underdevelopment: Aesthetics and Politics in Modern Brazilian Cinema* (Minneapolis: University of Minnesota Press, 1997); Rocha, *Século*, 7–31.

13. María Luisa Ortega, "El descubrimiento de América por los documentalistas viajeros," in *El cine documental en América Latina*, ed. Paulo Antonio Paranaguá (Madrid: Cátedra, 2003), 93–108.

14. *Punto final* (Chile), November 11, 1969.

15. Bill Nichols, *Representing Reality* (Bloomington: Indiana University Press, 1991), 167. Nichols describes how the fictional representation of "the time and space of lived experience," combined "the observational eye of the documentary with the intersubjective, identificatory strategies of fiction," and the prioritization of victims as subject matter (167). Nichols makes a particularly important point by referring to the connection between neorealism and the "observational" mode of the documentary while reminding us that documentarians boasted of their kinship with the Italian postwar movement. Louis Marcorelles finds that the most significant works of Italian neorealism served as a prelude to the direct cinema (*Élements pour un nouveau cinéma* [Brussels: UNESCO, 1970]). See also Robert Allen and Douglas Gomery, *Film History: Theory and Practice* (New York: McGraw-Hill, 1985).

16. See Parigi, *Carte d'identità*, 82–83. See also Stefania Parigi, "Neorealismo: Le avventure di una parola," in *Storia del cinema italiano*, ed. Callisto Cosulich, vol. 7 (Venice: Marsilio, 2003).

17. The award-winning Cuban films in Viña in 1967, *Now* (1965), by Santiago Alvarez, and *Manuela* (1966), by Humberto Solás, express the turning point of the Cuban cinema in the mid-60s, when it was pervaded by all the external influences that followed the strong initial neorealist presence. Neorealism was a strong influence on the learning stage of Cuban cinema, leaving seeds. See Juan Antonio García Borrero, *La edad de la herejía* (Santiago de Cuba: Oriente, 2002), 68–75. In the 1950s, Aristarco had appointed Alfredo Guevara as correspondent for his magazine, *Cinema nuovo*, tasking Guevara with writing about "neorealist initiatives" on the island. Still, what mattered most was Guevara's relationship with Zavattini and his work trips. In some way, neorealism helped to prevent Cuban cinema and culture from freezing. "In fact, Zavattini implicitly suggested that we should break once and for all with both the American cinema and the new reductionist tendency, i.e., Socialist Realism" (Julio García Espinosa, "Recuerdos de Zavattini," *Cine cubano* 155 [November 2002]: 62). In this regard, around 1963, the Cuban Institute was attacked by sectors of the PSP (Blas Roca) that supported socialist realism and opposed its heterodox policy in the matter of film distribution. See also Alfredo Guevara, *Ese diamantino corazón de la verdad* (Havana: Iberautor, 2002), 21–22; Alfredo Guevara, *Revolución es lucidez* (Havana: ICAIC, 1998); Michael Chanan, *The Cuban Image* (London: British Film Institute, 1985).

18. Paranaguá, *Tradición*, 212.

19. Alberto Ciria, "Notas sobre un cine latinoamericano," *Cinema nuovo: Edición Latinoamericana* 2 (Summer 1965): 176.

20. Paulo Gil Soares, *Memoria do Cangaço* (1965); Manuel Giménez, *Nossa escola de samba* (Our School of Samba, episode of *Brasil verdade*, 1968); Maurice Capovilla, *Subterraneos do futebol* (episode of *Brasil verdade*, 1968) (Capovilla had visited the Santa Fe School in 1963); and Geraldo Sarno's *Viramundo*, which was awarded the 16mm Documentary Film

Prize. See José Carlos Avellar, "A condição brasileira," in *Cine documental*, ed. Paranaguá, 304–8.

21. Sarno, *Glauber Rocha*.

22. Ugo Finetti, "Critica marxista e fautrice durante il neorealismo," *Cinema nuovo* 232 (1974): 430–40.

23. The materials published about the discussions at the 1974 conference included several documents from the Perugia and Parma conventions. See *Il neorealismo e la critica: Materiali per una bibliografia* (Pesaro: Mostra Internazionale del Nuovo Cinema, 1974); *Sul neorealismo: Antologia di testi e documenti (1939–1955)* (Pesaro: Mostra Internazionale del Nuovo Cinema, 1974).

24. The military coup in Chile is one of the facts on which Fredric Jameson bases his argument that "the 1960s" extend up to 1972–74. See Fredric Jameson, "Periodizing the 60s," in *The 60s, without Apology*, ed. Sohnya Sayres, Anders Stephanson, Stanley Aronowitz, and Fredric Jameson (Minneapolis: University of Minnesota Press, 1984), 178–209.

25. See Mariano Mestman, "From Algiers to Buenos Aires: The Third World Cinema Committee (1973–1974)," *New Cinemas: Journal of Contemporary Film* 1 (2002): 40–53.

26. Micciché proposes that "the neorealist cinema has not had a clear, identifiable *imaginary* of its own," which accounts for the variety of the bases of the post-neorealist "cinematic imaginary" (*Neorealismo*, 7–28).

27. While the NLAC was always present at events held during this stage, the Pesaro retrospective played a key role in promoting and articulating NLAC in the context of the unrest of 1968. The NLAC had begun to participate in Italian festivals in the early 1960s: at the Columbianum (Santa Margherita Ligure, Sestri Levante, Genoa) and the festivals in Porretta Terme and Pesaro.

28. Rossellini created San Diego Cinematografica in 1969. San Diego soon focused on Third World political documentaries fostering liberation movements (Renzo Rossellini, interview by author, September 2000).

29. Marco Bellocchio, "La révolution au cinéma," *Cahiers du cinéma* 176 (1966): 43, quoted in Alexandre Figueiroa, *Cinema Novo: A onda do joven cinema e sua recepção na Franca* (Campinas: Papirus, 2004), 164.

30. Such films included *Memorias del subdesarrollo* (Memories of Underdevelopment, 1968), directed by Tomás Gutiérrez Alea; *Lucía* (1968), directed by Humberto Solás; *La primera carga del machete* (The First Charge of the Machete, 1967), directed by Manuel Octavio Gómez; Santiago Alvarez's documentaries (*Now*, 1965; *Hanoi, martes 13* [Hanoi, Tuesday the 13th], 1967; *LBJ*, 1968; *79 primaveras* [79 Springs], 1969); *Valpaíso, mi amor* (Valparaiso, My Love, Aldo Francia, 1968); *El chacal de Nahueltoro* (Jackal of Nahueltoro, Miguel Littín, 1969); *Caliche sangriento* (Bloody Nitrate, Helvio Soto, 1969); *Tres tristes tigres* (Three Sad Tigers, Raúl Ruiz, 1968); *La hora de los hornos* (Solanas and Getino, 1968); *Yawar Mallcu* (Blood of the Condor, Jorge Sanjinés, 1969); *Chircales* (The Brickmakers, Marta Rodríguez and Jorge Silva, 1968–72); *Me gustan los estudiantes* (I Like Students,

Mario Handler, 1968); and *Liber Arce, liberarse* (Liber Arce, To Free Oneself, Mario Handler, 1969).

31. The Mérida conference took place in late 1968 and was organized by Carlos Rebolledo, who was also a member of the neorealist generation.

32. The jury members included Guido Aristarco, Rodolfo Eizaguirre, Agustín Mahieu, Marcel Martín, and José Wainer.

33. Oswaldo Capriles, "Mérida: Realidad, forma, y comunicación," *Cine al día 6* (December 1968): 6, reprinted in *Cine del tercer mundo* 1 (1969): 39–47.

34. Perhaps these filmmakers and critics should pay attention to Louis Marcorelles's warning about direct cinema: "Let us deal with the concrete on condition that we do not get lost in the concrete" (*Elementos para un nuevo cine*, trans. Loly Morán and Juan P. Millán [Salamanca: Sígueme, 1978], 140; translation by author).

35. Gutiérrez Alea, interview, in Julianne Burton, *Cinema and Social Change in Latin America* (Austin: University of Texas Press, 1986), 173.

IMPORTING NEOREALISM, EXPORTING CINEMA

Indian Cinema and Film Festivals in the 1950s

NEEPA MAJUMDAR

In 1946, when V. Shantaram made his war-effort film, *Dr. Kotnis ki amar kahani*, a biopic about a doctor who went with an Indian medical mission to China shortly after the Japanese invasion, he filmed it in two versions, Hindi and English, with the latter intended for the international film festival circuit or for release in the United States. He eventually sold the English version, *The Journey of Dr. Kotnis*, to Arthur Mayer and Joseph Burstyn, the top distributors of foreign films in the United States, who were also responsible for bringing to the American public the films of Roberto Rossellini and Vittorio De Sica. Shantaram's efforts came to nothing, despite some publicity in New York City, and the film eventually ended up, reedited and retitled, on the U.S. exploitation cinema circuit.[1] Shantaram's failed aspirations for international recognition were carried specifically on the conviction that his film was breaking ground in its concern with important contemporary subjects and its use of "authentic" cultural representation. But even on the home front, despite accolades about the film's "realism" and carefully reconstructed Chinese locations, *Dr. Kotnis's* thunder was stolen by *Dharti ke lal* (Children of the Earth, K. A. Abbas, 1946), on all counts: in terms of realism, its potential in the international market, and its ultimate place in the Indian cinema canon.[2] Shantaram gained international recognition for a later film, *Do ankhen barah haath* (Two Eyes, Twelve Hands, 1957), which was screened in San Francisco along with Satyajit Ray's second film in the Apu trilogy, *Aparajito* (The Unvanquished, 1956), in November 1958 and which won the Samuel Goldwyn International Film Award in 1959.[3]

Made by a Bombay director as a project for the Indian Peoples' Theatre Association (IPTA), *Dharti ke lal* was screened in Moscow and Budapest to much acclaim and was specifically mentioned by the Soviet and Hungarian

178

delegates to the first International Film Festival in India (IFFI), which was held January 24–February 1, 1952, in New Delhi, Bombay, Madras, and Calcutta. Both *Dharti ke lal* and *Dr. Kotnis ki amar kahani*, along with a few other films, among them *Chinnamul* (The Uprooted, Nemai Ghosh, 1950), anticipate the story of Italian neorealism's discursive role in debates about realism in India. Although the first IFFI is generally taken to be the point of origin for the influence of Italian neorealist aesthetics in India, the term *influence* only inadequately signals the amorphous forms that the urge toward "realism" took and to which Italian neorealism gave a name and identity in early 1952. In its most common retelling, though, the story of Italian neorealism in India is also inextricably bound to director Satyajit Ray, whose *Pather panchali* (Song of the Road, 1955) was consciously modeled on the humanist values and low budget of *Ladri di biciclette* (Bicycle Thieves, 1948), which he saw in London some years before it was screened at the IFFI.

As anywhere else in the world, the "realism" in Italian neorealism came to mean different things to different people in India. In the popular view of Indian cinema history, apart from its origins in India with *Pather panchali*, Italian neorealism finds its true incarnation only in the so-called Indian Parallel Cinema of 1975 onward, films that were state-funded in the hopes of producing a quality cinema that could represent India at film festivals. Here, I seek less to trace influences than to explore 1950s discussions of realism in India as catalyzed by what filmmakers and audiences described as the eye-opening experience of watching the three Italian neorealist films that were screened at the first IFFI. More specifically, I concentrate on this festival's impact and its echoes in cinematic and journalistic discourse in the early 1950s. Within the discourse of realism, one can find a continuum of films ranging from mainstream studio products such as *Footpath* (Zia Sarhady, 1953) to hybrid independent and studio films such as *Do bigha zamin* (Two Acres of Land, Bimol Roy, 1953) to state-supported independent films such as *Pather panchali*. The impetus behind these "realist" discourses was as much a concern with nation building as a concern with representing India's cinema abroad at film festivals. At the opening of the IFFI on January 24, 1952, Prime Minister Jawaharlal Nehru emphasized "the influence of films on people's lives and . . . the need for concentrating more on quality than on 'quantity production,'" thus implicitly using the occasion to chastise mainstream Indian films for failing at nation building.[4]

The IFFI spurred the highbrow *Times of India* to focus on Indian cinema, using the festival as an opportunity to take stock. Since film journalism had been dominated for decades by what I have elsewhere called the "What's Wrong with Indian Cinema?" genre of film criticism, no such assessment was really necessary.[5] But the films screened at the festival enabled discussion specifically of cinema's relation to everyday reality. One columnist, Adie, complained that the "shoddy melodrama and the suburban daydream world of the average Indian picture where no tramp or beggar, criminal or destitute, is without some cute teenager falling for him and breaking into a duet on the slightest provocation have nothing to do either with life or with art." He equally chastised Hollywood's "evasions and falsifications of reality," although in the 1930s and 1940s, Hollywood's technological expertise had usually been held up as a standard against which to examine what was wrong with Indian cinema. Reexamining realism, Adie remarked, "There is no viler heresy than to think that the nearer the filmic art approaches realism the more it loses in entertainment value. The success achieved by Italian directors like Rossellini and De Sica, some of whose pictures are to be exhibited during the festival, shows how imaginative treatment of social reality—men in desperate search of a living, their energy sapped by work in factory and life in the slums . . . can have as great a box-office pull as the frothiest of comedies." He concluded with the hope that the "Italians can certainly exercise a healthy influence on our film art."[6]

In March 1952, one month after the IFFI, a new bimonthly magazine, *Filmfare*, was launched, billing itself as "the first serious effort in film journalism in India." *Filmfare* saw the festival as an opportunity for Indian film stars to be exposed to quality films and to "assess the position India occupies in the film world today."[7] This shift in emphasis from filmmakers to film stars had much to do with a realignment of Italian neorealist methods in the context of Indian film production. In the first issue of *Filmfare*, Shantaram wrote a piece on realism as a defining characteristic of Italian films that provided a context for "a new wave of realism currently underway in Indian films, inspired by Italian cinema." In his typology of international cinema, the prosperity of Hollywood cinema's mode of production shows itself in the emphasis on spectacle ("show and splendour"), while in Italy, the ravages of war led to cinema's expression of realism and human values. In communist countries, according to Shantaram, an emphasis on increased production in all sectors had led to a cinema of mass propaganda and education.[8] Some of the films discussed in *Filmfare* as part of this Indian wave of realist films were *Awara* (The Vagabond, Raj Kapoor, 1951) and *Footpath*. *Awara*, released shortly before the film festival, was "India's choice for international Film Festival," according to a half-page ad that also claimed that the film was "smashing all records at all theatres."[9]

Differing approaches to realism are already apparent in the contrasting reviews of *Awara* in the *Times of India* and *Filmfare*. While *Filmfare* extolled the film's realist glimpse into Bombay slums and childhood poverty, the *Times of*

India critic complained about its "note of studied pose and stilted artificiality, a continuous contrivance for the effect which shatter realism [*sic*] in the story and rob the picture of its most essential quality"—that is, its critique of the social system that produces criminals. But the reviewer also conceded that "the immediate reaction of the average filmgoer is one of entertainment, though the more discriminating will question it later."[10] Thus, subject matter alone does not guarantee realism for this critic. In *Filmfare*, by contrast, Khwaja Ahmad Abbas, presumably a "discriminating" viewer of realism since he had made *Dharti ke lal* in 1946, had only praise for *Awara's* "social conscience" and "courage in tackling such a bold theme"; he even admired its fantasy sequences.[11]

Thus, within days of the festival, Italian neorealism provided a specific and concrete rallying point around what had been since the early 1930s an endemic Indian disavowal of popular cinema. Within the film industry itself, and certainly in intellectual discourses at large, cinema was the incorrigibly bad object, with only occasional exceptions, such as *Sant tukaram* (1936), which won an award at the Venice Film Festival in 1937. Many of the films associated with the realist impulse in India, such as *Dharti ke lal* and *Neecha nagar* (Lowly City, Chetan Anand, 1954), are now largely unavailable despite the far greater access to older films that the DVD boom has produced. The current unavailability of these films may be related to a disjunction between the nation-building project in which they were implicated and the contemporary globalized media economy.

If success abroad was the measure of pride in a national cinema, then 1954–57 were particularly good years for India's cinematic morale. At the Cannes Film Festival in each of these years, an Indian film won either an award or a special mention. In the chronology of these four years, *Do bigha zamin*, Roy's 1953 Bombay studio film, rather than Ray's *Pather panchali*, comes first, with *Do bigha zamin* winning one of the international prizes in 1954 and *Pather panchali* winning the Best Human Document award in 1956.[12] *Filmfare* consistently imagined Indian cinema and the publication's journalistic role in relation to cinema worldwide, despite its primary emphasis on Indian films. For *Filmfare*, "realism" as the defining characteristic of Italian films constantly came up in the context of discussing Indian films inspired by Italian cinema.[13] The magazine's interest in both realism and India's place in international cinema in its early 1952 issues signals a shift in attitudes toward Indian cinema. This shift is indicated not only by the state's hosting of an international film festival but also by *Filmfare's* creation of an annual award for the best Indian film in 1954. The first winner of the *Filmfare* prize was *Do bigha zamin*, India's first Cannes winner.

But what did the amorphous term *realism* signify in India in the immediate postindependence period, and what specific inflections did Italian neorealism bring to it? With regard to the theater and film productions of the IPTA, such as *Dharti ke lal* and *Neecha nagar*, the term meant primarily a form of social engagement and awakening, drawing also on left-oriented predecessors such as the Progressive Writers Association, whose literary work provided the scripts and song lyrics for many of these films. These artistic movements emerged out of the recent traumas of the Bengal famine in 1943 and the violent Partition of India prior to independence in 1946–47, which claimed millions of lives. As a style of theater, IPTA's "realist" social impulse did not preclude it from using a combination of song and folk performance styles, even while representing the horrors of the Bengal famine. Earlier in the century, a similar reliance on popular folk and theater styles arguably was also responsible in part for the much-vilified formal features of the Hindi sound film, with its fragmented narrative style, its dependence on song and other forms of spectacle, and its general aesthetics of frontality, in which moral values and emotional affect are externalized in mise-en-scène and performative gesture.

IPTA's mode of realism points toward a split between two ways in which Italian neorealist films were understood. First, they were seen as a form of social engagement, focusing on the urban and rural underclass and the problems of poverty and unemployment. Second, they provided a model for a mode of production that in turn left its trace in cinematic style. These two aspects of Italian neorealist films—their social critique and their mode of production and film style—explain the divide between the two trajectories of Italian neorealism in India, one in the Parallel Cinema (though not named as such then) beginning with Ray's work, and the other in the commercial Bombay and regional cinemas, where *realist* became quickly dissociated from a low-budget mode of production.

In accounting for the international success of Italian neorealist films, Ray pays less attention to film style than to sources and subject matter. According to Ray, the first reason for Italian films' success is their source in literature (as was the case for his *Pather panchali*), which meant that "the scripts turned out by these writers had superbly organized classical structures."[14] Although acknowledging that most of the scriptwriters for Italian neorealist films were "Leftists," Ray's second reason waters down social content to "deeply human . . . content."[15] Third, none of the filmmakers were amateurs; their years of cinematic experience meant that production constraints could be turned to aesthetic advantage.[16] Ray had no such cinematic experience when he made *Pather panchali*, and when he acknowledged the influence of De Sica's *Bicycle Thieves*, Ray invoked another set of characteristics of Italian neorealism, saying that he "knew immediately that if [he] ever made *Pather Panchali* [he] would make it in the same way, using natural locations and unknown actors."[17] In fact, the Indian reception of *Pather panchali* made much of those two factors, and this choice has set the film apart from other contenders to the neorealist mantle in 1950s India, such as *Do bigha zamin*.[18]

In the Indian imagination, despite exposure to other Italian films, *Bicycle Thieves* and De Sica very quickly came to stand for all of Italian neorealist cinema. Although *Sciuscià* (Shoeshine, Vittorio De Sica, 1946) had not yet been screened in India at this time, its narrative premise seems to have caught the Indian imagination, with Prakash Arora's *Boot Polish* (1954) being the most obvious imitation. Even Ray, in his chapter on "Some Italian Films I Have Seen," written well after the 1952 IFFI, says scathing things about most Italian films other than *Bicycle Thieves*. For example, he describes *Bitter Rice* as the only neorealist film, other than *Stromboli*, that "the Indian public has had a chance to see [but] if it failed to create an impression on our intelligentsia, it is because, in spite of all his striving after documentary conviction, De Santis is essentially a second-rate artist preoccupied more with showmanship than with social problems."[19] Here social problems and a documentary spirit collide with "showmanship" or presumably spectacle. Ray finds *La terra trema* (The Earth Trembles, Luchino Visconti, 1948) "a great bore, a colossal aesthetic blunder and a monumental confusion of styles" and even considers *Roma, città aperta* (Rome, Open City, Roberto Rossellini, 1945) overrated because of its excessively publicized production history: Ray pronounced the film squarely "within the conventions of melodrama," an aesthetic judgment that is all the more damning given his disdain for the melodramatic productions of the Bombay cinema industry.[20] In fact, Ray uses his glowing review of *Bicycle Thieves* to chide Indian directors: "The simple universality of its theme, the effectiveness of its treatment, and the low cost of its production make [*Bicycle Thieves*] the ideal film for the Indian filmmaker to study. The present blind worship of technique emphasizes the poverty of genuine inspiration among our directors. For a popular medium, the best kind of inspiration should derive from life and have its roots in it. No amount of technical polish can make up for artificiality of theme and dishonesty of treatment. The Indian filmmaker must turn to life, to reality. De Sica, and *not* De Mille, should be his ideal."[21] Here, Ray seems to be in accord with the *Times of India* reviewer of *Awara* but also analyzes the "artifice" criticized in that review in terms of a "worship of technique," which refers to both film style and to technical equipment. Citing De Sica's example of making good films with "faulty indifferent technical equipment," Ray seems to suggest a relation between austerity and creative inspiration.[22] In invoking De Mille's name here, apart from its symmetrical rhetorical flourish, Ray echoes Shantaram's discussion of Hollywood spectacle in opposition to neorealist restraint.

In the continuum between Ray's Bengali films and studio-based films such as *Footpath* and *Awara* that were nonetheless discussed as part of the new realist image that Indian cinema was projecting abroad, *Do bigha zamin* may be taken as an intermediary production. Filmed mostly on location in Calcutta and in a nearby rural area, the film used actors from the IPTA circuit rather than well-known film stars. Thus Balraj Sahni, who had performed the main role in *Dharti ke lal*, played a farmer, Shambhu, who comes to Calcutta to earn enough money to pay back his moneylender-landlord, who wants to take away Shambhu's land to build a factory. The first half hour and the final sequence of the film pack in all of its social analysis, while the bulk of the film shows his efforts at saving money as a rickshaw puller in Calcutta while his son earns money as a shoeshine boy. Much more than *Pather panchali*, this film directly evokes *Bicycle Thieves*. Other than narrative similarities such as the devastating theft of Shambhu's money almost as soon as he arrives in the city, there are also several visual echoes, such as in the early morning street scenes when Shambhu first takes out his rickshaw. The street scenes of Calcutta not only transfer the space of the film outside the studio but also perform a deft sound mixing in which dialogue is kept to a minimum except in closer shots, so that the city scenes have nothing other than an urban soundscape of car horns, trams, hawkers shouting, and the roar of trucks and buses. With the postsynchronized dialogue, city sounds recede, and we are back in the reverberating acoustic space of the studio, although the closeness of the shots appears to justify the change in sound signature. The difference between the Calcutta scenes in *Do bigha zamin* and studio-built city streets in other films is not only in their spaciousness, with most of the city scenes taken in extreme long shots, sometimes from a high angle and featuring well-known landmarks, but also in their attempt at reconstituting the urban soundscape.

Do bigha zamin also quotes more directly from *Awara*, as when the shoeshine kids do an impromptu version of the first line of the "Awara" song, and in other references to the film. Here, cinema constitutes a realm of luxury, as one of the boys can afford to go to the movies, proving to Shambhu's son that by polishing shoes, he might earn money to save their land. *Do bigha zamin* also includes a few of its own song sequences. It does not eliminate song sequences, as Ray did and as became the hallmark of the Parallel Cinema of the 1970s and 1980s. Rather, its music director, Salil Choudhury, draws on folk-derived musical forms, as he did in the IPTA plays for which he composed the music. Thus, *Do bigha zamin* brings together two streams of realist impetus, IPTA and Italian neorealism. However, the film's social critique and analysis of rural poverty, which remarkably recognizes the alignment of state, feudal, and economic interests against poor farmers, remain almost forgotten in the bulk of the film as the narrative transforms into an individual struggle to save a specific amount of money, seemingly suggesting that the story would have a happy resolution if only that magical number were reached. As if recognizing this situation, the film enacts a series of accidents and misfortunes that force the family to spend savings on medical expenses rather than on land. Here, "bad luck" rather than the rural cycle of exploitation becomes the narrative explanation for their plight. The final sequence shows first a montage of construction shots as a factory is built on their land and then a final scene in which the family, standing outside the factory fence, is roughly turned away by the guard. As a visual reminder of the cause of their plight, the factory returns the film to the social analysis with which it had begun, taking a startlingly different approach to Nehruvian development economy than Mehboob Khan's *Mother India* (1957), whose opening uses Soviet-style images of dams and factories to celebrate the new model of the nation.[23]

Two specific aspects of realism that the example of Italian films brought to the fore in India were the move to locations outside the studio and the use of nonstars. Although the shots of Calcutta in *Do bigha zamin* were startlingly new in the context of studio-lit street scenes, Balraj Sahni's rickshaw pulling garnered the most critical attention. Even while the narrative of the film exposed the ills of rural exploitation and the solidarity among the urban poor (unlike *Bicycle Thieves*), a secondary class-based narrative emerged in which the Western-educated, middle-class Sahni practiced pulling rickshaws as preparation for the role. As part of this story, of course, there was the important detail that the real *rickshaw wallas* of Calcutta could not tell the difference and took Sahni for one of their own. Such stories recast well-known actors and even stars as ordinary people who were just like the characters they were playing. Thus, the realism of *Do bigha zamin* derived, at least in India, as much from its location shots and its unrelenting look at poverty as from the almost ordinariness of its actors. Sahni's training in rickshaw pulling is incorporated into the film as a narrative detail when his neighbor who is too ill to pull his rickshaw shows Shambhu how to do it. The film includes numerous shots and montage sequences of Sahni pulling his rickshaw while carrying two or three passengers. This almost indexical trace of his physical link to the labor of the role effected for viewers the transformative leap from actor playing a role to real *rickshaw walla* doing his job and bypassed and even reversed the goal of using nonprofessional actors. Where nonprofessional actors might have to learn how to act, in this case, actors had to learn how to pull rickshaws or do other menial labor.

In the context of other films viewed as participating in the new realist aesthetic, acting now included training (usually lasting no more than a day or so) in underclass professions and behavior. Thus, film star Dilip Kumar, in preparation for *Kala admi* (Black Man), a film about miners, went (along with director Ramesh Saigal and some other crew members) to Jharia in the Bihar coal fields to learn about socioeconomic and cultural conditions of mine labor. Mistaken for a government official, Kumar learned "more about their condition than I could have as a film star studying the locale."[24] Similarly, Suraiya visited the Thane Mental Home to research her role as a "stricken girl" in P. L. Santoshi's *Pagal khana* (Insane Asylum);[25] on a later visit to another mental institution, she was confronted by a girl who could sing and dance and who wanted to know why she could not appear in the film since her beauty and talent matched Suraiya's. The girl's mental illness, it was suggested, derived from her thwarted desire to act in films, and Suraiya's director responded with a vague promise to try to find her a role. Even as *Filmfare* reported the incident as a sign of the labor of Suraiya's training and of the filmmaker's decency, it made no comment on the possibly missed opportunity to use a mentally ill person to play a mentally ill film character.[26]

Through news coverage and publicity such as these examples, the new discourse of realism in commercial Bombay films negotiated its alignment with Italian neorealism, with an implicit shift of interest from film directors to film stars. This context sheds light on actor Dev Anand's account of advising De Sica in 1952 simply to have his professional actors study their parts:

> "I have always picked up my players from the streets and feel out of sorts while directing sophisticated and famous stars." I was rather puzzled by De Sica's remark and asked for an explanation.
>
> "Stars seldom lead natural lives," De Sica said. "They live in a world of their own. They cannot portray the characters they never meet in real life." "But why not ask your stars to study their parts before acting them?" I asked.
>
> "I don't know. Perhaps that may improve things." This was the first time De Sica was handling professional actors.[27]

Anand says that he learned from De Sica that "one should study characters from real life before portraying them in films."[28] Cesare Zavattini, whom Anand met "in his tastefully decorated drawing-room," told the actor, "'We can make pictures anywhere we like—even discard the sets. We can pick up our heroes from the streets because they are the real characters.' He emphasized that 'Films must deal with burning problems of the day and should be low-budgeted. Plan them in outdoor settings.'"[29] Here was the formula of Italian neorealism laid out for *Filmfare*'s readers, even as its coverage of realist films such as *Footpath* prepared them for a hybrid form that could not bring itself to "discard the sets" or to "pick up our heroes from the streets." One film that used lesser-known actors, even if it did not pick them up from the streets, was *Boot Polish*, which had one memorable scene in a crowded commuter train, in which Bhola, the beggar child, momentarily forgets his blind act when he notices the star Raj Kapoor dozing in a corner. Even before Bhola recognizes the actor, the film points him out aurally by playing a snatch from the title song of *Awara*. In keeping with the move to infuse stars with the everyday, Bhola's younger sister insists that the man is just a look-alike since "everyone looks like Raj Kapoor these days." For her skepticism to be credible, the sleeper on the train needs to look the part of an ordinary, tired commuter who cannot be the real Raj Kapoor in the diegesis, even though he is Kapoor in nondiegetic terms. The insertion of stardom here works as a reminder that this is a realist film with no major stars.[30]

If *Do bigha zamin* combines IPTA and Italian neorealist aesthetics, Zia Sarhady's *Footpath*, made for Ranjit Movietone Studio, epitomizes the hybrid Bombay neorealist film, remaining resolutely with stars within studio sets and includes all of the heterogeneous attractions of Bombay entertainment, including song and comic sequences. This film, set in an urban slum, shows the transformation of a writer and journalist into a racketeer because his newspaper work brings in no income. More than anything else, the film's publicity gave it a reputation for realism. Starring Dilip Kumar and Meena Kumari, two of the biggest stars of the 1950s, the film nevertheless became associated with the new realist aesthetic primarily through its focus on poverty and its mise-en-scène. *Filmfare* gave a lot of coverage to this film while it was being shot, and Sarhady wrote an essay on realism for the magazine. He defines realism as "the portrayal of a given state of affairs after a comprehensive scientific analysis of the cause and effect. Realism *does not* distort the image that is visible to all. Its essential character is to retain everything offered by life, but, at the same time, it has to interpret this life in terms of past, present, and future."[31] While evoking the precision of science, Sarhady leaves room for the creative negotiations in the practice of filming. He distinguishes realism from what he calls "actualism" and "naturalism"—the former a direct transcription of life to the screen, "without adapting it to suit the film medium," and the latter a mechanical and superficial portrayal of life, "ignoring the deeper impulses and values which inspire the activity, struggle and progress of mankind."[32]

He rejects both, distinguishing his practices from those of other directors, for whom he claims naturalism as the more common style. In making these distinctions, he also leaves much room for what in his practice constitutes the representation of reality. *Footpath* combines the high-contrast shadowed look of film noir with settings reflecting its interest in the urban poor. The publicity about the film's realism rested on shots of staged squalor, such as littered alleys. Two sequences in particular stand out. In one, a conversation between two of the main characters is framed by two men in the background who are bathing under faucets lined up on a wall in the street. The standard studio set of a street corner, with its stairs and streetlamp, is modified to include visual and aural markers of the everyday.[33] On the soundtrack, we hear, in addition to the voices of the speakers, the scrubbing sound of the men soaping themselves, exemplifying the lengths to which the film's creators went to establish the film's realist pedigree.

Filmfare ran a full-page photo spread showing the set-up for a film shoot in which Kumari bathes under a faucet in a slum courtyard, describing her actions as "the uninspiring daily ritual of city dwellers." Moreover, according to the report, "realistic films are not made by characters in torn clothes" but are made by other details in the setting as well, such as the scrubbing sound of men washing themselves.[34] Nothing in this coverage mentions the fact that this is to be a song sequence. Kumari's bathing sequence points to another function of the rhetoric of realism surrounding this film. In several shots that test the 1950s limit for modesty, Kumari is shown bare-shouldered, washing herself as she sings. These shots are intercut not only with close-ups of the gutters and drains through which the dirty water is running but also with shots of sky, trees, and birds, a conventional visual substitute for sex scenes. In a later interview in *Filmfare*, Kumari used the framework of realism to "excuse" her bare appearance in this scene. She would like to play all parts except those "which are unnecessarily sexy and vulgar," because "I refuse to show my bare legs and uncovered shoulders. I consented to appear in a brief one-minute bathing scene in 'Footpath' because Zia Sarhady said that it would lend a 'realistic' touch to the song that I had to sing."[35] This statement points to a possible appeal of the Italian films that remained unspoken at least in India, which is their relaxation of taboos in visual representation. In the United States, for example, the high-art distribution circuit for foreign films brushed against the exploitation cinema circuit, and many of these films played in both. As one account puts it, "In Joe Burstyn's and Arthur Mayer's 1947 pressbook for *Open City* . . . blocks of textual praise for the film were balanced with less lofty sentiments and imagery that built up the sexual angle: hints at lesbianism, 'violence and plain sexiness,' link the marketing of this film in uncanny ways to that of American exploitation films of the same period."[36]

Mayer said that "the only sensational successes" he and Burstyn scored "in the fifteen years in which we were engaged in business were the pictures whose artistic and ideological merits were aided and abetted at the box-office by their frank sex content."[37]

While no such publicity took place for the Italian and other foreign films screened at the international film festival in India, realism functioned as an explanatory framework for stretching the boundaries of what could be shown. In fact, *Do bigha zamin* explicitly references an even more daring scene in *Awara* in which the heroine changes clothes behind a towel after she has been swimming with the hero and he runs off with her clothes. *Do bigha zamin* shows the street urchins commenting on this scene when they see a man wearing a shirt printed with images from that scene. In the discourse of realism, enabled in part by the Italian films shown at the IFFI, we see by the end of the 1950s two strands in the afterlife of Italian neorealism in India, one that enabled it to showcase its films at festivals abroad and another that could experiment with boundaries and conventions at home. In the example from *Footpath*, the limits of screen representation are tested on the body of a woman.

The publicity *Filmfare* devoted to this sequence points to a new celebration of stardom and sexuality made possible by the renegotiated discourse of realism in the early 1950s. In *Awara*, too, the scene of the heroine changing her clothes tested these unspoken limits and became so celebrated that it is even referenced in clothing fashions, as indicated in the *Do bigha zamin* sequence. While Indian cinematic discourse from the 1920s through the mid-1940s remained mired in the reformist language of improving the moral reputation of cinema, thereafter and especially after the first IFFI and India's representation at Cannes, realism provided a new framework of self-critique that replaced morality as a criterion of evaluation. A part of this multidecade self-scrutiny was a seemingly perennial language of crisis that manifested itself in the recurrent discussions of what was wrong with Indian cinema.[38] The "crisis" in Indian cinema in the early 1950s, as Shantaram, Sarhady, and others saw it, was the Indian government's contradictory attitude toward the cinema: hosting international festivals on the one hand and on the other refusing industry status, with all of its tax benefits, to India's film industry.[39] The Italian delegate to the 1952 IFFI, Vinicio Marinucci, spoke of the economic support given by the Italian government to film producers. Turning to the state of Indian cinema, he noted "the strong call for realism" in Indian films that would "assure a wider market for Indian productions. Indian films with a complete Indian background, Indian theme and Indian talent—that was what was required. . . . 'A truly national picture makes an international picture,' he added, and said that Indian films should not be 'American-like.'"[40]

In this statement was a formula by which the Indian government would come to support a new Indian cinema while continuing to tax the commercial cinemas that could not or would not invest in themes and talent "national" enough for international success. At this point, interest in realism became inextricably tied to the expectations of the international cinematic market, which defined cinematic quality in terms of cultural "authenticity," in contrast to the "American-like" hybridity of the Bombay studio film. In this context, Ray's Apu trilogy films came to carry the mantle of the Italian neorealist legacy in India.

Such cinematic hierarchies were also echoed by film practitioners working in Bombay studios. Writing in *Filmfare* in April 1952, Shantaram, for example, noted a "crisis" in Indian cinema that went beyond finances and was tied to film form. This "crisis in values" was expressed in Indian cinema's inability to produce cinematic realism. This failure, he argued, did not result from technological failings, such as the inability to take the camera out of the studio, but rather from failings in stories and themes and the "undue importance given to stars." He concluded, "Our films reflect the lethargy and purposelessness that characterize our country today. Like the masses in our country, the film-makers too are groping in the darkness."[41] The connection between technology and realism, a concern that recurs in the writings of both Shantaram and Ray, among others, brings out some of the contradictions between filmmakers working in the industry and those, like Ray, who were outside it. One of the events at the 1952 IFFI was an exhibit in Bombay and Calcutta of the latest film equipment. Various foreign manufacturers "displayed projectors, tape-recorders, studio lights, transformers, rectifiers, a model of sound stage and the working model of a processing plant."[42] In aspiring to international status, Indian filmmakers and government officials clearly tied technological advancement to cinematic quality. But quality, in turn, was discussed in terms of a restraint in stylistic flourish and the outward show of technique. As in the case of the reconfiguration of film stars to become like ordinary nonactors, technology was reshaped to serve the impression of reality, so that film locations might remain in the controlled space of the studio, as in *Footpath*'s "street" bathing sequences. In its negotiations and compromises in grafting Italian neorealist aesthetics to an Indian studio-based realism, mainstream cinema lost the historical battle of neorealist status to state-supported filmmakers such as Ray. In later accounts of the history of Indian cinema, the influence of neorealism tends to be relegated almost exclusively to the Parallel Cinema, so that neorealism's impact on mainstream filmmakers has become obscured. In fact, the encounter with Italian cinema at the 1952 film festival illuminates the extent to which Bombay cinema's self-image depended on a careful negotiation of the dual but contradictory imperatives of realism and a star- and production-values-based economy.

Notes

1. The film was retitled *Nightmare in Red China* (1955) and reedited to become an anticommunist propaganda film, where the original had represented Dr. Kotnis fighting alongside the communists. For more details, see Neepa Majumdar, "Immortal Story or Nightmare? *Dr. Kotnis* between Art and Exploitation," *South Asian Popular Culture* 6.2 (October 2008): 141–59.

2. See, for example, Sardi, "Indian Films on Foreign Screens," *Bombay Chronicle*, October 12, 1946.

3. *New York Times*, November 16, 1958, March 6, 1959.

4. *Times of India*, January 25, 1952.

5. See Neepa Majumdar, *Wanted, Cultured Ladies Only! Female Stardom and Cinema in India, 1930s–1950s* (Urbana: University of Illinois Press, 2009).

6. Adie, "Life and Letters: Focus on Pictures," *Times of India*, January 25, 1952.

7. *Filmfare* 1.4 (April 18, 1952): 19.

8. V. Shantaram, "The Real Film Crisis," *Filmfare* 1.4 (April 18, 1952): 32–33.

9. *Times of India*, January 5, 1952.

10. Ibid.

11. Khwaja Ahmad Abbas, "Indian Films in 'Fifty-one,'" *Filmfare* 1.1 (March 7, 1952): 21–23.

12. Other winners at Cannes included Prakash Arora, the director of *Boot Polish* (1954), which got a special mention for the acting of Baby Naaz in 1955 (and was released in New York in 1958, to very positive reviews), and a special mention for *Gotama the Buddha*, a documentary by Rajbans Khanna, in 1957. *Neecha nagar* beat them all to it in 1946 (the same year as *Rome, Open City*), when it became the first Indian film to win a prize at Cannes.

13. *Filmfare* 1.7 (May 30, 1952).

14. Satyajit Ray, *Our Films, Their Films* (Calcutta: Orient Longman, 1976), 85.

15. Ibid,.

16. Ibid., 86.

17. Ibid., 9.

18. Ray saw *Pather panchali*'s connection to Italian neorealism mainly in terms of its film style, which he polemically contrasted with the melodramatic style of commercial Indian

cinema. But his narrative form and cinematic style are equally indebted to the visually emphatic style of Bombay films, favoring visual images over spoken words and transferring emotion to external objects and locations. See Neepa Majumdar, "*Pather Panchali*: From Neo-Realism to Melodrama," in *Film Analysis: A Norton Reader*, ed. R. L. Rutsky and Jeffrey Gieger (New York: Norton, 2005), 510–27.

19. Ray, *Our Films*, 121.

20. Ibid., 122–24.

21. Ibid., 127.

22. Ibid., 68.

23. Although *Mother India* does appear to celebrate dams and factories as economic progress, its occasional close-ups on the muddied red river, very deliberately analogous to the blood of the poor, arguably enact a visual critique of development. *Mother India*, an epic-scale melodrama with a staggering and enduring box-office record, points to the importance of film style in Indian readings of neorealism's influence, since its focus on rural exploitation, though widely appreciated, did not qualify it for discussion in terms of realism except in the case of the performance of its star, Nargis, who, at the peak of her career, played an old village woman. This focus on the role's potential risk to her career is also another example of the realignment of stars in the production of a discourse of realism. Despite the closer cinematic ties to the Soviet Union following Nehru's visit in 1955 and *Mother India*'s Soviet-style iconography, socialist realism seems to have had little discursive impact in India at this time.

24. "The Fortnight in Films," *Filmfare* 1.18 (October 31, 1952): 6.

25. "The Fortnight in Films," *Filmfare* 1.15 (September 19, 1952): 6.

26. "The Fortnight in Films," *Filmfare* 1.17 (October 17, 1952): 6.

27. Dev Anand, "Realism and Low Budgets Keynote Film Making in Italy Today," *Filmfare*, 1.21 (December 12, 1952): 16. This account suggests even more strongly how much the reception of Italian films in India was tied to its neorealist image, since Anand seems clearly to have been unaware of De Sica's decades-long experience with professional acting and actors.

28. Ibid., 17.

29. Ibid.

30. The *New York Times*'s fairly positive review of *Boot Polish* is partially based on the idea that Kapoor plays the main adult role in it and that he wrote the script, neither of which is true (*New York Times*, August 18, 1958).

31. Zia Sarhady, "True Realism in Our Films," *Filmfare* 1.5 (May 2, 1952): 32.

32. Ibid., 32–33. It is possible that he may have derived the term *actualism* from its associations with fascist ideology in Giovanni Gentile's philosophical system of *attualismo*. See, for example, Claudio Fogu, "Actualism and the Fascist Historic Imaginary," *History and Theory* 42 (May 2003): 196–221.

33. For more on shifts in mise-en-scène with the influence of Italian neorealism, see Moinak Biswas, "In the Mirror of an Alternative Globalism: The Neorealist Encounter in India," in *Italian Neorealism and Global Cinema*, ed. Laura E. Ruberto and Kristi M. Wilson (Detroit: Wayne State University Press, 2007), 72–90.

34. *Filmfare* 1.8 (June 13, 1952): 35.

35. *Filmfare* 1.17 (October 17, 1952).

36. Mark Betz, "Art, Exploitation, Underground," in *Defining Cult Movies: The Cultural Politics of Oppositional Taste*, ed. Mark Jancovich et al. (Manchester: Manchester University Press, 2003), 206.

37. Eric Schaefer, *Bold! Daring! Shocking! True! A History of Exploitation Films, 1919–1959* (Durham, N.C.: Duke University Press, 1999), 336.

38. Even Ray starts *Our Films* with the chapter "What Is Wrong with Indian Films?"

39. For more on the role of the state in shaping a "good" Indian cinema geared toward film festivals and awards, see Sumita Chakravarty, "The Authenticity Debate," in *National Identity in Indian Popular Cinema, 1947–1987* (Austin: University of Texas Press, 1993), 235–68.

40. *Times of India*, January 31, 1952.

41. V. Shantaram, "The Real Film Crisis," *Filmfare* 1.4 (April 18, 1952): 32.

42. L. L. Khandpur, "First International Film Festival of India," in *70 Years of Indian Cinema (1913–1983)*, ed. T. M. Ramachandran (Bombay: Cinema India–International, 1985), 583.

NEOREALISM AND NATIONALIST AFRICAN CINEMA

SADA NIANG

African cinema emerged in the second half of the twentieth century. The first African film, *Mouramani*, a short narrative on a man and his dog by Mamadi Touré, appeared in 1955. It was followed by an explosion of films in the 1960s. All were informed by an aggressive nationalism couched in political imperatives for authenticity. To a large extent, Manichaean stylistics framed the first African images, yet by the circumstances of its emergence, African cinema practice was as much a child of various postwar Euro-American film schools and trends. The narrative of liberation notwithstanding, films made by the first generation of African filmmakers have drawn both from African modes of artistic construction and from the aesthetics of Italian neorealism,[1] the French New Wave,[2] Latin American filmmaking, and genres such as Western,[3] gangster,[4] and crime films.[5] This essay examines the impact of Italian neorealism on the Francophone African cinema of the nationalist period (1960–75). Affinities exist between these practices on three levels: historical, institutional, and aesthetic. In style and content, African cinema has been part of world cinema from the very beginning.

Historical Affinities

Italy and most of its former African colonies partially shared many historical experiences at the end of World War II. The year 1945 had witnessed the end of difficult periods in both places: brutal repression (fascist and colonial); a reinvention of local indigenous histories by political systems eager to find legitimacy in a discourse of omissions and half-truths; and finally a general impoverishment of populations grappling with unemployment and the consequences of long years of monoculture, respectively. In Africa, most territories had been under colonial domination for the better part of the twentieth century. Their history had been retold in terms that were disparaging

to African peoples, their civilizations denied and their populations declared
less than human. Starting in 1854, a system of forced labor, derived from the
practice of Atlantic slavery, had been instituted throughout the African continent.[6] Literary figures and filmmakers have delved into this experience. In the
latter half of the twentieth century, women writers such as Malika Mokeddem
and Assia Djebar dramatized the brutality of the conquest and the experience
of displacement caused by outright confiscation of ancestral lands fertile in
crops of citrus fruits, vegetables, and other products prized in France yet not
suitable for French soil.[7] The cloak of violence that veils Mohamed Lakhdar's
Chronique des années de braise (Chronicle of the Years of Fire, 1975) finds its
roots in such widespread usurpation and processes of marginalization.

Such acts in West and North Africa rested on a discourse of denial and self-
aggrandization. Such discourses purported locals to be much less industrious
than their colonizers, much less inclined to appreciate the value of hard work,
and thus worthy of western "benevolence." The legitimizing discourse also
cast doubt on their intellectual abilities. In short, most African populations
experienced the years prior to the end of World War II as a time of negative
mystification, usurpation, and marginalization through racial discrimination
and arrogance. These, as Aimé Césaire noted in *Discours sur le colonialisme*,
could hardly be construed as legitimate signs of the West's supposed humanist
zeal.[8]

The colonial cinema that developed out of this situation was a paternalistic
propaganda tool that used "figures of . . . ridicule" to mime films made in
Europe.[9] These mimeses were deliberate and incomplete, made to reflect the
purported intellectual inferiority of colonized Africans. These films' narratives,
mostly articulated by metropolitan voice-overs, posited an ignorant, unedu-
cated audience unable to distinguish between real and imagined experience.
Citing the Laval Decree of 1934 and using censorship of Paulin Soumanou
Vieyra's *Afrique sur Seine* (Africa on the Seine, 1958) as proof, Melissa Thackway
argues that "colonial authorities actively sought to discourage the development of any African filmmaking activity, thus implicitly acknowledging the
potentially subversive nature of film."[10]

The chronology of the fascist Mussolini regime (1922–43 and, as the
Republic of Salò in Northern Italy, 1943–45) was much less extensive, but
its effects on the locals through repressive legal and discursive practices
proved just as traumatic. As in the African context, historical revisionism figures prominently in the fascist experience of remodeling Italian society. The
African wars attracted several important profascist directors: Augusto Genina's
Lo squadrone bianco (The White Squadron, 1936), filmed on location in Libya,
contains beautiful sequences underlining the vastness and solemnity of the

African desert; Goffredo Alessandrini produced a film on the Ethiopian war, *Luciano Serra, pilota* (Luciano Serra, Pilot, 1938), starring Amedeo Nazzari, a popular actor, and with postproduction supervised by Vittorio Mussolini, Il Duce's son.[11]

As described in other essays in this volume, postwar Italy saw the rise of a new kind of cinema, generally associated with the term *neorealism*, that purported to be more in tune with the preoccupations of the common citizen, more reflective of the present challenges faced by urban masses throughout the peninsula, and totally averse to the pompous rhetoric of Italian fascism. Institutional and aesthetic linkages existed between this cinema and the cinema of Francophone Africa in the second half of the twentieth century.

Institutional Linkages

The first identifiable linkages between neorealism and the emerging African cinema of 1960–75 took the form of the transmission of the scholarship of filmmaking. Starting in the early 1960s, several filmmakers, mostly from North Africa, studied at the Centro Sperimentale di Cinematografia,[12] which in time trained neorealist directors from all over the world. Among the most notable from the African continent were Morocco's Ben Barka Souheil; Algeria's Haddad Moussa, who also served as a production assistant to Luchino Visconti; and Senegal's Ababacar Samb Makharam, who later produced *Jom, histoire d'un peuple* (Jom, 1981).[13] In addition, a smaller group of African filmmakers trained at Moscow's Vsesoyuznyi Gosudarstevennyi Institut Kinematografii (All-Union State Cinema Institute), while the majority of African filmmaking graduates attended the Institut des Hautes Études du Cinéma and other French schools of cinema, including the École Supérieure des Études Cinématographiques, the École Louis Lumière, and the Institut National de l'Audiovisuel, all located in Paris.[14] These new graduates, including those trained at the Centro Sperimentale, constituted a critical mass of knowledge, producing films from their own perspective, telling their stories with the tools of realist filmmaking, and more often than not rebutting the colonial master narrative. They frequently collaborated with each other and created an explosion of African films in the nationalist era.

In 1973, African and Latin American filmmakers, along with Jan Lindquist from Sweden and Salvatore Piscicelli from Italy, met in Algiers to draft a set of resolutions to guide the practice of African cinema.[15] The majority of the participants came from Algeria, but filmmakers from other African nations and elsewhere who had trained at the Centro Sperimentale and were familiar with the aesthetics of neorealism also played a major role in crafting a new—albeit ideal—aesthetic charter for the emerging African cinema. Their presence tilted the debates toward a greater social realist approach buttressed by partisan and at times recriminatory politics. The committee that drafted the resolutions was chaired by Algerian Mohamed Lamine Merbah and included filmmakers who remained active into the twenty-first century, such as Guinea's Flora Gomes.[16] Membership was also open to filmmakers from outside the continent. All participants were critical of the Hollywood tradition. Piscicelli provided a direct link to the practices of neorealism. His cinema, exemplified by his working-class drama, *Immacolata e Concetta* (Immacolata and Concetta: The Other Jealousy, 1979), "signaled his affinity with . . . lower-class, southern setting, and simultaneously claimed his place within a tradition of regional cinema." Like the neorealist classics, *Immacolata e Concetta* shunned nostalgia in favor of the hic et nunc (here and now) of 1970s Italy. It deliberately articulated the need for greater authenticity in Italian cinema by featuring a Neapolitan story and "local actors familiar with Neapolitan dialect"; Piscicelli thus aligned himself with Visconti's and De Sica's approaches.[17]

Two of the largest groups on the committee drafting the resolutions came from Latin America and the host country, Algeria. The most prominent member of the Latin American contingent was Fernando Birri.[18] As Mariano Mestman documents in his essay in this volume, Birri had studied at Rome's Centro Sperimentale before returning to his native Argentina in 1956 and directing several films that are widely considered to be in a clear neorealist vein.[19] By 1973, Birri's Bolivian counterpart at Algiers, Humberto Rios, had produced five shorts with a realistic and political flair—*Faeno* (1960), *Pequeno illusion* (Little Illusion, 1961), *Argentina mayo 1969* (Argentina May 1969, 1969), and *Eloy* (1969)—as well as one feature-length film, *Al grito de este pueblo* (To the Cry of These People, 1972). Bolivian cinema was undergoing a complete, albeit controversial, revival under the leadership of Jorge Sanjinés, who had returned from Chile in 1959 and joined with a group of radical filmmakers.

Many of the African filmmakers had been involved in their countries' nationalist struggles. Algerian Mohamed Lakhdar Hamina studied at the Prague film school, FAMU, and worked briefly at the Czech studios before joining the Algerian resistance fighters at the border with Tunisia. After 1962, he became the head of the Office des Actualités Algériennes.[20] Algerian Mohamed Slim Riad was imprisoned in France as a Front de Liberation Nationale supporter,[21] and Moustapha Badie was an autodidact who shot the first feature film (*La nuit a peur du soleil* [The Night Is Afraid of the Sun, 1965]) in independent Algeria.[22] Mustapha Kateb was a professional actor on stage and screen;[23] Tewfik Farès had collaborated on short films and wrote scripts;[24]

Ahmed Rachedi was the first director of the Office National du Commerce et de l'Industrie. He also produced five feature films, among them the celebrated *L'opium et le baton* (Opium and the Stick, 1969).[25]

Aesthetic Affinities

The aesthetic proposals drafted by the committee headed by Merbah and later adopted by the Federation Panafricaine de Cinéastes (Fepaci) match almost point by point the major positions of the Italian neorealists: Film becomes an argument for action on persons, social processes, and social conditions. Film language, narrative, dialogues, music, and costumes are informed by the relevant features of the local context and combine to ground the meaning of—mostly linear—narratives, actions, and character types in reality. The art of filmmaking, no longer lifted from its context of creation, draws inspiration and finality from this very context. It is a means through which the lives of African men and women can be improved if not changed. The resolutions urge African filmmakers to search for "new forms taking into account the means and possibilities of third countries," to foster "films which bring about disalienation and . . . information for the peoples," and creatively to "favor a cinema in the interests of the masses."[26] These precepts conceptually echo Giuseppe De Santis's concern for an authentic use of the landscape, De Sica's insistence on imaging spaces of suffering, humiliation, and survival for poor Italians (for example, the hotels and the hospices in *Umberto D* [1952]) as well as places of leisure for the well-off and the rich (the restaurant scene in *Ladri di biciclette* [Bicycle Thieves, 1948]). These guidelines also echo Lattuada's insistence that film should be didactic. The principles also lay the groundwork for an authentic use of exterior locations, as in a few neorealist films: the park scenes in De Sica's *Umberto D*, the long countryside shots in Luchino Visconti's *Ossessione* (1943), and the street and stadium scenes in De Sica's *Ladri di biciclette*. Italian neorealists, however, enjoyed an infrastructure set up by the now defunct fascist regime; most African filmmakers, in contrast, worked on a shoestring. Nonetheless, the strength of the images in *Ladri di biciclette* and Sembène's *Borom Sarret* (1963) reveals "convergence in necessity,"[27] as concisely articulated by Lattuada: "The desire to shoot everything on location was above all dictated by the desire to express life in its most convincing manner and with the harshness of documentaries."[28] Both groups felt the need to reimage things, people, and places without embellishing or distorting them. Honest self-definition became a governing ethical imperative. For both Italian neorealists and African filmmakers, everyday authentic dialogue supplanted exalted voice-overs. Images spoke to audiences with the starkness of familiarity. The film's explicit or implied discourse exposed real and vital issues facing the locals and the inventive ways various characters attempted "to interpret and transform" those issues.[29] In the films of De Sica, Rossellini, and Zavattini, the devastating effects of World War II, the ensuing partisan struggle, unemployment, and poverty loomed large; among African directors such as Ousmane Sembène, Souleymane Cissè, and Safi Faye, the encroachment of the city on traditional social spaces, the challenge to ancestral values, World War II, the war in Indochina, and the Algerian War of Independence provided much substance for filmmaking.

In the films of the African directors, depictions of the effects of World War II took a particularly acute tone. The imposition of the war effort program was denounced, its victims celebrated. The Senegalese infantryman provided various films with a forerunner type to the character of the student/immigrant returning home from France in films of the 1980s. Mental illness, the traumas of concentration camps, and the horrors of war are starkly depicted in Momar Thiam's *Sarzan* (1963). In Sembène's *Borom Sarret* (1963), Oumarou Ganda's *Cabascado* (1968), and even the more recent Sanou Kollo's *Tasuma* (1997), Senegalese infantrymen bear the painful marks of the relatively short time spent in the French/British army or in German POW camps. All of these men speak a bastardized form of French derided as *français petit nègre*; all display a worldliness limited to bars and seedy red-light districts. Some, like the soldier in *Cabascado*, enjoy a material ease that evaporates quickly at late-night parties. In the end, all return to the land, are unemployed, or suffer from mental illness. With characters in Italian neorealist films, they share an earthiness embodied by their clothes, their gait, their language and mannerisms, their unchanging modest-to-poor condition, and their vulnerability and daily tribulations to avoid hunger, homelessness, and utter despair. Citizenship in their new or renewed societies is riddled with insecurity, anxiety, and fear of the ruthlessness of the powerful. The cinema that builds them into major, typical characters, rests on an uncompromising—albeit Manichaean—discourse that offers no concession to the Other and critiques complacency. Both neorealists and first-generation African filmmakers made "poor but strong cinema, with many things to say in a hurry and in a loud voice, without hypocrisy, in a brief vacation from censorship; and it was unprejudiced cinema, personal and not industrial, a cinema full of the real faith in the language of the film, as a means of education and social progress."[30] The Algiers resolutions echoed Lattuada's ideas by defining the new African cinema as a necessarily didactic and socially engaged practice. Films produced between 1960 and 1975 abide by this recommendation to a large extent. Many not only focused on the heretofore conflicted relationship between African societies and their former colonial dominators but tackled the unease caused by internal conflicts in newly independent countries. Sembène's *La noire de* . . . (Black Girl, 1966) belongs among the former, while his *Borom Sarret*; his masterpiece of nationalist cinema, *Mandabi* (The Money Order, 1968); and his *Emitai* (God of Thunder, 1971) belong to the second category. Two of Souleymane Cissé's films, *Den muso* (The Girl, 1975) and *Baara* (Work, 1979), cast a critical look at internal Malian/African social values and practices. Med Hondo's early works, *Soleil O* (1971) and *Les bicots nègres vos voisins* (Black Wogs Your Neighbors, 1973), center on issues of immigration yet refute any romanticization of the issue. Instead, they confront the experiences of black migrants in monolithically French urban environments. Oumarou Ganda's *Le waazou polygame* (The Polygamist Morale, 1970) plays in tandem with Moustapha Alassane's *Femme, villa, voiture, argent* (Woman, Villa, Car, Money, 1972) to portray and denounce abuse of self and others. Both films seek to educate their audiences about corruption as well as unproductive and self-serving tendencies in the newly independent Niger.

In all these films, the setting is local, and most of the action takes place outdoors. Film studios were (and still are) rare on the African continent; thus, filming on location was not only economically sound but culturally pertinent. The few interior scenes of nationalist African cinema obey the controlling precept of authenticity. For example, the bedroom and nightclub scenes in Vieyra's *Afrique sur Seine* accurately reflect the usual places patronized by recently arrived African migrants. The camera movement in Sembène's *La noire de* . . . buttresses the progressive objectification of the maid by focusing on her nervous pacing inside the apartment. An overwhelming majority of African films of the nationalist era selected locations in villages, small concessions, city streets, cemeteries, and markets. Both Ababacar Samb Makharam's *Et la neige n'était plus* (And Snow Was Not Anymore, 1965) and *Jom*, as well as Sembène's *Mandabi*, *Emitai*, and *Ceddo* (Outsiders, 1977), take place mostly outside. Djibril Diop Mambéty's *Contras City* (1969) features no interior scenes. His *Touki bouki* (Journey of the Hyena, 1973) is shot almost entirely on location save for the slaughterhouse scene at the beginning and the robbery scene inside Charlie's apartment. In *Touki bouki*, even the scenes of intimacy between Mory and Anta take place outside, on a cliff or by the seaside. Moustapha Alassane's *La bague du roi Koda* (King Koda's Ring, 1962) explores the open spaces of the village. Souleymane Cissé's *Baara* moves among various apartments, a factory, and the streets of Bamako, with the most intense moments of the film (the women's march) located in the latter spaces. Med Hondo's *Soleil O* is a reenactment of major defining moments of Africa's encounter with the

West. Its interior church, interviews, and hotel scenes are carefully matched by location scenes depicting war experiences of Africans, public transport stations, and busy Paris streets. Interior settings, the film seems to suggest, deal violence to the African immigrant, unlike open public spaces, where a general indifference of the local French population offers the newly arrived a semblance of tolerance. In this and other respects, *Soleil O* (1971) stands very much as a forerunner to Sembène's *Emitai*, *Ceddo*, and even *Camp de Thiaroye* (The Camp at Thiaroye, 1988). Ababacar Samb Makharam's *Kodou* (1971), produced by the only Senegalese film director trained at the Centro Sperimentale di Cinematografia, includes wide shots of urban and rural spaces as the camera follows a young woman. Momar Thiam's *Baks* (Cannabis, 1974) includes a few interior bar and bedroom scenes but is mostly shot along the rocky cliffs of the Dakar coast and in the green fields of cannabis on the outskirts of the city. Finally, Safi Faye's *Kaddu beykat* (Letter from My Village, 1975) is shot entirely under a baobab tree used as meeting point by village elders.

Interior scenes in nationalist films were generally designed as dramatic moments. Sembène's *Mandabi*, for example, features a bedroom, Dieng's, with all the amenities of this intimate space in areas such as the Medina, Colobane, Rebeuss, or Pikine of the 1960s. The furniture comprises a bed, an earth pot for water, a metallic bed frame, a grass-stuffed mattress, and posters glued on the flammable wooden wall panels: Dieng, this setting indicates, is a man living on the verge of poverty, spending the better part of the day outside hustling to feed his family. Mbraka's store is a central point in the film. It sits in an open space surrounded by several concessions. Its dark interior is a torture chamber in waiting. Here Dieng is slowly robbed of his newfound freedom, further impoverished, and threatened with physical violence. Later in the film, Dieng is defrauded and beaten in a photographer's studio.

Most actors in nationalist African films are nonprofessionals selected for their ability to exude authenticity without artifice, naturally to personify reality and to suggest "all that there is within a man,"[31] and trained on the spot. Their costumes are those of the man on the street, their language and diction, however imperfect, reproduce everyday generational, regional, semantic, and prosodic features. De Sica's statement on this improvised mode of direction fits perfectly the practice of Sembène, Cissé, Alassane, and Ganda:

It is not the actor who lends the character a face which, however, versatile he may be, is necessarily his own, but the character who reveals himself sooner or later, in "that" particular face and in no other. . . . [T]heir ignorance is an advantage, not a handicap. The man in the street, particularly if he is directed by someone who is himself an actor, is raw material that can be modeled at will. It is sufficient to explain to him those few tricks of the trade which may be useful to him from time to time; to show him the technical and, in the best sense of the term, of course, the histrionic means of expression at his disposal. It is difficult—perhaps impossible—for a fully trained actor to forget his profession. It is far easier to teach it, to hand on just the little that is needed, just what will suffice for the purpose at hand.[32]

Character development and creating a "specific" language to help define African identities became two of the major goals of the first generation of African films.[33] In *Borom Sarret*, Sembène diligently fashions a costume for Modou that is congruent with the dress code of his profession and social condition. He is likely a newcomer to the city, with an aura of strangeness hanging over him. Modou lives off the crumbs of institutions hidden from the images of the film and wears clothes discarded by members of these institutions to partially shield his body from the sun, the rain, and the ambient heat. His khaki shirt is a staple of used clothes markets; its flapping shoulder straps suggest a (surplus) military uniform, possibly his own, since he is a retired serviceman. Time and frequent use have turned it into a tattered piece of cloth with tears showing as he bends over during his early morning prayer. His hat suggests the elegance of urban dandies of the time but is too small and too faded adequately to protect him from the sun. His pants partially cover his legs, suggesting a Moorish influence, with their long leather strings as a belt. They leave his legs vulnerable to objects that fall from his cart. Finally, his shoes leave the better part of his feet bare and exposed to falling bricks and sand and the feet of passengers on his cart.

Such carts are sold at bargain-basement prices in the slums and popular markets of Dakar. The cart, still a staple of transportation in villages and some cities, is made of a discarded truck axle (with wheels attached) topped by a wooden base and with sides joined by a single two-by-eight-foot piece of wood. Modou's identity, just like his clothing, is a composite. It draws from traditional, Western, and Asian influences without fully espousing any of them. Neither nationalist exalted discourses nor past ontological reductions have a hold on him. Instead, his tribulations and the pain and short-lived contentment they bring reflect a life where past and present are at odds, the future fearful. Like most of Sembène's major characters, Modou is a type: A peasant at heart, he has been dragged into modernity through wars, conflicts, and colonial domination before morphing at the edge of a postcolonial city divided by power, culture, and race. A citizen of the new nation, he knows little about the rights and obligations of his new status. Fear of hunger, humiliation, and the powerful govern his present life. His daily ordeals to eke out a livelihood mirror the dilemmas of many of his passengers and neighbors. His experiences also provide a measure of the challenges facing a country required to integrate various external political, cultural, and economic structures yet subjected to historical divisions of space, language and power, widespread poverty and corruption. Indeed, *Borom Sarret* could very well have been titled *Borom dekk* (the owner of a country, the native). By featuring a character who sets out to conquer his daily fears of hunger and humiliation but fails, Sembène invites all who appear in the film and those hidden behind the glass windows of high-rises to confront the ills facing the new country: poverty, superstition, vanity, and lack of political courage.

In 1963, Modou was hailed as the first black African character who occupied center stage in a feature film, yet the actor playing the role never again appeared in one of Sembène's films. Most likely, the actor had been recruited and trained on the spot. In fact, professional actors were rare in Africa in the 1960s. Many, including Mambéty, Mansour Diouf, Langouste, Makhoureydia Gueye, Douta Seck, and James Campbell, had some training in dramatic arts. The dearth of cinema infrastructure meant that few if any Africans were trained as film actors. In the case of Sembène, evidence indicates that professionalism was not a criterion in the casting of roles. In *Borom Sarret*, none of the actors, Sembène included, is a professional. In *La noire de . . .*, numerous onlookers crowd the scenes shot in Colobane, a popular district of Dakar. The shop from which Diouana's brother walks out at the end of the film is filled with young unemployed men. In *Mandabi*, Sembène stated that the actors "weren't professionals. The old man who plays the main role, we found working near the airport. He had never acted before. I had a team of colleagues and together we looked around the city and country. . . . [W]e rehearsed for a month in a room very much like this lecture hall. *Mandabi* was the first film completely in the Senegalese language and I wanted the actors to speak the language accurately. There was no text, so the actors had to know what they were going to say, and say it at the right moment."[34] Filming on a shoestring also meant more forceful direction for would-be actors as far as costume, diction, and space management were concerned. Here, knowledge of the craft of acting, as suggested by De Sica, was key. Sembène might have had an edge in this area, as he performed several roles in his films. Working with nonprofessionals also requires a familiarity with the language and culture of the actors. *Emitai*'s characters speak the Jola language, an idiom in which Sembène was not fully competent, a situation that raised a few challenges: "I had to fight against a particular disbelief in the beginning. The people feared not being paid according to the agreements. But little by little the cooperation was turning out to be good, mainly with the women who were much more obedient than the men. They were trained by Thérèse Mbissine Diop [the lead actor of *La noire de . . .*]. I only had to give explanations when needed depending on the situation. I felt a bit uncomfortable about the language because while I speak Wolof, Mandingue and Bambara, I only understand a bit of Diola."[35]

As has often occurred in the history of art, Italian filmmakers intended the break from the recent past to be total, perhaps because of an aversion to Mussolini's regime. The neorealist filmmakers advocated—but, contrary to the Fepaci group, did not impose—respect for an "ontological wholeness of reality," whatever that reality might be.[36] This covenant bestowed on films such as the three discussed here as well as De Robertis's *Uomini sul fondo* (SOS Submarine, 1941) a documentary quality later adopted both by African and Latin American filmmakers. The combination of this ontological factor with simplicity in the narrative, coupled with everyday themes and the typology of actors as epitomized by *Borom Sarret*'s Modou, suffused these films with an immediacy that has become one of the hallmarks of African filmmaking. In fact, fiction and documentary filmmaking were joined at the hip from the beginning. Documentary filmmaking indeed preceded fiction on the continent, with the former serving as a launching pad for the latter. France, through its ministry of cooperation, signed contracts with African agencies to produce monthly and later weekly newsreel films on local political and cultural events in the new republics. Diawara reports that "Senegal was the first Francophone country to sign a newsreel program," followed soon thereafter by Ivory Coast, Cameroon, Dahomey, Togo, Madagascar, and Upper Volta.[37] These films of varying lengths were shown at local theaters before or between feature films—usually American, French, or Italian B movies. But these newsreels were important in that they provided cash-strapped budding African filmmakers with an opportunity to practice their craft before embarking on their own projects. At times, work on the newsreels was the only training a filmmaker received before initiating a big project. In Senegal, the agency responsible for these documentaries was led by Paulin Vieyra, who directed *Afrique sur Seine*.

Out of these experiences grew a desire for more autonomy in creation. Fiction films were planned under Vieyra, and a few shorts were produced.[38] Whereas, as Diawara notes, "the emergence of Senegalese cinema in the late sixties with Sembène and Mahama Traoré was due less to the availability of a structure provided by the Service du Cinéma and more to France's willingness to produce African films,"[39] the widespread local diffusion of the African newsreels created a stock of skills and experience that would permeate fictional films produced from 1960 to 1975. For example, the newsreels enabled urban

African audiences to experience for the first time the image of themselves and people they knew in positions of power.

As a result, very few first-generation films have narrative and stylistic configurations that do not include a documentary aspect. Sembène's *La noire de . . .* is drawn from a real event reported in a French newspaper. He later learned that the story of *Mandabi* had happened to a Cameroonian police officer.[40] *Emitai* recounts events and conditions experienced by villagers, their families, their enlisted sons, and the French colonial officers during World War II in Casamance. In fact, almost all of Sembène's first-generation films include scenes that could have been drawn straight out of the current events sections of daily newspapers. In *Borom Sarret*, the scene in which the corrupt police officer steals Modou's medals would qualify. The maids' labor market in *La noire de . . .* reproduces a real place, a street corner and recognizable power relations between female black job seekers and their potential white upper-class employers. The first shot in *Mandabi* features a Hausa-looking hair cutter shaving Dieng's nostril hair with great dexterity, a scene that can be witnessed in the vicinity of any market in any Senegalese city. Finally, *Mandabi*'s wedding scene, party scene, and even the drama surrounding the first nuptial night represent common occurrences. Oumarou Ganda's *Cabascado* is located in a village with stretches of concessions backed by wide expanses of cultivated lands; even Moustapha Alassane's parodic and somewhat fantastic *Le retour d'un aventurier* (Return of an Adventurer, 1968) features shepherds leading their herds to the grazing lands, village elders meeting to discuss daily events, and messengers on horseback. Likewise, ritual scenes abound in the first-generation films. The rituals distinguish between male and female modes of resistance in *Emitai* and structure the drama of Jean Pierre Dikongué Pipa's *Muna moto* (Somebody Else's Child, 1975), Sembène's *Xala* (The Curse, 1973), and Tidiane Aw's *Pour ceux qui savent* (For Those Who Know, 1971). Documentary aspects are so widespread in these fictional films that as far as African cinema is concerned, genre boundaries are at most tenuous. These fictional films ground themselves in the immediacy of place, current events, and issues pertinent to spectators.[41]

These affinities between two cinemas separated by such geographical distances point to similar conditions, comparable histories, and a "convergence in necessity."[42] They show that African cinema did not become global in one fell swoop. Its globality was present from the beginning, nurtured by scholarship, aesthetic choices, and the cinema culture of the filmmakers. These influences proved unshakable in spite of vigorous nationalist discourses and images in the 1960s. African films, much like African music and costume styles, have seen their fair share of *métissage* through contact with the West as well as the East. The forms that have ensued have helped dramatize the continent's particular political and cultural situation while remaining hybridized and open to the world.

Notes

1. Sada Niang, "Du neorealisme en Afrique: Une relecture de *Borom Sarret*," *Presence Francophone* 71 (2008): 76–90.

2. Anny Wynchank, "Djibril Diop Mambéty fondateur d'un cinéma nouveau," *Cinémaction* 6 (2003): 93–98.

3. Niang, "Neorealisme en Afrique"; Dyana Oscherwitz, "Of Cowboys and Elephants: Africa and the Nouveau Western in Djibril Diop Mambéty's *Yenas*," *Research in African Literatures* 39.1 (Spring 2008): 224–38.

4. Niang, "Neorealisme."

5. Alexie Tcheuyap, "De la fiction criminelle en Afrique: Relecture des films d'Ousmane Sembène," *Présence Francophone* 71 (2008): 56–75.

6. Myron Echenberg, *Colonial Conscripts: The Tirailleurs Sénégalais in French West Africa, 1857–1960* (London: Heinemann, 1991); Alice Conklin, *A Mission to Civilize: The Republican Idea of Empire in France and West Africa, 1895–1930* (Stanford: Stanford University Press, 1997); Adam Hochschild, *King Leopold's Ghosts* (New York: Macmillan, 1998); Elikia Mbokolo, *L'Afrique au XXe siècle: Le continent convoité* (Paris: Seuil, 1985); Ferdinand Oyono, *Une vie de boy* (1956; Paris: Pocket, 1970); Ousmane Sembène, *Les bouts de bois de dieu* (Paris: Pocket, 1960).

7. Assia Djebar, *L'amour, la fantasia* (Paris: Lattès, 1985); Malika Mokeddem, *Le siècle des sauterelles* (Paris: Ramsay, 1992).

8. Aimé Césaire, *Discours sur le colonialisme* (Paris: Présence Africaine, 1955).

9. Homi K. Bhabha, *The Location of Culture* (London: Routledge, 1994), 85.

10. Melissa Thackway, *Africa Shoots Back: Alternative Perspectives in Sub-Saharan African Film* (Oxford: Currey, 2003), 7.

11. Peter Bondanella, *Italian Cinema from Neorealism to the Present*, 3rd ed. (New York: Continuum, 2001), 19.

12. Ibid. See also Laura E. Ruberto and Kristi M. Wilson, *Italian Neorealism and Global Cinema* (Detroit: Wayne State University Press, 2007).

13. Roy Armes, *Dictionary of African Filmmakers* (Bloomington: Indiana University Press, 2008), 44, 72, 116.

14. Ibid.

15. See Imruh Bakari and Mbye B. Cham, eds., *African Experiences of Cinema* (London: British Film Institute, 1996), 17–24.

16. See Armes, *Dictionary*, 94, 70.

17. See Àine O'Healy, "Violence and the Erotic in Salvatore Piscicelli's *Immacolata e Concetta*," http://tell.fll.purdue.edu/RLA-Archive/1999/Italian/OHEALY.HTM (accessed August 20, 2009).

18. "Fernando Birri, el alquimista poético-político: Por un nuevo cinema latinoamericano, 1956–1991," *Cuadernos hispanoamericanos* 560 (February 1997): 140–41; Julianne Burton, ed., *The Social Documentary in Latin America* (Pittsburgh: University of Pittsburgh Press, 1990); Jose Agustin Mahieu, "Fernando Birri, el profeta," *Cuadernos hispanoamericanos* 561 (March 1997): 115–17; Anton Giulio Mancino, "Birri, Fernando: L'Alatramerica," *Cineforum* 34.11 (November 1994): 93–94; Anna Maria Piccoli, "Fernando Birri: Un viaggiatore nella Roma neorealista," *Veltro: Rivista della civiltà italiana* 38.5–6 (September–December 1994): 417–21; Michael T. Martin, *The New Latin American Cinema* (Detroit: Wayne State University Press, 1997).

19. Birri's goal, similar to Piscicelli's, was to portray the drastic living conditions of Argentina's urban and rural poor. Early in his career, he founded the Film Institute of the National University of the Litoral in Argentina, the first film school in Latin America. With his students, he created the first in a long series of influential documentaries, *Tire dié* (Throw Me a Dime, 1960), which showed children in a poor town sprinting along train tracks to beg passengers for money, and a neorealist feature film, *Los innundados* (Flooded Out, 1961).

20. Armes, *Dictionary*, 87.

21. Ibid., 111.

22. Ibid., 37.

23. Ibid., 82.

24. Ibid., 64.

25. Ibid., 107.

26. Bakari and Cham, *African Experiences*, 20, 21.

27. Julianne Burton, ed., *Cinema and Social Change in Latin America: Conversations with Filmmakers* (Austin: University of Texas Press, 1986), 7.

28. Roy Armes, *Patterns of Realism* (South Brunswick: Barnes, 1971), 67.

29. Burton, *Cinema and Social Change*, 11.

30. Armes, *Patterns*, 66–67.

31. Bondanella, *Italian Cinema*, 32.

32. Quoted in ibid., 56.

33. See Josef Gugler, *African Film: Re-Imagining a Continent* (Bloomington: Indiana University Press, 2003); Thackway, *Africa Shoots Back*; Nwachukwu Frank Ukadike, *Black African Cinema* (Berkeley: University of California Press, 1994).

34. Annett Busch and Max Annas, eds., *Ousmane Sembène: Interviews* (Jackson: University Press of Mississippi, 2008), 46.

35. Ibid., 21.

36. Bondanella, *Italian Cinema*, 32.

37. Manthia Diawara, *African Cinema: Politics and Culture* (Bloomington: Indiana University Press, 1992), 58.

38. Ibid., 59.

39. Ibid., 60.

40. See Olivier Barlet, "La leçon de cinéma d'Ousmane Sembène au festival de Cannes 2005," http://www.africultures.com/php/index.php?nav=article&no=3854 (accessed September 25, 2009).

41. Conversely, Jean Marie Téno's *Afrique je te plumerai* (Africa, I Will Pluck You Clean, 1992) starts as a documentary but quickly resorts to fiction to better express "frustration . . . people's disarray" and to attempt to "dismantle a system that locks people into things that they don't want" (Thackway, *Africa Shoots Back*, 206). Téno told Thackway, "When I begin to think about a subject, there are things I can find on the ground and others that don't exist. So I express myself through writing, through fiction, through the desire to tell a story that is really couched in peoples' realities" (206).

42. Burton, *Cinema and Social Change*, 7.

DOCUMENTING THE SOCIAL REALITY OF BRAZIL

Roberto Rossellini, the Paraíban Documentary School, and the Cinema Novistas

SARAH SARZYNSKI

There is only one heroism in the world: to see the world as it is, and to love it.
—ROMAIN ROLLAND, Epigraph in Josué de Castro's *Geografia da fome*

Roberto Rossellini visited Brazil in August 1958 after the Brazilian government invited him to plan a semidocumentary about Northeastern Brazil. Josué de Castro's books on the politics of hunger, specifically *Geografia da fome* (The Geography of Hunger, 1946), piqued Rossellini's interest.[1] According to Rossellini, "The book is extremely easy to translate into a cinematographic image and is also easy to show in the form of a documentary the world's hunger and misery."[2] Although the local Brazilian press highlighted Rossellini's dramatic personal life (which at the time was divided between Ingrid Bergman and Somali Das Gupta), Rossellini focused on his intentions for the film. He told interviewers that his experience of filming in India would "bring a contribution to how the Northeast is seen."[3] He mentioned that a major theme of the film would be the heroism of the Nordestino (person from the Northeast),[4] who was heroic because it took great courage and strength to survive in an underdeveloped area.

Rossellini claimed that his films took no political position. He believed that art must be connected to social problems, and film was a means to "artistically—and scientifically—document" social reality.[5] He explained that neorealism was not an expired cultural movement but was experiencing a "crisis," as were all the world's major film industries in the late 1950s.[6] Rossellini had just returned from India, where he had filmed a television documentary that would be broadcast in 1958 as well as *India matri bhumi* (India Motherland, 1958), productions that combined "documentary and poetry" in short, unrelated segments.[7] For a brief period, Rossellini had departed from Europe and turned to the Third World, inspired by "underdeveloped areas" that were the "countries of realism," where people lived "only in the concrete."[8] Rossellini viewed underdeveloped areas as a "battlefield" where traditional culture clashed with modern technology and science.[9] Whereas many directors might have seen a drastically different battlefield forming in the Third World in 1958, Rossellini's mission was to "show" reality and portray what he considered the "great problems of humanity": hunger, water, energy, and science.[10]

The meeting that took place in August 1958 between the father of neorealism and the eminent Brazilian politician famous for his studies on poverty and hunger is significant in that it symbolizes the idealism of broader political and artistic movements of the late 1950s and early 1960s.[11] During this period, the Third World, its "revolutionary" poverty, and the contradictions of modernity rose to the forefront of international Cold War politics. Neorealism in Italy provided the basic language for filmmakers around the globe to express these social issues in a realistic way, granting them a power of depicting what they claimed and what audiences recognized as the "truth" or "reality" of a compelling social or political issue. As a consequence of increased rural social activism in the impoverished Northeastern region of Brazil and a historical legacy of realist novels and images that portrayed Northeastern Brazil as a nonmodern, feudal, miserably poor region, Brazilian filmmakers interested in depicting the reality of the Third World flocked to that region. In 1963, the newspaper *O norte* claimed that Paraíba had turned into a mecca for filmmaking.[12] This essay connects the transnational language of neorealism with the nascent Northeastern film movement of the Paraíban documentary school and the early radical cultural movement known as the Cinema Novo movement to trace the development of the aesthetics and politics of filming the social reality of the Third World.

Historical Precedents to Linduarte Noronha's *Aruanda* (1960)

One Northeastern documentary in particular, *Aruanda* (1960), caught the attention of well-known Brazilian filmmakers. It is quite possible that at any other historical moment the films of the Paraíban documentary school would have drifted into obscurity—in fact, most of the films have almost disappeared, with the exception of *Aruanda* and *Romeiros da guia* (Pilgrims of Guia, 1962). In this section, I sketch the language and politics of neorealism and outline the historical developments occurring in Northeastern Brazil in the late 1950s and early 1960s. I contextualize the emergence of Cinema Novo within the scholarship on neorealism to suggest why certain debates emerged in Brazil during this time. In other words, what led the Cinema Novistas not only to watch films such as Linduarte Noronha's *Aruanda* but also to use the Paraíban documentaries as an inspiration for the Cinema Novo movement?

According to Alberto Farassino, one of the problems in defining Italian neorealism stemmed from the idea that in the postwar period, "in short, everything Italian is everything neorealist." Thus, it is difficult to define neorealism as a specific film genre or connect it to a specific director.[13] The films often had low budgets and were nonstudio productions, and many focused on political and social themes related to the period of the war or after the war. The "low budget effect" supposedly gave the films a "look of authenticity."[14] Attention to regional accents and to filming on location also produced an effect of reality. Although all of the Italian neorealist films appear "professional" when compared to their Cinema Novo counterparts, similar arguments were used in Brazil to connect the "low budget effect" to authenticity and reality.

Neorealist films were shot throughout Italy in an attempt to create a new sense of Italian identity by incorporating the regional into the national. Rossellini's *Paisà* is the most obvious example, with its map of Italy and stories that illuminate the outline of the Italian nation from the south to the north. Many neorealist films were shot in Naples, Livorno, and Sicily, providing a contrast with the films made during fascism, which focused on Rome. Scholars have argued that this change helped to construct a new sense of national unity and identity: Italy was not just Rome; rather, the other regions lay claim to and had a stake in Italian national identity. Drawing from these ideas about the connection between neorealism and nationalism, Angelo Restivo argues that Italian neorealism was the "most visible" national cinema to question modernization and the uneven development of capitalist societies.[15] Neorealist films from 1959 to 1968 often focused on the contradictions between the modern, industrialized Italian North and the underdeveloped South, depicting the contradictions of modernity within the Italian economic "miracle."

Brazilian cinema explored similar themes in the 1950s and 1960s, using an aesthetic of Third World realism to portray the contradictions of modernity in the Brazilian nation.[16] The Cinema Novo movement shifted to filming the Northeast in the early 1960s; 1950s neorealist films had largely been urban and shot in the South.[17] Not only did the Northeast challenge traditional Brazilian national images,[18] but it also became the quintessential Third World of the Cold War in the era of the Cuban Revolution, with rural social activism, radical cultural movements, U.S. Alliance for Progress projects, and a repressive military coup in 1964.

Linduarte Noronha,
Aruanda (1960).

Northeastern Brazil had long been known as a region of contrasts, and in the 1950s and 1960s, it was often compared to India in terms of misery, traditional culture, and inequalities. A contrast was often drawn between Brazil's modern, urban South—São Paulo and Rio de Janeiro—and the rural, backward Northeast, a distinction commonly referred to in this period as Brazil being "Bel-India" (Belgium/India). By the late 1950s, rural social movements in Northeastern Brazil led by peasant leagues, communist parties, and the Catholic Church had dramatically expanded, demanding revolutionary change and the incorporation of rural workers into the Brazilian nation. Leaders of these social movements claimed that Brazil's revolution would emanate from the Northeast, the true heart of the Brazilian nation, not yet corrupted by the foreign modernity of the urban South. Stereotypes with a historical legacy reappeared in the Brazilian media, portraying Nordestinos as a backward, ignorant, and nonmodern species with a tendency for violence.

In the early 1960s, Northeastern Brazil often took center stage in world news and politics. For example, the largest U.S. Agency for International Development office in the world was located in Recife, the first Alliance for Progress funds were allocated to Northeastern Brazil, and the U.S. consulate in Recife tripled in size in 1961, employing sixteen vice consuls.[19] This focus resulted from an expansion of rural social movements such as the *ligas camponesas* (peasant leagues) and the fear of the spread of communism in Brazil. Cold War politics linked poverty and rural activism to social revolutions such as the Cuban Revolution, and local and international politicians and journalists labeled Northeastern Brazil "the next Cuba." Within this milieu of Othering representations of Nordestinos, rural social activism, and Cold War political struggles, Linduarte Noronha's documentary on a poor community in Northeastern Brazil screened in Rio and São Paulo, provoking filmmakers and critics to debate a new aesthetic for filming the Third World.

Screening *Aruanda*

Promising offspring, rebellious child, fruit of the unheard of union between consciousness and action in the breast of the cinematographic class, this makes the multiple tendencies and passions the blood of its development. It chews that which falls upon its
plate—neorealism, Nouvelle Vague, French political auteur cinema, "Cahiers du Cinéma,"
chanchada, Vera Cruz, Eisenstein. The frail "underdeveloped" cinema swallows the fat and
healthy theories on ordinary dishware with our meager technical resources. Shazam! The
radiographic image of the X-ray reveals the guts of poverty without a solution.
  —MARILIA FRANCO, describing *Aruanda*

From the moment of its release, Noronha's documentary, *Aruanda*, shot off
sparks in the Brazilian cinema world. Filmmakers and cultural critics gathered
to watch the short documentary on a *quilombo-remanescente* (maroon) community in the mountains of Paraíba in Northeastern Brazil. The documentary
starts with a historical reenactment of a slave seizing his liberty by fleeing
to the mountains of Serra Talhada, forming a community of runaways. The
twenty-minute documentary then shifts from the historical dramatization of
a family walking to the hills to a scene of women making clay pots by hand
and firing them in a rustic kiln. Community members then load the pots on
the backs of burros to sell at the weekly market, and the documentary ends
at the close of market day with the community members returning to their
home in the hills.

As film critic Jean-Claude Bernardet wrote, the film "provoked violent debates" when it was shown at the first Convenção da Crítica Cinematográfica
in São Paulo in 1960 and at the São Paulo Bienal of 1961.[20] *Aruanda* raised
questions such as, "What should Brazilian cinema say? How do we make films
without equipment, without money, and without a popular exhibition circuit?"[21] Many critics and filmmakers classified *Aruanda* as "primitive" cinema
or as a "savage" cinema of the Third World. The poor quality of the film
and the filming technique, such as drastic lighting contrasts, editing, sound
quality, and filmography, were not necessarily seen as defects. Instead, these
problems were classified as "a reality of underdevelopment filmed in a underdeveloped way."[22] *Aruanda*, with all its technical defects, became the symbol
of Third World or underdeveloped filmmaking, sharply contrasting with the
European and U.S. film industries.

Cinema Novo director Glauber Rocha was particularly inspired by
Aruanda, supposedly because it reflected the language of a Third World cinema for which he had been striving. Rocha repeatedly referred to the filmmakers as primitive, as making savage cinema, unskilled and emblematic of

the underdevelopment of the Third World. For Rocha, *Aruanda* was "a creation of hunger and blood" that marked a new line of cinema, much like Jean Vigo's *L'Atalante* (1934) or Rossellini's *Roma, città aperta* (Rome, Open City, 1945).[23] As Rocha wrote in 1963, "Noronha and Vieira are close to that fantastic Rossellini; realism from the material of misery itself, in its polluted character of the superficies of the earth and in the famished faces of men. We are sure that *Aruanda* wants to be the truth before it is a narrative; a language that is a language of the real is the real."[24] Rocha emphasized what he called the real, the truth, a realism derived from misery and hunger, and a language of the Third World.

Other critics argued that *Aruanda* was primitive because of the underdeveloped training and skills of the provincial filmmakers. Critic David Neves focused on how the film "reflected the primitivism of the means and cinematographic conceptions born in the Ciclo Paraíbano." According to Neves, the Nordestino filmmakers grew up in an antimodern, conservative society that feared and prohibited modern cinema technology.[25] Film assistant João Ramiro Mello supposedly had not seen his first film until he was fifteen years old because his family thought that cinema was immoral. According to Neves, Noronha was overwhelmed by the debates that his film provoked in São Paulo, unaware that *Aruanda* could be seen as a new type of narrative and technique introduced by Third World. In other words, Neves saw *Aruanda*'s reception in São Paulo as unintended and unexpected by the Paraíban filmmakers.

The perception of Northeastern Brazil and Nordestinos in the South in the late 1950s and early 1960s influenced *Aruanda*'s reception. The region and its people were seen as revolutionary in their poverty but also as inherently backward and nonmodern. Furthermore, even though the published commentary about *Aruanda* in São Paulo and Rio emphasized the technical merits of the film and the filmmakers, the film's theme and images explain the reaction it engendered. In other words, this film became an emblem of Third Cinema not only because of its aesthetics but also because of its images, story, and music, which, alongside the technical defects, represented the Third World.

The Cinema Novo directors and film critics had seen Italian neorealist films, and by the late 1950s a number of films with an urban setting had been produced in Brazil in line with the aesthetic and social themes of neorealism. But, in *Aruanda*, the Cinema Novo directors and film critics saw what was not in the European films or the Brazilian films of the 1950s: the Other. *Aruanda* depicted the black, the savage, the primitive. The film showed a desertlike area, seemingly isolated, with naked and barefoot black children running and hiding in trees. It showed women hand-building clay pots and then firing them in traditional kilns. Families ate bowls of the sandlike *farofa* with their hands, and burros carried the pots to the local market, where pythons of tobacco were bartered as an old man played a wooden flute. These images and sounds belonged to the imagined Third World: India, Africa, and Northeastern Brazil. For the Cinema Novistas and film critics, the interior region of Northeastern Brazil was as far removed from Rio de Janeiro and São Paulo as Africa or India. The people and places in *Aruanda* were the Other, the nonmodern, illustrating a reality about which the Cinema Novistas knew little—perhaps only what they had read in novels about Northeastern Brazil.[26]

Yet the Cinema Novo directors and film critics saw in *Aruanda* what they wanted to see because it illustrated their version of the "real" Third World and the possibilities for non-Hollywood/European cinema. Claims of authenticity were premised on the idea that the Nordestino filmmakers were primitive and thus connected to their savage subjects. Although the filmmakers were from the Northeast, they were not as untrained or savage as portrayed by the Cinema Novistas and critics in the South. While the power attributed to portraying the "reality" and authenticity of Third World poverty in Brazilian cinema opened doors for certain films and filmmakers, it was not an actual movement toward new types of alternative regional film movements. The fact that the documentaries and the school faded into obscurity must be read as a story of nationalism versus regionalism and Cold War politics.

The Northeast as a Filmmakers' Mecca

The debates about *Aruanda* allude to the broader questions being raised about the development and direction of the Brazilian national film industry. In the mid-1950s, the studio systems that had previously held so much influence (Atlântida, Vera Cruz) had ceased to exist, replaced by state-run agencies and institutes.[27] Filmmakers and critics were aware of Italian neorealists' domestic and international successes in creating a national film industry outside of the studio system. And, as Stephanie Dennison and Lisa Shaw argue, one of the main successes of Cinema Novo was its ability "to put Brazilian cinema on the world cinematic map . . . increasing its international dissemination and popularity ever since."[28] Célia Aparecida Ferreira Tolentino claims in her book on the rural in Brazilian cinema that one of the greatest accomplishments of the revolutionary era was the production of great cinema.[29] Two film movements developed after *Aruanda*'s screening in 1960: the well-known Cinema Novo movement, and the more obscure Paraíban documentary school.[30] The trajectory of the two movements sheds light on cultural politics in Brazil during the Cold War and raises questions about the aesthetic of Third World realism.

The Cinema Novo aesthetic of hunger became masterful cinema, whereas the Paraíban documentaries exemplified underdevelopment.

The first-wave Cinema Novistas strove to provide a realistic image of the misery and poverty of the Third World in contrast to exoticized or romantic versions of the Third World. The fundamental trilogy of the radical cultural movement known as Cinema Novo—Nelson Pereira dos Santos's *Vidas secas* (Barren Lives, 1963); Ruy Guerra's *Os fuzís* (The Guns, 1963); and Glauber Rocha's *Deus e o diabo na terra do sol* (Black God, White Devil, 1964)—were shot with the aesthetic of hunger in mind. In theory, therefore, filmmakers employed handheld camera shots as a style and used direct sound and non-professional actors. The films were supposed to make the viewer feel uncomfortable by depicting the misery and hunger of the Third World with static shots held for too long, with confusing plots and narratives that were not structured in a linear fashion, and with Nordestinos portrayed as miserable victims who lacked all power, even the power to speak. From the directors' perspective, the Nordestino was a victimized Other. For the most part, these films used well-known themes associated with Northeastern Brazil, such as epic stories of maroon communities such as Canudos and Palmares, religious fanaticism, drought, misery and poverty, and exploitation of rural workers by the landed elite.

Vidas secas drew from Graciliano Ramos's 1927 novel, which is often compared to John Steinbeck's *The Grapes of Wrath*. The film takes place in 1940 and starts with the declaration that "more than anything, [this film] is a testament to the dramatic social reality of these times and of the extreme misery that has enslaved twenty-seven million Nordestinos." The films tells the story of the members of a Nordestino family who struggle to survive in spite of drought, exploitation by large landowners and government officials, and hunger and ignorance. The story unfolds in the rural *sertão*, a desertlike area with thick, prickly bushes, and a few scenes take place in a small town supposedly typical of the Northeast. The characters lack the ability to communicate, both with each other and with authorities, and they often talk without communicating. The family's dog, Baleia, is portrayed as more human than any of the family members, relating the common perception of Nordestinos as animal-like. Pereira dos Santos shot in black and white, often using handheld shots and direct sound. The lighting is the light of the *sertão*, with great contrasts and a blinding sun. Pereira dos Santos frequently held shots for extended lengths without any action or movement in the scene, accentuating the idea that life is static and unchanging in Northeastern Brazil.

Os fuzís is set in a small town in the *sertão*. It has been described as being shot in a documentary style, and Guerra used similar techniques to those

Pereira dos Santos employed in *Vidas secas*. Guerra tied together a story of a pilgrimage of messianic Nordestinos with a story about the Brazilian military taking control of a town to protect the local store and guard the food from the members of the local population, who were sacking the establishment. The soldiers do nothing but exploit the population and commit acts of violence. The film's contrast between the images of the townspeople and the messianic pilgrims and the truck driver and the soldiers leaves a strong impression. The Nordestinos do not talk. They are portrayed as famished and ignorant, turning to religion as a way to hope for survival. The only characters with agency are Gaucho, the truck driver, and the soldiers. For example, in one of the final scenes, a man carries his dead baby with an entirely passive attitude; Gaucho then revolts, getting angry and turning to violence out of frustration with the situation.

The themes of violence, misery, messianism, and backwardness also mark *Deus e o diabo na terra do sol*. Unlike Guerra and Pereira dos Santos, Rocha used a music track, varying between classical music by Brazilian composer Heitor Villa-Lobos and the song of a *cordelista*, the popular pamphlet poetry commonly associated with Northeastern Brazil, which is used as a narrative tool. Rocha uses handheld shots and sharp editing cuts that at times create a dizzying effect, commenting on the circular history of the Northeast and the trapped feeling of Nordestinos. The film starts in the late 1930s in the *sertão* with a cowhand killing his boss in reaction to being exploited. The cowhand and his wife then become a part of a messianic cult. But, as Rocha suggests, this course does not provide an answer for Nordestinos, only a continuation of the violence and ignorance typical of the Northeast. The couple flee the messianic community and join a band of *cangaceiros* (backlands bandits). The bandits violently attack the estate of a large landowner, torturing and murdering him and his family. But such actions also are not the answer for Nordestinos. As the *cangaceiros* are stalked and eventually shot and killed, the cowhand and his wife run toward the sea, where they will find liberation. The combination of the location, the historical situations and figures (*cangaceiros* and messianic cults), the violence, and the music of the *literatura de cordel* emphasized the most common symbols associated with Northeastern Brazil, consolidating a visual image of this region, its people, and its problems.

Through an aesthetic of hunger and violence, Cinema Novo directors strove to portray the authentic, nonexotic—or miserable and poor—Third World with the goal of provoking revolution through art. The foundational films of Cinema Novo have had a enduring influence on cinematic representations of Northeastern Brazil. As Walter Salles Jr., director of *Central do Brasil* (Central Station, 1998), has claimed, the films of the early 1960s created a visual memory of Northeastern Brazil that continues to influence representations of the region in film today. The Cinema Novo directors coded Northeastern Brazil as *O Nordeste*, or the traditional, backward Other. It is the dry *sertão*, a land of impoverished, oppressed people who can barely communicate and who suffer as perpetual victims of the wrath of large landowners, soldiers, politicians, and messianic leaders. The techniques and aesthetics used to create a realistic image of Northeastern Brazil helped to reinforce certain popular notions of this region and its people.

While the Cinema Novo directors developed the aesthetic of hunger as a means of expressing the reality of the Third World, the Paraíban school documentarians strove to depict the social reality of the Northeast and used an aesthetic similar to the Cinema Novo style. Although the films of the Paraíban school have been labeled documentaries, the distinction between these films and those of the Cinema Novistas was not a drastic division between documentary and fiction. Both the Paraíban school and the Cinema Novistas used "fictional" narratives and nonprofessional actors and filmed on location. But the Cinema Novistas were always described as filmmakers, whereas the Paraíban school filmmakers were often seen as journalists or nonprofessional filmmakers. The division between the two movements also came from the perception that the Northeastern filmmakers did not comprehend the power of their aesthetic, whereas the Cinema Novo directors defined it as Third Cinema.

In addition to *Aruanda*, films associated with the Paraíba school include Linduarte Noronha's *Cajueiro nordestino* (Northeastern Cashew Tree, 1962) and *Fogo, salário da morte* (Fire! Death Wages, 1970); Vladimir Carvalho's *Romeiros da Guia* (Pilgrims of Guia, 1962), *A bolandeira* (Grinder, 1967), *A pedra da riqueza* (Stone of Riches, 1975), and *O país de São Saruê* (The Land of São Saruê, 1971); Ipojuca Pontes's *A poética popular* (Popular Poetry, 1970) and *Os homens do caranguejo* (Men of the Crabs, 1968); and Rucker Vieira's *A cabra na região semi-árida* (The Goat in a Semi-Arid Region, 1966). All of these films were shot in the Northeast in rural locations either in the interior or along the coast. While many of the films portrayed how people lived and survived in their environment—the birth of a goat, an Afro-Brazilian pilgrimage, the hunt for crabs in the mangroves—the themes often tied people's lives to the region's history. Thus, when *Romeiros da guia* portrays the residents of a fishing community traveling to a site for an Afro-Brazilian ceremony, the underlying narrative is a history of slave resistance and survival in the colonial era.

The films used symbols associated with Northeastern Brazil to show the region's poverty and isolation from modern Brazil as well as to stabilize ideas of regional identity. The documentaries often used traditional music: For example, *Cajueiro nordestino* lacks a narrative voice but is narrated by the *coco praieiro*, a type of music associated with Afro-Brazilian culture. All of the films depict the marginalization of Northeastern communities and how they survive by way of traditional means connected to the land. Whereas the people depicted in *Aruanda* make pots from the earth, in *Romeiros da Guia*, the community members cast nets into the sea from the shore or from small, canoelike boats; in *Homens do caranguejo*, Pontes focuses on people digging through mud in search of crabs.

While these films were documentaries showing current reality and ways of life in Northeastern Brazil, they posed the question of how long these communities would remain untouched by modern Brazilian fishing or agricultural practices. The directors emphasized this message by suggesting the communities' isolation from urban areas, or modern civilization. Even in *Cajueiro nordestino*, when the documentary shifts to showing the consumption of cashew by-products in urban areas, the juxtaposition with the people who pick the fruit/nut emphasizes their isolation. Yet in most cases this isolation was probably an intended representation rather than a reality. Many of the areas are close to cities, and community members likely interacted with urban, modern society. Moreover, some of them probably moved to cities in the Northeast or in the South during the period when the documentaries were filmed, since these years saw mass migrations from rural to urban areas. The political message was not that the communities were revolutionary but that they were poor, nonmodern, and isolated.

Although the filmmakers were Nordestino and claimed to be the authentic and perhaps "primitive" voice of the Northeast, they were educated professionals with training in filmmaking, photography, and/or journalism. Noronha started his own theater as a teenager, learning how to set up a projector and display films. Rucker Vieira, the cameraman for *Aruanda*, spent years in São Paulo employed as a filmmaker and receiving fellowships to attend film school. The Paraíban school filmmakers were also educated in film theory and film history. Before *Aruanda*, the filmmakers had seen many of the classic films, including Robert Flaherty's *Man of Aran* (1934).[31] They also participated in *cineclubes*, where they read and discussed film theory. As Ipojuca Pontes remembers, the *cineclubes* had access to *Cahiers du cinéma* and many other European publications via priests coming from Italy.[32] Many filmmakers were employed as journalists, suggesting their social background and their inability to survive financially solely as filmmakers—they needed to make a living. The Paraíban school's Vladimir Carvalho and Pontes continued their professional careers in filmmaking. Carvalho still holds a position at the Universidade de Brasília, and Pontes served as minister of culture in 1990 and 1991.

In the series of interviews that José Marinho de Oliveira conducted with the Paraíban documentary school filmmakers,[33] most of the filmmakers described the Third World conditions of the communities and the isolation of their subjects, emphasizing how the subjects of the documentaries were the nonmodern Other. Pontes described how he got malaria while filming *Os homens do caranguejo*, a documentary adapted from Josué de Castro's *Homens e caranguejos* (Of Men and Crabs, 1966). Echoing Noronha's description of the hardships encountered by the filmmaking team in Santa Luzia, Pontes described how the filmmakers on location for *Os homens do caranguejo* spent hours in the mud flats, cutting their feet on clamshells, waiting for the tides to be right for filming.[34] While the conditions required the filmmakers to interact with poor people in poverty-stricken environments, the filmmakers were not from the communities and knew that they were telling the story of the Other.

Noronha's comments on the savageness of the community in *Aruanda* also exemplify his awareness of his outsider perspective. Noronha had difficulty convincing some of the community members of Santa Luzia to participate in the film, especially one little boy: "I had serious problems in the area of finding the boy that I wanted for the film. And he has a strange name. Even though he was from such an isolated group, the name of the boy was Henrique. The boy, like all of the people that lived isolated there, was a real little animal [*verdadeiro animalzinho*], five years old and he would never come close to us."[35]

Noronha supposedly enticed the boy with a large bag of candy. Even though Noronha was from Paraíba and had previously spent time with this community, he still used a language that distinguished community members as the Other, animal-like and isolated from the modern world. Perhaps Noronha would have found the name Zumbi more appropriate for the child than Henrique.[36]

The Paraíban documentary school filmmakers shared the goal of denouncing the social reality of Northeastern Brazil, in which Nordestinos were seen as needing (and possessing) superhuman strength to survive in a Brazil that was closer to the Middle Ages than to modernity. The filmmakers were not associated with any one political party or with the Catholic Church *cineclube* movement, but all believed themselves the most entitled to film the "reality" of the Northeast since they were Nordestinos. When describing their films, the filmmakers cited their personal histories and their intimate contact with sugarcane workers, fishermen, cattle ranchers, and other rural Nordestinos to indicate their legitimacy to document the reality of this region. Their ideas, goals, and techniques resembled those proposed by Rossellini and the Cinema Novo directors, yet the school's trajectory differed markedly.

Conclusion

After the 1964 military coup, Northeastern Brazil experienced immediate repression. Rural social movement leaders and participants were arrested and tortured, sometimes disappeared, and were forced into exile. With the April 1 coup, a film crew making a film about the *ligas camponesas* and the death of peasant leader João Pedro Teixeira immediately fled the location where they were filming, hiding in the rural areas and traveling by foot back to Recife or elsewhere to go into hiding.[37] The military invaded the recently founded University of Paraíba in João Pessoa, closing it down for a time. At the university, the military particularly focused on the Paraíban school, seizing a "Russian" camera and arresting many of the filmmakers. This action constituted a major blow to the Paraíban school, which had limited resources and whose members had been proud of the donation of the camera. It was never seen again.

Rossellini never returned to Brazil and never filmed his project based on *Geografia da fome*. According to one scholar, the plan was abandoned in 1958 because Brazilian government officials prohibited Rossellini from filming because they thought it would portray an exceptionally negative view of Brazil. Such an explanation is unlikely since Rossellini originally had been invited by the Brazilian government.[38] Other sources suggest that Rossellini could not find funding to make the film. Another possibility lies in Rossellini's possible lack of interest in the project after facing harsh criticism for his TV series and film on India. The case of Rossellini's film also suggests the boom and bust in terms of the popularity of producing films to document poverty and inequality in the Northeast.

The idea of documenting the social reality of Northeastern Brazil received enormous national and international attention in the early 1960s, particularly inspired by *Aruanda*. After the coup, many directors continued to make films about Northeastern Brazil, and some *cineclubes* continued to exist throughout the dictatorship (1964–85).[39] But after 1964, repression and popular consent created a sense of failed revolution that swept the "social reality" of Northeastern Brazil off the national political agenda and out of the general public's view. The reality of the region and its people depicted in the films of the early 1960s emphasized backwardness, passivity, and a lack of agency. The social reality of the films contradicted the military government's promises of "progress" and an "economic miracle," and films that portrayed the Northeast's poverty threatened to destabilize the image the military government wanted to promote domestically and internationally to maintain its power and legitimacy to rule. While certain "social reality" films and documentaries were produced about the Northeast after 1964, the majority of these films either focused on the "folkloric" Northeast, such as the high-production-quality documentaries of the Caravana Farkas,[40] or faced censorship, as in the case of Vladimir Carvalho's *O pais de São Saruê*, censored until 1979, and Olney São Paulo's *O grito da terra* (1965), which had a limited release and endured major cuts.[41]

Thus, exploring the idea of neorealism as a transnational political and cultural movement involves the need to take into consideration the historical context of movements such as neorealism and Cinema Novo. All of these filmmakers were watching each other's films, reading criticism, and engaged in transnational conversations about cinema. In many ways, only minor aesthetic or technical differences exist among Italian neorealism, cinema verité, and Cinema Novo. What made neorealism Italian is that it communicated a political message based on portraying a reality of postwar Italy, and Cinema Novo expressed a political message based on the "reality" of Brazil and/or the Third World. The attempt to construct new ideas of national identity through these film movements in the early Cold War period as well as the theme of depicting the contradictions of modernity connects the film movements. A second issue that must be considered when evaluating these cultural movements is the meanings, purposes, and consequences of claims to portraying reality. As in the case of Brazil, the reality depicted in these films had precarious consequences. While on the one hand, these films raised people's awareness about the problems of Northeastern Brazil, on the other hand, the images reinforced certain already preconceived stereotypes about Nordestinos. These stereotypes furthered the idea of Nordestinos as the Other and may have helped to legitimize the type of repression that occurred in Northeastern Brazil during the military regime. One way to read the situation is that the portrayal of the reality of these nonmodern, animal-like, or slavelike communities was swallowed by the promises of modernity associated with the military government. With a few whips and shackles and the disappearance of the rebellious leaders, poverty could be erased from the popular imagination and replaced by progress and order.

Notes

1. Josué de Castro was one of Brazil's most prominent international political figures in the 1950s as the president of the United Nations Food and Agriculture Organization.

2. "Rossellini (no Rio) não quis falar sobre Ingrid Bergman," *Diario de Pernambuco*, August 20, 1958, 6.

3. "Rossellini: Um 'homen isolado' alvo da imprensa sensacionalista," *Diario de Pernambuco*, August 23, 1958, 3.

4. The identification of Nordestino and regionalism in Brazil is particularly strong, and certain physical and cultural traits are ascribed to the Nordestino identity.

5. "Rossellini é esperado hoje no Recife," *Diario de Pernambuco*, August 22, 1958, 3.

6. For the Brazilian journalists reporting on Rossellini's visits, this notion translated into one of the main ideas associated with neorealism: Rossellini would use local actors, artists, and extras in his film on Northeastern Brazil.

7. Sam Rhodie, "India," in *Roberto Rossellini: Magician of the Real*, ed. David Forgacs, Sarah Lutton, and Geoffrey Nowell-Smith (London: British Film Institute, 2000), 112–25. As Rhodie claims, "It was precisely Rossellini's almost uncinematic, certainly humanist, and often naïve search for reality, which he equated with truth, that resulted in a cinema that dismantled many of the procedures that had constituted the existing cinema" (121).

8. Ibid., 112; Roberto Rossellini, *Fragments d'une autobiographie* (Paris: Ramsay, 1987), 164. His Third World efforts included trips and filmmaking in Africa, India, Jamaica, and Brazil (Peter Brunette, *Roberto Rossellini* [New York: Oxford University Press, 1987], 195). Perhaps Rossellini went abroad in response to Cesare Zavattini's 1952 call for neorealism to shift to an "analysis of the world" (Angelo Restivo, *The Cinema of Economic Miracles: Visuality and Modernization in the Italian Art Film* [Durham, N.C.: Duke University Press, 2002], 51).

9. Brunette, *Roberto Rossellini*, 196.

10. Tag Gallagher, *The Adventures of Roberto Rossellini* (New York: Da Capo, 1998), 503.

11. *Diário de Pernambuco*, August 22, 1958, 3; *Jornal do Brasil*, August 20, 1958, 7. Rossellini was but one of the many international figures who traveled to Northeastern Brazil during this period to witness, study, or document the (revolutionary) misery of the Third World. Other international figures included Jean-Paul Sartre, Simone de Beauvoir, Celia Guevara (mother of Ernesto "Che" Guevara), Robert Kennedy, Arthur Schlesinger Jr., and Helen Rogers of ABC News, who filmed a one-hour news feature on the region.

12. Wills Leal, *O discurso cinematográfico dos Paraíbanos ou a história do cinema da/na Paraíba* (João Pessoa: A União, 1989), 80.

13. Alberto Farassino, ed., *Neorealismo: Cinema Italiano, 1945–1949* (Turin: EDT, 1989), 23.

14. P. Adams Sitney, *Vital Crises in Italian Cinema: Iconography, Stylistics, Politics* (Austin: University of Texas Press, 1995), 34.

15. Restivo, *Cinema of Economic Miracles*, 8.

16. In one of the only scholarly works on the Paraíban documentary school, José Marinho argues that filmmakers sought mainly to provide sociological studies on the socioeconomic problems of the Northeast, such as land reform (*Dos homens e das pedras: O ciclo*

do cinema documentário paraíbano [1959–1979] [Niteroi: Editora da Universidade Federal Fluminense, 1998], 25–26).

17. Mariarosario Fabris, *Nelson Pereira dos Santos: Um olhar neo-realista?* (São Paulo: UDUSP, 1994).

18. Célia Aparecida Ferreira Tolentino claims that the 1960s films of the Northeast radically shifted the ideas of "true national identity" of the 1950s by showing the "real" country: poor, backward, and lacking modernization (*O rural no cinema brasileiro* [São Paulo: Editora UNESP, 2000], 142).

19. Sarah Sarzynski, "History, Identity, and the Struggle for Land in Northeastern Brazil, 1955–1985" (Ph.D. diss., University of Maryland, 2008).

20. Jean-Claude Bernardet, *Brasil em tempo de cinema: Ensaio sobre o cinema brasileiro de 1958 a 1966* (Rio de Janeiro: Civilização Brasileira, 1967), 19.

21. Ibid., 19–20.

22. Ibid., 21.

23. Glauber Rocha, *A revolução da Cinema Novo*, quoted in Marilia Franco, "Liberdaruande," *Communicação e artes*, São Paulo 17 (1986): 85–90, Folder 004430, Museum de Arte Moderna Archives, Rio de Janeiro.

24. Leal, *Discurso cinematográfico*, 106: "Noronha e Vieira estão próximos àquele fantástico Rossellini; realismo da miséria material com ela mesma, em seu caráter poluído da superfícies da terra e na cara faminta dos homens. Fiquemos certos de que *Aruanda* quis ser verdade antes de ser narrativa: a linguagem como linguagem nasce do real, é o real."

25. Ibid., 107.

26. The only Cinema Novo director from Northeastern Brazil was Rocha, who was from Bahia, and while he had a personal connection to the region, the interior region where *Aruanda* was filmed remained a distant place. But Rocha's fascination with *Aruanda* also tapped into his perceptions of the Third World and the type of filmmaking required to portray it.

27. The Executive Group of the Cinema Industry began in 1961 to study the national film industry and increase exhibition. In 1966, the National Film Institute placed quotas on theaters to promote national films.

28. Stephanie Dennison and Lisa Shaw, *Popular Cinema in Brazil, 1930–2001* (Manchester: Manchester University Press, 2004), 132.

29. Tolentino, *Rural no cinema brasileiro*, 135–36.

30. A third film movement during these years was connected to the Center of Popular Culture of the National Student Union and the Brazilian Communist Party, but it produced only two films, and only one was released in 1960. *Cinco vezes favela* included five short films about Rio de Janeiro's urban poor. The military coup interrupted the filming of Eduardo Coutinho's documentary, *Cabra marcado para morrer*, on the Northeast and its rural social movements. It was released as *Twenty Years Later* (1984).

31. Marinho compares Noronha's process of filming, scriptwriting, and casting to Flaherty's (*Dos homens*, 149–50).

32. Ipojuca Pontes, interview by José Marinho de Oliveira, Depoimentos Cinema Brasileiro, tema Nordeste, Copia de trabalho, orientação de Maria Rita Galvão, São Paulo, ECA/USP, s.d. Cinemateca Brasileira, D22416. The emphasis on materials being brought from Italy also recalls the connection between Italian filmmaking and Northeastern Brazil.

33. The interviews included Vladimir Carvalho, Manoel Clemente, Eduardo Coutinho, João Ramiro Mello, Paulo Mello, Linduarte Noronha, Ipojuca Pontes, and Rucker Vieira.

34. Pontes, interview.

35. Linduarte Noronha, interview by José Marinho de Oliveira, Depoimentos Cinema Brasileiro, tema Nordeste, Copia de trabalho, orientação de Maria Rita Galvão, São Paulo, ECA/USP, s.d. Cinemateca Brasileira, D22417.

36. Zumbi was the name of the leader of Brazil's most famous *quilombo* community, Palmares.

37. The film was Coutinho's *Cabra marcardo para morrer*.

38. Gallagher, *Adventures*, 503.

39. Marinho's work describes a few of these films and associations, such as the Association of Cinematographic Critics of Paraíba (1964–68), and short films such as Vladimir Carvalho's *A bolandeira* (1967) and *Sertão do Rio do Peixe* (1968). Vladimir Carvalho and Ipojuca Pontes are the Paraíban school filmmakers who continued to produce films with a national market (Marinho, *Dos homens*, 261–80).

40. Caravana Farkas was a documentary film movement filming Northeastern popular culture, religion, and artisanal labor.

41. A Super 8 film movement in Recife, Pernambuco, emerged in the 1970s as an important form of resistance against the dictatorship (Alexandre Figueirôa, *Cinema Pernambucano: Uma história em ciclos* [Recife: Prefeitura da Cidade do Recife, Secretaria de Cultura, Turismo e Esportes, Fundação de Cultura Cidade do Recife, 2000]).

NEOREALISM IRANIAN STYLE

HAMID NAFICY

Neorealism has had a long and distinctive history in Iranian cinema. Some of the best filmmakers were influenced by its philosophical tenets and stylistic features, and domestic and foreign critics made much of the impact of Italian neorealism on Iranian authorial cinemas both before (New Wave) and after the revolution (art house cinema). There has been some controversy in film studies about what constitutes neorealism, even among its defenders. For the purpose of this study, I invoke Georges Sadoul's definition, one of the first to call neorealism a "school" and one that offered five reasonable prerequisite characteristics:

- geographically bounded (concentrated in Rome, Italy);
- temporally bounded (post–World War II phenomenon, 1945–51);
- existence of masters (for example, Roberto Rossellini, Vittorio De Sica, Cesare Zavattini, Luchino Visconti);
- existence of disciples (for example, Luigi Zampa, Pietro Germi, Renato Castellani, Giuseppe De Santis);
- formation of a set of rules (location shooting, long takes, invisible style of filming and editing, predominance of medium and long shots, use of contemporary true-to-life subjects, open-ended plots, working-class protagonists, nonprofessional cast, vernacular dialogue, implied social criticism).[1]

Applying these criteria, I make clear both the similarities and differences between Iranian neorealism and its Italian progenitor. In addition, I demonstrate that Iranian-style neorealism has not been homogenous, exhibiting itself in two different styles under two different political systems, and that it has been neither a fully formed film school nor a movement but a moment of convergence in the social history of cinema.

Prerevolutionary New Wave Cinema
Realism and Neorealism as Counters to Official Culture

Beginning during Mohammad Reza Shah Pahlavi's rule in the late 1960s, New Wave filmmakers forcefully introduced some of neorealism's characteristics into Iranian cinema, which at the time was dominated by escapist song-and-dance, melodrama, and stewpot movies. The spark that social-realist filmmakers Farrokh Gaffary (*Jonub-e shahr* [South of the City, 1958] and *Shab-e quzi* [Night of the Hunchback, 1964]) and Ebrahim Golestan (*Khesht va ayeneh* [Mudbrick and Mirror, 1965]) ignited with their films was fanned by Feraidun Rahnema's modernist *Siavash dar takht-e jamshid* (Siavash in Persepolis, 1965) and Davud Mowlapur's realist *Showhar-e ahu khanom* (Ahu's Husband, 1968) and finally burst into full flame with Masud Kimiai's *Qaisar* (1969) and Darisuh Mehrjui's *Gav* (The Cow, 1969). *Qaisar* gave rise to the modernized tough-guy movie genre, the *jaheli* (urban toughs) movies, while *The Cow* led to the New Wave films. The New Wave and the urban tough movies competed in the marketplace for audiences and financing, which received them unequally, and they benefited unequally from government largesse and censorship. The urban toughs movies garnered large nationwide audiences composed of people from average and lower-class backgrounds, while the New Wave films attracted smaller but intellectually inclined spectators only in large cities. The former genre traveled primarily within the nation and in some neighboring countries, while the latter traveled abroad far and wide to major film festivals and brought with it celebrity and controversy. In one of the peculiarities of Iranian cinema, the state bestowed more funding on the New Wave films (as prestige projects for festivals) while the films often criticized and challenged the government on political grounds. In turn, the state tended to censor these films more emphatically than the urban toughs and other popular genre movies.[2]

The Pahlavi-era New Wave cinema was limited to fictional films (features and short subjects) made inside Iran. However, even though a majority of the filmmakers operated from Tehran, the diegetic locations of their movies were not always Tehran but were often villages and rural countryside, as in Mehrjui's ur-neorealist *The Cow*. This film, both funded by and then banned for one year by the Ministry of Culture and Art, tells the story of a farmer who loses his cow, which is the sole source of his livelihood and of the village's milk, and then begins to embody the animal in spirit and body. Its focus on villagers was regarded as a return to Iran's roots in a different genre from the urban toughs films' return to the authentic bedrock of Iranian society and psychology. *The Cow*'s honest treatment and truthful portrayal of village life using a sparse if somewhat primitive realistic style was regarded as a breath of fresh air, linking it to the Italian neorealist cinema. The powerful idea of a return to indigenous roots was energized not only by foreign and domestic Marxist thinkers, who interpreted this approach as return to "the people," but also by contemporary intellectuals such as Jalal Al-e Ahmad and Ali Shariati, who conceptualized the film as a return to cultural and religious traditions.[3] The idea of return was also being promulgated abroad in the writings of Frantz Fanon, later reinterpreted for cinema by Teshome Gabriel.[4] Finally, Mehrjui's adaptation of a story by a leading leftist dissident writer and psychiatrist, Gholamhosain Saedi, became a harbinger of a new alliance between educated filmmakers (Mehrjui received a bachelor's degree in philosophy from UCLA) and contemporary oppositional writers. This alliance proved to be an important pillar of the New Wave cinema.

Unlike the commercial stewpot and urban toughs movie genres, the New Wave films did not constitute an urban cinema, with Tehran as its locus, although they did deal with the clash of premodernity and modernity in other ways. Temporally, the New Wave lasted for approximately one decade—between Mehrjui's *The Cow* in 1969 and the revolution in 1979. The last New Wave films before the revolution shut down movie houses and the film industry were Parviz Sayyad's *Bonbast* (Dead End, 1977), Bahman Farmanara's *Sayehha-ye boland-e bad* (Tall Shadows of the Wind, 1978), and Parviz Kimiavi's *O.K. Mister* (1978), all of which in retrospect seem uncannily to have predicted the preconditions for the revolution and the revolution itself.

In terms of the master-and-disciple structure, the situation was more complicated in Iran than in Italy, partly because no generational hierarchy separated masters from disciples. Almost all of the New Wave filmmakers belonged to the same generation, with some directors a few years older than others or with a few more years experience in cinema. As such, it is difficult to establish the master-discipline hierarchy during the Pahlavi period alone. However, if a longer historical perspective is taken by including the postrevolution period, New Wave filmmakers of the Pahlavi period may be regarded as the masters for the art house cinema disciples of the Islamic Republic period. In that case, the masters would include Mehrjui, Abbas Kiarostami, Sohrab Shahid Saless, Farrokh Gaffary, Ebrahim Golestan, Parviz Kimiavi, Masud Kimiai, Kamran Shirdel, Bahram Baizai, Naser Taqvai, Bahman Farmanara, and Amir Naderi—basically all of the New Wave filmmakers. Both their courageous precedence during the Pahlavi state and their status as elder filmmakers—most remained active after the revolution—gained them respect and influence among the younger generation. Even here, however, problems arise, as some of the New Wave filmmakers—Mehrjui, Kiarostami, Kimiai, Baizai, Kimiavi, Naderi, Taqvai, and Farmanara—became instrumental in the rise of the art house cinema, fighting in the same trenches as the postrevolution neophytes. And there were some in-between filmmakers, such as Nosrat Karimi, who made commercial movies but did so with a nod and a wink to the thematics and aesthetics of neorealism, particularly in his comic sendoffs of Iranian traditions, *Doroshgehchi* (Carriage Driver, 1971) and *Mohallel* (Interim Husband, 1971).[5]

In terms of a set of stylistic rules, the textual and authorial features present in Mehrjui's *The Cow* became influential guideposts for the New Wave movies. They employed realism, surrealism, representational acting involving character subjectivity, and an invisible style of continuity filming and editing. Thematically, these films dealt with ordinary peoples' lives, religious and popular beliefs, pervasive fear and anxiety, social criticism, hostility and intolerance toward outsiders, and the often disturbing and destructive impact of strangers and intruders on society. Like many art cinema filmmakers in authoritarian states, the liminal position of the filmmakers as intellectuals kept them between rocks and hard places—the state, which both supported and banned them; the public, which demanded political commitment; and the film industry, which was bent on maximizing profits.

Some Iranian filmmakers' textual and thematic characteristics resembled those of Italian neorealism, but they also benefited from what I call the domestic "hybrid production mode," which combined improvisational and industrial practices, governmental and private sector funding, Western and native expressive styles.[6] For example, the use of the invisible style ensured realism and integrity of and respect for the continuity of time, space, and causality—in short, reality. However, because of Iranian-style improvisation, causality in the New Wave movies was somewhat looser than in neorealist films. Camera positions and camera movements both were regulated and enjoyed creative improvisation. Conversely, as in Italian neorealism, long shots and long takes were prevalent. Locations were often exterior and natural instead of interior and artificial (studio-based). Artificial lighting was used minimally, and outdoor sequences were generally filmed entirely with natural light. The cast consisted not only of nonprofessional nonactors but also of seasoned actors. Postdubbing was de rigueur, although it was tighter than in the commercial cinema. The protagonists were mainly members of the working or lower classes or rural folk. Many stories were contemporary. New Wave fiction films often contained slice-of-life sequences that were documentary-like. The endings were often unhappy, ambiguous, and open and sometimes circular.

Humanism, hunger for unvarnished reality, social criticism, antiauthoritarianism, and moral and ethical considerations were strong themes.

Despite critical disagreement about the specific textual features of Italian neorealism and whether it was a school, a movement, a style, or a tendency, observers generally concurred about its general philosophy. According to this philosophy, neorealism was principally a moral statement about the world told with a moral poetics, and it sought to promote true objectivity and thus "force viewers to abandon the limitations of a strictly personal perspective and to embrace the reality of the 'others,' be they persons or things, with all the ethical responsibility that such a vision entails." It was hoped that this shared moral commitment would eliminate filmmakers' individual, personal, and authorial differences and unite them on larger social issues.[7]

In the case of Iranian New Wave directors, this moral commitment to reality and to a poetics of realism also involved a political commitment to society, which meant criticizing not only traditions but also government actions. And since they could not directly inscribe these criticisms without inviting censorship, banning, and sometimes incarceration, they resorted to symbolism, surrealism, mysticism, abstraction, and indirection, thereby tending to subvert the other tenets of neorealism, particularly those that emphasized reality, clarity, and realism. As a result, Iranian New Wave neorealism was an amphibolic movement, style, school, or filmmaking moment. In addition, neither Iran's sociopolitical and ideological formations nor its industrial film formations resembled those of post–World War II Italy, nor was foreign cinema's impact on the New Wave limited only to neorealism. The 1970s Iran was not postwar Italy, when turmoil prevailed, social and economic structures were destroyed, film industry facilities were in disarray, and the importation of foreign movies was restricted to encourage local productions. Nonetheless, modernity, industrialization, capitalistic relations, and the Pahlavi culture of spectacle had brought on many sociopolitical and psychological disruptions and turmoil to make both Iranian filmmakers and their spectators hunger for unvarnished reality and for something new—a new order of things and a new cinema. In addition to the Italian neorealism, the French New Wave (*Nouvelle Vague*), which gave its moniker to the Iranian authorial cinema, was highly influential, as were the American art house cinema and those of other world cinemas, particularly India, Japan, and Eastern bloc countries. Iranian filmmakers were nothing if not highly cine-literate and cosmopolitan; even those who had not studied filmmaking abroad had been exposed to and trained by the many movies they had seen in commercial cinemas, cineclubs, film festivals, cultural offerings of various Western embassies, and universities.

New Wave: A Movement or a Moment?

Film movements emerge under favorable sociopolitical conditions and require the coalescence of certain institutions, practices, tendencies, formations, and creative individuals. However, they do not generally last long. As sociopolitical, cultural, and film industry conditions and individual filmmakers undergo changes, film movements also undergo transformations, either metamorphosing into other movements or ceasing to exist. The New Wave films emerged in the contexts of the second Pahlavi official culture and culture industry and were both enabled and enchained by this culture and industry. The New Wave did not die entirely in 1979; instead, it metamorphosed into the art house cinema of the mid-1980s, under the Islamic Republic, thanks to the continuity provided by several key filmmakers—the New Wave masters—and other enabling state institutions. During its decadelong existence, however, the New Wave was neither homogenous nor harmonious. And the separation of the two film camps, the commercial cinema and the New Wave cinema, was not hermetic. Some filmmakers—for example, Masud Kimiai and Amir Naderi—made both commercial movies and New Wave films, and some commercial cinema filmmakers at times made New Wave–type films: Parviz Sayyad with his *Dead End*, Feraidun Goleh with his *Zir-e pust-e shab* (Under the Skin of the City, 1974), and Mohammad Motovasselani with his *Sazesh* (Compromise, 1974).

In addition, despite the fact that many of the New Wave films were financed or aided by the state, they were far from being panegyric odes to the regime, like the newsreel documentaries. Instead, they usually implicitly and sometimes explicitly criticized prevailing social conditions, including the government, for which these filmmakers paid a price and by which they gained a degree of prestige as oppositional, intellectual cineasts. Both state sponsorship and filmmakers' political commitment to "the people" proved to be doubleedged swords. Moreover, no master-disciple hierarchy existed among New Wave filmmakers.

As such, the New Wave filmmakers did not, strictly speaking, constitute a cohesive film movement. Instead, they formed a group of ambitious intellectuals with diverse class backgrounds, film training, and ethnoreligious affiliations and with individualistic tastes, aspirations, and styles. They maintained competitive and at times even antagonistic relationships. Film and cultural magazines discussed and promoted the New Wave films; however, unlike the Italian and French movements, which featured publications that promoted neorealism and the Nouvelle Vague, no organ of the New Wave was published on a sustained basis. These factors and the divisive politics of the government and the commercial stranglehold of major distributors, importers, and exhibitors discouraged these and other film industry members from forming sustained independent civil society organizations, such as professional unions, pressure groups, and media, through which to freely discuss issues, represent themselves, and exert collective influence. The majority of the New Wave filmmakers were leftist in their political outlook and opposed the Shah's government, but a majority also benefited from its largesse, even if they bit the hand that fed them—like many great Eastern European filmmakers of the same era, whom the Iranians admired. Thus, they remained largely atomized and somewhat compromised. As a result, the New Wave cinema was not so much a filmmaking movement as a filmmaking moment of convergence.

Postrevolution Art House Cinema
Hybrid Textuality, Subverting Realism and Neorealism

A second moment for the Iranian iteration of neorealism emerged in the form of an art house cinema within a decade after the revolution of 1978–79, later dubbed the Islamic Revolution. The revolution brought to an end some twenty-five hundred years of monarchic rule, removing Shah Mohammad Reza Pahlavi and ushering in an Islamic theocratic state, the Islamic Republic, headed by Ayatollah Ruhollah Khomeini. The revolution was fed partly by targeting the institutions that revolutionaries considered to be promoting moral corruption, economic and political exploitation, and unbridled Westernization: bars, banks, and movie houses. All in all, some 180 cinemas nationwide— nearly a third of the country's venues—were destroyed or burned. In one rare and horrific arson incident, 377 spectators were burned alive while watching Kimiai's *Gavaznha* (The Deer, 1975) at Rex Cinema in the city of Abadan. In a fit of iconoclasm after the success of the revolution, many entertainers, moviemakers, actors, and film stars were "purified," in the parlance of the time: They were sidelined, silenced, banned, imprisoned, or tortured, or they lost their properties to expropriation. Many others escaped the country or chose what turned out to be a painful permanent exile. Yet within three years, a new postrevolution film industry and cinema began to emerge inside Iran,[8] while a thriving pop culture, television, and cinema flourished in exile.[9]

Periods of major social turmoil and transition seem to produce some of the most innovative cineasts and cinematic movements. The formalist Soviet films of Eisenstein and Vertov followed the Russian Revolution; the British realist documentaries immediately preceded and followed World War II; the Italian neorealists emerged during and immediately after World War II; and the

Polish "black films" emerged during the Spring Thaw of de-Stalinization in the mid-1950s. Concurrent with the worldwide social turmoil of the 1960s and 1970s, too, several innovative film movements surfaced, including Cinema Novo in Brazil; New Wave in Iran; cinema vérité in the United States, France, and Canada; and Third Cinema in Latin America and elsewhere. Thus, there was good cause to expect that the 1978–79 revolution in Iran and its preconditions and aftermath would produce a new cinema. The result was an Islamicate cinema and film culture (more culturally than religiously Islamic) that produced several different types of cinemas, including popular genre movies, war movies, women's movies, and the most widely known type outside Iran, the art house cinema. The same medium whose purported corrupting, poisonous, and immoral products had been employed to discredit and dismantle the Pahlavi regime was now deployed to legitimize the new Islamist regime, but only after films had been "purified" and reoriented away from sex and violence and toward Islamicate values.

Within three years of the revolution, this process was well under way, and conditions for a new cinema and film industry converged into fruition. The Ministry of Culture and Islamic Guidance, headed by an educated midlevel cleric, Hojattoleslam Mohammad Khatami (later to become president), was put in charge of cinema, and the cabinet passed rules and regulations governing the financing, production, exhibition, distribution, and importation and exportation of movies. Importing of foreign movies was severely curtailed, leaving the domestic film industry without unbeatable foreign rivals. Similar to the Pahlavi state's funding of quality (New Wave) films, the Islamic state began financing art house films. As in the case of the New Wave, intellectuals made these films, and they grew to become an important oppositional force. The Islamic regime, like the previous regime, sought to channel and control this dissident cinema through funding and through its vast apparatuses of censorship and coercion.

The art house cinema filmmakers experimented most deeply, widely, and successfully with neorealism's philosophic and stylistic tenets. However, this experimentation sought to reify neither the tenets of neorealism nor those of the Islamic Republic; rather, it questioned and critiqued and even sought to achieve a kind of universal critical humanism. This humanism, which countered the Islamic state's violent intolerance and policies, was a primary reason for the art house films' success and attractiveness abroad.

These films were produced according to the logic not only of the hybrid production mode (consisting of public and private sector funding and semiindustrialized and artisanal practices) but also of a hybrid textual mode consisting of realist and counterrealist narrative strategies.[10] Much has been made of Kiarostami's debt to Italian neorealism, to which he readily admits;[11] however, his relationship to it is quite complex. He is both the embodiment of classic neorealism and its most exemplary exception. His career and cinema embody the features of classical neorealism: The stories of his films are socially and geographically bounded to the middle- and lower-class milieu and are temporally bounded to contemporary times (no future-tense narratives or historical subjects). However, with success, Kiarostami's works began to exceed this classic tenet, as he began receiving coproduction funding from Europe and started working abroad, with such films as *ABC Africa* (2001) and *Tickets* (2005).

Classic neorealism as a school needed the presence of masters and disciples. Kiarostami has been a sort of master whose works influenced disciples, either indirectly (the disciples emulate the master) or directly (the disciples work as his assistants or use his film ideas and screenplays for their own films). Ebrahim Foruzesh, Jafar Panahi, Alireza Raisian, Mohammad Ali Talebi, Iraj Karimi, and Niki Karimi made films inspired by specific ideas from Kiarostami or used his screenplays. Others who worked for him as assistants but did not use his screenplays, such as Bahman Ghobadi, were nevertheless influenced by his style. Ghobadi subsequently almost single-handedly created a Kurdish national cinema with his powerful and widely distributed films, *Zamani bara-ye masti-ye asbha* (A Time for Drunken Horses, 2000), *Lakposhtha parvaz mikonand* (Turtles Can Fly, 2004), and *Niwemang* (Half Moon, 2006). Even actors working with Kiarostami made films in a style he inspired: Mania Akbari, for example, made a daring directorial debut with *Bist angosht* (20 Fingers, 2004). However, as demonstrated by the recent public spat between Kiarostami and Ghobadi over *Kasi az gorbehha-ye irani khabar nadarad* (Nobody Knows about the Persian Cats, 2009), the latter's film about the vibrant and counterhegemonic underground music scene in Iran, the master-disciple dyad is not a lasting configuration in the creative arts. The government banned the film inside Iran, partly because it was filmed without official permission, causing Ghobadi to leave the country in protest. When Kiarostami publicly criticized his former protégé's filming and departure, Ghobadi responded with an unusually emotional public letter: "On what basis do you give yourself permission to ridicule the efforts of filmmakers who stand with the oppressed people, using unacceptable words and, worse than that, speak with the same voice as religious dictators?"[12]

Finally, through his films, Kiarostami developed a set of "rules" that both paid homage to the realist aesthetics of Italian neorealism and developed a new Iranian and Kiarostamian rendition of neorealism—ironically, a deconstructed version of the original.

The spirit and style of untrammeled neorealism is strongly present in Kiarostami's early short films, such as *Bread and Alley* (1970) and *Traveler*

(1974), in which his actors are ordinary people untrained in the art of acting. The protagonists are often male children on dogged true-to-life quests or journeys to get something, to redress a wrong, or to prove something. Kiarostami shows himself to be an artist of the everyday but not of everydayness, for he does not seek the tediousness, repetitiveness, and degradation of the everyday but instead searches and discovers the moments of rupture, tension, and glory hidden in the quotidian. These Pahlavi-era films placed him within the New Wave category. Inspired by the neorealist style and ethos, almost all of his films were shot on location in cityscapes and in the countryside—not in the studio—and in available light, using a small crew and simple equipment (and now digital cameras), with vernacular dialogue that is often devised on the spot. The filming style generally consists of long shots and long takes.

However, at the same time that his films treat these ordinary social worlds and encounters with the ethos and aesthetics of realism and neorealism, they embody certain deconstructive practices that counter or problematize realism and neorealism, resulting in formally rigorous works that are quietly operatic in their humanism and in their celebration of life's small victories and filmmaking. In his playfulness, expansiveness, indirection, and blurring of reality and fiction, Kiarostami is more like Kimiavi than like Shahid Saless, whose strict, recessive, closed-form aesthetics and adherence to codes of realism border on superrealism. The mixing of fiction and nonfiction elements has a long history in Iranian cinema, dating back to Ovanes Ohanians's *Haji aqa, aktor-e sinema* (Mr. Haji, the Movie Actor, 1933), Kimiavi's *Bagh-e sangi* (The Stone Garden, 1976), and Shirdel's *Unshab keh barun umad . . . Ya hamaseh-ye rustazadeh-ye gorgani* (The Night It Rained . . . or The Epic of a Gorgani Peasant, 1967). But that mixture came into its own only in the 1990s, creating creative vistas as well as problems both for the authenticity of the documentary and for the reality of the fictional. Kiarostami's deconstructive and counterrealistic practices include self-referentiality, self-inscription, and self-reflexivity as well as ironic blending of reality and fiction, forms of distancing, indirection, and sly humor. By these means, the most well known practitioner of neorealism is also the best violator of what Kamran Shirdel aptly called "the dictatorship of neorealism."[13] Other art house cinema directors employed some of these neorealist and counterrealist strategies; however, Kiarostami always keeps the spectators in an ambiguous position, constantly parsing the truth of fiction from the fiction of realism.

This ambiguity is driven partly by Kiarostami's personality and style and partly by Iranian hermeneutics and psychological orientations of veiling (*hejab*), dissimulation (*taqiyeh, ketman*), ritual courtesy (*taarof*), cleverness (*zerangi*), inner purity (*safa-ye baten*), and indirection—in short, by strategies that demonstrate distrust in manifest surface values and instead valorize latent core meanings, which endow authorial cinema and arts in Iran, in Bahram Baizai's words, with "visual duplicity." He refers not so much to their duplicity and hypocrisy in terms of lack of morality and truthfulness but to their penchant for duality, ambiguity, complexity, evasiveness, playfulness, relativity, and hedging their bets. The realism of neorealism is thus contingent and is continually deferred and problematized. Instead of practicing clarity and frankness, which can cause problems in a highly collective, dual, and hierarchical society, Iranians have learned to engage in "saying things without appearing to have said them . . . , but in such a way that those who should, understand that you have said it. Many Iranian filmmakers live this visual duplicity, as they have to follow unerringly the various written and unwritten supervisory [censorship] regulations without believing in a single one of them. And the supervisory office knows this."[14] This is another dimension of the Iranian art and style of improvisation, which permeates all the arts.

While Baizai tends to see these strategies moralistically and modernistically as duplicity, they can also be regarded as artfulness necessitated by collective, hierarchical, and authoritarian formations. As Lebanese American anthropologist Suad Joseph rightfully notes in an autobiographical essay, "I learned many things about indirection. I learned that fulfillment of my desires usually required the active involvement and compliance of others. Desire was not to be satisfied through my autonomous actions. I could hint, imply, and create situations for others to read, interpret, and act upon, but others needed to act for my wishes to be realized. . . . It also taught me that action on my part was a necessary condition of the fulfillment of the desires of significant others."[15] Indirection not only fits the ethos of collective formations but also necessitates a hyperawareness of one's surroundings and a keen power of observation, important traits for filmmakers. Kiarostami's films as well as those of his school are filled with instances of such indirection—apparently simple movies with deep meanings, saying things without appearing to say them—not only in the films' plot, character behavior, and theme but also in the films' visuality and aesthetics. The problem is that in less deft hands, everything is made to be hermeneutically too complex, interpretable politically, and narratively slow to the point that even if a filmmaker engages in clarity and openness, neither the censors nor the spectators believe it. Baizai's movies, too, are hermeneutically complex but in a different, historically aware, mythically informed, linguistically eloquent, and palimpsestical manner.

Even when Kiarostami uses the continuity filming and editing schemes of the classic realist (and neorealist) cinema, such as shot–reverse shot, he undermines them. Many of his films, particularly his later road movies, such as *Tám-e gilas* (Taste of Cherry, 1997), in which a driver and a passenger are filmed in a moving car, talking for long periods, contain not only long takes but also shot–reverse shots. However, while using shot–reverse shot exchanges between the two characters in the car, there is no over-the-shoulder shot that places them both in the same visual space. Kiarostami told me in an interview that these shots are filmed without the driver and the passenger ever being present together in the car. Each time that one person is on camera, Kiarostami occupies the other front seat. In a sly subversion of codes of realism and neorealism, the protagonists are forced to react not to each other, as is customary in those styles, but to the director's presence, which insinuates Kiarostami's authorial control into each profilmic scene, as he coaches the cast and feeds them lines of dialogue. Thus, the apparent casualness and improvisation in his visual style, which consolidate his connection both to Italian neorealism and to French New Wave films, is illusory. Nevertheless, the film is to a large extent improvisational, as Kiarostami did not use a traditional screenplay and written dialogue for the actors. These are manufactured impressions of casualness and realism that he has strived hard to invoke, not innocent recordings of unfolding reality, as many believe. They conceal his considerable planning and tinkering with locations, prop arrangements, acting, dialogue coaching, and filming.

Considered the engine of classical realism, shot–reverse shot filming and editing, often involving over-the-shoulder shots, creates audience identification with characters by suturing them into the diegesis. As such, the classical realist style is highly psychological and fictional; while Kiarostami's sparing use of these strategies and his undermining of them when he uses them render his films more social and realistic, even didactic. In this manner, his techniques may work against cinema's identificatory mechanism of individualized subjectivity, which is a hallmark of modernity; instead, his approach promotes distantiation and collective identity, which are hallmarks of premodernity—or of an emerging postmodernity.

His works tend to be didactic because the understated characters in many of them do not appear to discover much in their quests, and if they do, they seem unaware of the discovery. They are determined but often not transformed by their own discoveries, the way the characters in modernist novels and films are. We get this impression because they rarely have subjectivity, which is usually signaled by point-of-view filming and by shot–reverse shot editing. Instead, Kiarostami's primary filming style, involving long shots and long takes, tells us more about his subjectivity than that of his characters. This technique strengthens his authorial grip on his works. However, this didactic structure means that the audience discovers something universal by which it is potentially transformed. Hence, his films have a gripping power on spectators, particularly non-Iranians. In addition, because Kiarostami breaks the fourth wall and self-reflexively inserts the process of filmmaking into his stories, the focus of inquiry is shifted from the characters to the camera, the cinema, the director, and ultimately the spectators, who become aware of their own act of film watching. His later films, therefore, constitute a trompe l'oeil cinema,[16] for they mix illusion and reality and create uncertainty and ambiguity about which is which—a far cry from the classic neorealist concerns and style. These dualities, distances, ambivalences, and uncertainties—characteristics of late modernity, inscribed in both content and form—along with critical humanism have propelled Iranian art house cinema onto the world stage. It is perhaps the most postmodern of all national cinemas, for it captures and expresses postmodernity's zeitgeist.

Notes

1. Cited in Millicent Marcus, *Italian Film in the Light of Neorealism* (Princeton: Princeton University Press, 1986), 21–22.

2. Hamid Naficy, "Iranian Cinema," in *Companion Encyclopedia of Middle Eastern and North African Film*, ed. Oliver Leaman (London: Routledge, 2001), 130–222.

3. Jalal Al-e Ahmad, *Occidentosis: A Plague from the West*, trans. Robert Campbell, ed. Hamid Algar (Berkeley: Mizan, 1985), published in Persian as *Gharbzadegi* (1961); Ali Shariati, *Bazgasht* (Tehran: Amir Kabir, 1355/1976).

4. Frantz Fanon, *The Wretched of the Earth*, trans. Constance Farrington (New York: Grove, 1963); Teshome Gabriel, "Towards a Critical Theory of Third World Films," in *Questions of Third Cinema*, ed. Jim Pines and Paul Willemen (London: British Film Institute, 1989), 30–53.

5. Jamal Omid, *Tarikh-e sinema-ye Iran, 1279–1375* (Tehran: Entesharat-e Rowzaneh, 1995/1374), 582–83.

6. Hamid Naficy, *A Social History of Iranian Cinema*, 4 vols. (Durham, N.C.: Duke University Press, forthcoming).

7. Marcus, *Italian Film in the Light*, 23.

8. Naficy, "Iranian Cinema."

9. Hamid Naficy, *The Making of Exile Cultures: Iranian Television in Los Angeles* (Minneapolis: University of Minnesota Press, 1993); Hamid Naficy, *An Accented Cinema: Exilic and Diasporic Filmmaking* (Princeton: Princeton University Press, 2001); Hamid Naficy, "Iranian Émigré Cinema as a Component of Iranian National Cinema," in *Media, Culture, and Society in Iran: Living with Globalization and the Islamic State*, ed. Mehdi Semati (London: Routledge, 2008), 167–92.

10. Naficy, *Cinema, Modernity, National Identity.*

11. Philip Lopate, "Interview with Abbas Kiarostami," in *Totally, Tenderly, Tragically: Essays and Criticism from a Lifelong Love Affair with the Movies* (New York: Anchor, 1998), 352–53.

12. Quoted in Michael Slackman, "Iranian Filmmakers Keep Focus on the Turmoil," *New York Times*, January 3, 2010, http://www.nytimes.com/2010/01/04/world/middleeast /04iranfilms.html?partner=rss&emc=rss (accessed January 26, 2011).

13. Mohammad Tahaminejad, "Kamran Shirdel, coeur de lion," *Forum des images* (Paris), program notes, September 10–October 19, 2003, 37.

14. Bahram Baizai, "Pas az sad sal," *Iran nameh* 14.2 (Summer 1996/1375): 379.

15. Suad Joseph, "Eyes of Indirection," in *Remembering Childhood in the Middle East: Memoirs from a Century of Change*, ed. Elizabeth Warnock Fernea (Austin: University of Texas Press, 2002), 306–7.

16. Laura Mulvey, "Kiarostami's Uncertainty Principle," *Sight and Sound*, June 1998, 26.

EPILOGUE

Neorealism, Cinema of Poetry, and Italian Contemporary Cinema

SILVIA CARLOROSI

As this collection of essays on international cinema demonstrates, neorealism demands a new reading that frees it from the few reassuring rules on which it was supposedly based. The dangers of creating -*isms* are well known. Even the most unconventional movement risks becoming captive to its own critical legacy, a process Roland Barthes figuratively called "inoculation." As he stated, "One immunizes the contents of the collective imagination by means of a small inoculation of acknowledged evil, immunizing it against changing; one thus protects it against the risk of generalized subversion."[1] After years of international resonance, historical neorealism, then, had been inoculated and protected against subversions, coming to its official end. *Umberto D* (1952) usually marks the end of the historical period of Italian neorealism: In Millicent Marcus's words, "The film is at once a celebration of neorealism and a lament to its death."[2] This volume makes clear, however, that neorealism continued its process of transformation both nationally and internationally well beyond that film. As a continuous process, neorealism did not die, and its core characteristic, an incessant vital search to express a different approach to reality, allowed it to revive itself and protected it against the impeding danger of inoculation. A floating notion of reality kept neorealism alive in different forms and across borders, allowing it to survive, expand, be exported, and be revisited in contemporary Italian filmmaking. As Marcus puts it, "The survival of classical realism goes far to explain the inconsistency and contradictions of modern realist theory, which demands that art be at once objective and politically *engagé*, that it be disinterested yet didactic, limited to the phenomena of empirical experience yet attuned to the underlying patterns that determine it, a styleless record of material reality yet formed and harmonized by human reason."[3]

The two films on which I focus here, Andrea and Antonio Frazzi's *Certi bambini* (A Children's Story, 2004), and Matteo Garrone's *Gomorra* (Gomorrah,

2008), are just two examples of how contemporary Italian cinema is dealing with its neorealist legacy, pushing it in the direction of what we can call, using Pier Paolo Pasolini's intuition, a "cinema of poetry." Even if it would be difficult to mark these films entirely as neorealist, they certainly echo neorealism and its core themes. Moreover, they are engaged in the representation of a dark side of reality, a reality of the Other, or a reality seen from the Other's side—that is, from a perspective that is not constricted in the borders of narration but expanded in the poetic form of cinema. As Garrone's remarkable international success testifies, by so doing, these filmmakers are also making neorealism internationally relevant again.[4] I analyze these films, investigating how their "cinema of poetry" can rightly be considered the contemporary legacy of neorealism, with its main interest in representing the real, even in its multifaceted expressions.

Scant attention to rules has always been part of neorealism's history, characterizing the movement even in its earlier stages. This absence of rules also has always made defining neorealism difficult.[5] By the 1960s, Michelangelo Antonioni, Pier Paolo Pasolini, and Federico Fellini, just to name a few Italian directors who started their careers at the heart of neorealism, were already surpassing its model to highlight the notion of a reality that was floating and difficult to grasp. They expanded the limits of the classical neorealist movement to include a "metaphysical reality" (Fellini), a "recreation of reality" (Antonioni) and a "certain realism" (Pasolini).[6] According to the maestro, Fellini, one of the shortcomings of neorealism was to limit itself to show only what was happening in the daily struggle of the common man, failing in this way to evolve with the reality itself, to look at the real without prejudice. "It's a question of having the feeling for reality. Italy was in ruins; you could say everything you felt just looking around. Later, the leftist press capitalized on this inadvertent one-sidedness by saying that the only valid thing to do in films is to show what happens around you. But this has no value from an aesthetic point of view, because always the important thing is to know *who* sees the reality."[7] In broad terms, the maestro believed that making film with a neorealist perspective meant to show a reality in its entirety (*a tutto tondo*), inclusive not only of its social but also of its spiritual and metaphysical aspects—"all that there is within man," as Fellini put it.[8] In this way, everything becomes realistic, including imagination. Hence Fellini's camera focused on all aspects of the human existence and its problematics. Critic André Bazin labeled Fellini's neorealism "the neorealism of the person"; Amédée Ayfre termed it "phenomenological realism"; Marcus underlined its "transcendent" connotations.[9] All agree that to mature and adapt to the social, political, and aesthetic changes of reality, making films with a neorealistic approach meant evolving beyond the movement's critically established limits.

In the same line, Antonioni's filmmaking was labeled "interior neorealism."[10] Having started his career working for the journal *Cinema*, the intellectual place of neorealism's conceptualization, and after his initial documentary phase as a director, Antonioni moved on to an existential phase during which he investigated the inner reality of his characters, who suffered from the mal du siècle of the 1960s. His existential trilogy (or *tetralogy*, if we wish to include *Deserto rosso* [Red Desert, 1964]) included *L'avventura* (1960), *La notte* (1961), and *L'eclisse* (Eclipse, 1962) and stemmed directly from his neorealist perspectives, bringing them to a new form. The director strove to be truthful regarding reality and to depict it objectively. He trusted his subjectivity to express his understanding of the concept. "I began," Antonioni explains, "as one of the first exponents of neorealism, and now by concentrating on the internal of character and psychology I do not think I have deserted the movement, but rather have pointed a path towards extending its boundaries. Unlike early neorealist filmmakers, I am not trying to show reality, I am attempting to recreate realism."[11]

Pier Paolo Pasolini's new neorealism also tended to represent a subjective realism while remaining indebted to historical neorealism. Like Antonioni, Pasolini's cinema sought to provoke reactions from viewers and increase their awareness of present social conditions. Unlike neorealist authors, however, Pasolini limited himself to illustrating reality without proposing a proactive solution or predicting a better future; rather, he highlighted reality's contradictory, ambivalent value. As Maurizio Viano puts it, Pasolini's cinematic text is imbued with "a certain realism that, in its turn, may affect the spectator in such a way the s/he feels motivated to adopt a realistic attitude (ideological self-awareness). . . . Thus, the ideological view of reality prompts the subject to investigate what cannot be seen, the dark side, the forbidden."[12] Pasolini's new neorealism, brought to life in oxymoronic terms, constituted a form of resistance against the social establishment. It acted by raising awareness, calling for viewers' interpretations and constantly renewing its forms of expression via a stimulating contamination of forms, images, and sounds.

Much like these classic directors, many contemporary Italian filmmakers are expanding the formal limits of neorealism but staying true to its core concern, the representation of reality. They experiment with new forms of visual representations that go beyond simple narration toward a more sophisticated use of the film form, which Pasolini called "poetic" as early as the 1960s. In fact, Pasolini as writer, critic, and director was the first to theorize an encounter between cinema (an audiovisual medium) and poetry (a purely verbal medium). He expressed his ideas in his talk, "Cinema of Poetry," delivered at the 1965 Pesaro Film Festival.[13] The author offered an analysis of cinematic language and explained that it contains the potential to develop the poetry of images through the use of visual signs, which he called "im-signs," and a "free indirect subjective" camera.[14] According to Pasolini, then, cinema is an expressive, subjective, metaphorical, oneiric representation: the filmmaker chooses the im-sign from the chaos of all possible images, which are prehuman, pretextual, and irrational, and adds to it an individual expressive quality represented through a "free indirect subjective" camera.[15] This is "the cinematic compromise between free indirect speech and interior monologue that could end the dominance of prose."[16] A free indirect camera re-creates the author's subjectivity via the characters' minds, thus visualizing the overall poetic of a film and re-creating it with maximum independence, free from any causal, temporal, or spatial logic. If the eye behind the camera can merge with the protagonist's mind and be guided by his/her irrational thoughts, subjective visions, and interior feelings, the film will gain the power to provoke and disrupt the linear logical and illustrative proceedings of a prosaic cinema and begin to unveil the profoundly poetic nature of cinema.

According to Pasolini, such a cinema of poetry would provide the freedom of expression necessary to reproduce the subjective shades that constitute reality.[17] Poetry is an intrinsic characteristic of the cinematic language that only poetic authors can bring into their work, either consciously or unconsciously. Only by using the cinematic language in all its potentialities can filmmakers disrupt the linear logic of a prose cinema and thus begin to unveil an alternative dimension of the real.[18] In a more conventional cinema of prose, on the contrary, narrative imposes an order that superintends the film's signification and that develops a sequential logic of events and of straightforward meanings, as classic Hollywood cinema exemplifies.[19] In some sense, Pasolini was continuing the project of historical neorealism, which had transgressed from the predominant prose form. Neorealism differentiated itself from the purely logical and illustrative proceedings of a proper cinema of narrative, as it sought to create a narrative structure different from that of Hollywood films, using repetitions and modules that disrupt the linear sequence of events, as theorist Gilles Deleuze explained in his *The Movement-Image*.[20] A cinema of poetry, then, carried the legacy of neorealism but differed from the earlier cinematic tradition in its fully theorized engagement with a new language of poetry rather than the poetic inner lyricism inherent in traditional neorealist films.

Like neorealist directors, auteurs of cinema of poetry were to strive to portray social reality as it unfolded before their eyes, but unlike the neorealists, these auteurs did not believe in the existence of an objective reality to be depicted. If historical neorealism was founded on the belief in the univocal meaning of the image, supposed to evoke the same feelings to everyone in the audience, a cinema of poetry was instead focused on giving ambivalent and ambiguous images to the public, buoyed by the belief that a universal point of view from which to look at the real did not exist. In so doing, the cinema of poetry perfectly inscribed itself in a rapport of continuity with historical neorealism in its characteristic of a nonstatic mode of representing the real.

While they shared neorealist authors' fundamental love for reality, the auteurs of cinema of poetry could not embrace either their faith in objectivity or their ideological optimism for the future. A cinema of poetry also proposed the highlighting of the aesthetic power of the film form. Indeed, the focus on the form connected the cinema of poetry to neorealism. A cinema of poetry thus shared with its predecessor an ethical and aesthetic basis, on which it elaborated and which it brought to sophisticated results. As the Frazzis' *Certi bambini* and Garrone's *Gomorra* show, a cinema of poetry is perfectly inscribed in such an aesthetic search while also engaged in the representation of the dark side of reality, a reality observed and represented from a perspective that is not constricted in the borders of narration but expanded in the poetic form of cinema.

At the level of content, the continuity between some of the recent Italian films and historical neorealism is striking. In its early years, neorealism often employed the perspective of the child to look at the social reality of Italy in the post–World War II period. Contemporary Italian cinema draws on the legacy of these neorealist children. "A recurrent trope in the national cinema during the postwar years," comments Àine O'Healy, "the image of the child as observer of a society that is out of control has been revived during the past [two] decade[s] in the works of several Italian filmmakers, suggesting an implicit homage to the legacy of neorealism."[21] Romoletto and his friends in Roberto Rossellini's *Roma, città aperta* (Rome, Open City, 1945), little Pascà of *Paisà* (Paisan, 1946), Giuseppe and Pasquale in *Sciuscià* (Shoeshine, 1946), and young Bruno in Vittorio De Sica's *Ladri di biciclette* (Bicycle Thieves, 1948) find their counterparts in many child protagonists of films in Italy's most recent cinema.[22] This recurrence signals not only how contemporary directors still feel compelled to pay homage to the legacy of neorealism but also how the figure of the coming-of-age young boy can be used as a metanarrative instrument and a mirror of reality. As Nicoletta Marini-Maio points out, "On one hand, the child is the active subject as well as the (often) abused object of the action; on the other hand, he or she provides the narrative point of view of the film, usually from an oblique and low perspective."[23] However, if the classical neorealist films used the child specifically for his condition as powerless and helpless spectator to reveal crude reality in all its brutality, in today's films, children are active protagonists of the film narrative as well as metanarrative tools revealed by formal poetic cameras.[24]

In *Certi bambini*, Andrea and Antonio Frazzi's camera highlights the condition of the protagonist, Rosario. The film tells the story of how the eleven-year-old street urchin is initiated into adulthood and the criminal life.[25] Set in a Neapolitan neighborhood, *Certi bambini* uses Rosario as an exemplar for the many children who live at the margins of legal society and whose initiation into adulthood is regulated not by the school or legal social system but rather by the criminal society governing the city. Most likely an orphan, Rosario lives with his old and sick grandmother. The care he takes of her contrasts markedly with the moral carelessness with which he joins the criminal groups of the area, ultimately even committing murder. The film advances by means of multiple flashbacks from Rosario's mind, as he travels on a metropolitan train to complete his first mission as a killer. The audience thus ultimately comes to better understand the child and his friends, their social condition, and the events that bring the eleven-year-old thoughtlessly to kill a man and soon thereafter go to play soccer with the same careless attitude.

As Rosario is the main focalizer of the film, the character through whom the world makes sense, the Frazzis make great use of subjective shots, or semi-subjective shots, frequent and sudden camera cuts, close-ups and in- and out-of-focus details, all of which become central formal elements that highlight the film's message. Images seem to be born in the child's mind and directly presented to the viewers through the use of a Steadicam that enhances the effect of the instability and alinearity of Rosario's mind as well as the high speed at which the world and Rosario are moving.[26] "The most relevant feature of the Steadicam," explains Marini-Maio, "is the fact that it can move anywhere and does not anchor the characters; indeed, it follows them even into the most impervious places. The Steadicam is a shooting human body, and its fluid motion and vision correspond to human motion and vision."[27] The Steadicam's formal characteristics thus make the Frazzis' camera best suited to highlight Rosario's confusion of mind and the speed of his life, as it follows him in a neorealist style, shadowing (*pedinamento*), modeling the cinematic form to its narrative content. Like Pasolini's free, indirect camera, the Frazzis' Steadicam re-creates the authors' subjectivity via the protagonist, visualizing the overall poetic of a film freely re-created, unbound by any logical, causal, or temporal assets. Such a camera is, then, the proper instrument of a cinema of poetry, which places itself in opposition to a mere imitation of the real and, rather, visually represents the real in its complicated, emotion-laden, subjective experiences.

High speed and confusion are the main formal cinematic elements that are highlighted in *Certi bambini*'s first scene and remain dominant throughout the film. The Frazzis' camera moves quickly as a group of children climbs some ideally beautiful marine white cliffs. From high-angle to low-angle shots, the camera records the children as they quickly move up the cliffs, dressed alike, thus giving a whole view of them as a group whose members' background and future might be also alike. Their figures are in focus, while everything else increasingly blurs. The editing is essential, too: sudden camera cuts from one child to the other suggest that the kids are like pieces of the same puzzle to be put together. They are indeed the subject of the film. The four boys soon make their way to the highway rail, through an uncultivated field of tall grass, a scene shot frontally with very tight close-ups. In the meantime, the soundtrack is imbued with the roaring of the cars on the highway: a whole world of confusion, chaos, and speed that the children cannot control and that is largely opposed to the calm suggested by the first shot of the sea, which instead symbolizes the peacefulness that childhood should embrace. Playing a dangerous prank on death, three of the four urchins decide to cross the road, and one by one they make it to the other side, while the fourth rambunctiously decides not to go. Thematically unconnected to the scene's narrative content, the Frazzis' visual aesthetic choices emphasize the speed, confusion, and mystification of the environment, which is the main force that guides the children's lives. The ideal peacefulness of the sea and the actual disorder of the kids' condition are in striking contrast, an element that is largely evidenced by the camera movements that frame the whole scene from nearby. The Frazzis often try to shoot close up on the kids, but the images are in part obscured by rocks, tall grass, or passing cars, which occupy the foreground of the shot.

Similarly, once we enter the train with Rosario, the narrative loosens its temporality, and the central element of the scene is the speed of the train. Speed becomes a formal and aesthetic ingredient, the main focus of the camera, which emphasizes it with frontal shots of the train, frequently cutting to lateral shots of the train in motion. The main subject of the various scenes on the train is the speed of Rosario's life: Like many children in similar circumstances, he must grow up faster than others. As the memories are played out in the boy's head while on the train, the Frazzis' camera, mostly driven by binary associations, cuts to temporally and spatially different planes. Making extensive use of subjective or semisubjective shots, the camera cuts from shots of the boy on the train to shots of his life in flashbacks: Rosario is in fact trying to make sense of his life, replaying his memories in his mind. The two parallel

Certi bambini (2004): An aerial shot of the neighborhood on the periphery of Naples showing boys (including Rosario) playing soccer. The inclusive shot seeks to give the neighborhood a universal value.

moments (present and past) are shown subjectively from Rosario's point of view, interacting and intersecting in an often alinear time frame, as evidenced by the appearance of people from his memory (such as the begging musicians) on the train. Memories of Rosario at home with his grandmother appear as if the two were seen through the windows of a high-speed train. The most evident example of how the Frazzis' camera can break temporal and spatial co-ordinates is the scene in which Rosario talks about his age with a girl he likes, Caterina. This scene is played twice with slightly different endings.[28] Rosario's life can be played and replayed, with the same actors and extras or with different protagonists, but the story will be the same, like a play that runs every day or night. The common and universal status of Rosario's life is evident in the last shot, the first and only aerial shot in the film. The camera captures a group of children at play, while an ambulance siren echoes the man's death. The editing cuts to a series of three long-distance shots that show Rosario as an integral part of the group of boys playing soccer, then part of the neighborhood square, finally part of a larger environment. The neighborhood lies on the periphery of Naples, but the inclusive shot aims to give it a universal value.

More than on the narrative content of scenes as such, the focus is on the Frazzis' formal aesthetic choices. The whole film is intended to underline Rosario's specific condition: He is, after all, an adolescent, with an improper sense of time and space and with little life experience, making him an unreliable narrator. Broaching definitions of childhood elaborated by critic Giuliana Minghelli and philosopher Giorgio Agamben as well as Zygmut Bauman's concept of liquid modernity, Marini-Maio suggests that Rosario's psyche is represented as both liminal and liquid. Adolescence, a liminal state between the dependence of childhood and the autonomy of maturity, also embodies the liquid, ever-mutating status of modern contemporary society.[29] Marini-Maio explains how "the permutations taking place in liquid modernity, as Bauman calls postmodern society, find their quintessential site in adolescence."[30] Shaped by Rosario's liminal and liquid status, the events, images, and emotions of his life are represented as intermittent and accumulated fragments. Only in the final climactic scene of the murder and its soccer epilogue are viewers able to make sense of how and why Rosario's two lives can coexist. Rosario's liminal and liquid state indeed allows him to have a chameleon-like personality—simultaneously to be a kid, a merciless gangster, and a compassionate caregiver. Most important, these two characteristics of Rosario's psyche are aesthetically rendered by the Frazzis' Steadicam, as Marini-Maio notes: "In *Certi bambini* the Steadicam has a place, a role, and a perspective: its fluidity is particularly apt to render the dynamic energy—the *liquidity*, in Bauman's terms—of Rosario's motion, feelings, memories, and a-linear thoughts."[31] The aesthetic exploration of the Frazzis' camera, then, visually codifies the meaning of Rosario's life, and that exploration becomes the formal and aesthetic central moments of their film. The narrative of the story is thus modified, and its most intimate subjective substance is captured by Frazzis' poetic camera. Their specific aesthetic choices are then significant per se, as they highlight the film's visual content, mirroring its main message but without mimicking the narrative progression.

Similarly to the Frazzi brothers, Garrone's camera works to amplify the liminal and liquid function of children as agents of reality. His internationally renowned *Gomorra* brought attention to the works of this contemporary Italian director and his poetic camera. The film is a coherent development of the cinematic discourse Garrone has been formulating for the past fifteen years, still linked to the same impulse that guided his camera at the beginning of his career, which defines his cinema of poetry: an aesthetic exploration of reality, not its mere representation. *Gomorra* contains a provocation that goes beyond its disquieting content to engage the form and object of the same filmic text to which the director applies, in an original and atypical way, the film's principle, or modus operandi. The film is a visual interpretation of Roberto Saviano's courageous and critically acclaimed book (*Gomorra*, 2006), which revealed and denounced Naples's criminal underbelly. If Saviano uses written narrative to make his specific accusation, placing himself in the line of the most famous Pasolinian "I know [*Io so*]," Garrone's form of statement of accusation and act of resistance are shaped within a cinematic and intellectual aesthetic.[32] In a departure from the journalist Saviano, Garrone does not claim objectivity or authenticity for his stories. As a matter of fact, the director explained that he did not want to achieve an authentic representation of the stories of his protagonists. He used Saviano's work as a point of departure to create his verisimilar world of the Camorra, imagining things as they could be, as if he were making an impressionist picture that seeks to give viewers a perceptible idea of that world. Garrone's *Gomorra* is focalized in only five of the stories or events that Saviano condemns and denounces in his work, at times enriched by imagined anecdotes: the stories of the tailor Pasquale, who sells his knowledge of couture by teaching a group of Chinese workers and therefore is punished by the Camorra; of the young Totò, who gradually enters the clan; of Ciro, who brings the stipends to the families protected by the Camorra but whose life becomes complicated thanks to the group of secessionists; of Franco and Roberto, implicated in the black market of eliminating toxic garbage; and finally of the naive teenagers, Marco and Cirowho, who want not to be part of any clan but rather to constitute their own and are eventually killed by the Camorra system. In the film world, reality is linked to the eye of the directors who represent it and to their capacity to transform it: All depends on where they choose to look, since the act of looking is always subjective, always has to do with a creative process. As an auteur of the camera, Garrone visually represents what he sees and imagines—as Pasolini said, "everything that is not known or is silenced."[33] Garrone's cinema can thus be considered a cinema of poetry that tries to liberate itself from the imitation of the real while going beyond it, surprising the viewer while offering an emotional impact.

Exemplary of Garrone's careful attention to the image is the opening scene of *Gomorra*, which seems a visionary surrealistic painting. This particular scene was not even in the original screenplay, but Garrone decided to shoot it after researching the Neapolitan area, observing it firsthand, and noticing how the value of beauty was profoundly rooted in the style of the new *camorristi*.[34] The setting is not immediately understandable, and the bloody shooting comes at first as a shock. From a black screen the viewers are introduced into the film with a disturbing noise. Little by little, the scene is illuminated by an unnatural fluorescent light; it is then shot in negative, slowly losing definition. The difficulty encountered in depicting colors, of gaining definition, is the formal aesthetic representation of the difficulty of focalizing the problem, the difficulty of seeing, understanding, and analyzing such a complicated world as that of the Camorra. This world seems to come from a different and distant galaxy, and it does not seem to make any sense. But the violence of the shooting, which spreads out of the scene, makes everything clear and puts everything in the right light. This is Naples, this is the way the Camorra lives and acts. Through the use of close-ups and extreme close-ups, the shifting in and out of focus, the swift movement of the camera on details, the refusal of deep focus, and the extensive use of narrative synecdoche and ellipsis, Garrone's *Gomorra*

In the initial scene of *Gomorra* (2008) the *camorristi* are depicted in a beauty salon. The setting is initially difficult to recognize because it is partially shot in negative, slowly losing definition, before all is made clear and a gunfight starts.

brings viewers inside this world, inside the scene, makes viewers witness the stories firsthand. Along the same lines, Garrone uses sharp focus and out-of-focus shots to show the confusion felt by various characters. Significant is the image of the young Totò, who wanders through the labyrinth-like building of Le Vele in Scampia: Garrone's camera, in another clear homage to neorealism, shadows the boy but always keeps his figure in focus as he moves around and brings deliveries to the families, in the same place where the groups of *camorristi* are talking, acting, or simply investigating, while everything around him appears out of focus, unrecognizable, confused.

The eye of the camera—and hence the eye of Garrone and the eye of the viewer—is always inside the scene, part of the scene but invisible, as if it is scrutinizing without intervening. The director seeks to make each scene a privileged point of observation from where he can witness the scene and capture its innermost core. For this reason, Garrone prefers to shoot his films himself with a handheld camera, as if it were part of him and he were part of the scene, as if he existed in symbiosis and empathy with it, so that he can gain a privileged perspective on what is happening.[35]

While investigating the scene so closely, Garrone thus can look beyond the image: He transforms it, capturing its most intimate substance, its pure form, which does not necessarily correspond to its naturalistic one. Rather, his image represents the object's most abstract value, which goes beyond the representation, becoming subjective interpretation on the part of the director and calling for a personal and sudden recognition on the part of the viewers. Garrone's cinema is therefore quite distant from the reproductive logic of contemporary cinema of prose or of cinema in general. His aesthetic resistance to a pure narrative format shocks viewers, affecting them at a physical level while offering an alternative vision of the real, created with his poetic camera.

Garrone's film never offers an exhaustive and detailed vision of the Neapolitan world, as Saviano does. On the contrary, the point of view from which Garrone and his viewers witness such a world is never complete. The camera's proximity to the scene and its objects distorts these objects and refuses to offer a clear, comprehensive vision. It is significant that the two teenagers, Marco and Ciro, spy on the *camorristi*, but their vision is always obfuscated or blocked by an obstacle: their perception of the Camorra, like that of viewers, is not clear. Their use of weapons, their thefts, burglaries, and violence make them feel as if they live in a film—perhaps the protagonists of their beloved *Scarface*, participants in a game that casts them as the heroes who succeed at everything. In the same vein, Garrone alternates sharply focused and out-of-focus shots to show the confusion felt by various characters. The only clear element is the invasive and threatening acoustic presence of voices from offscreen, which suggest a world populated by groups organized by the Camorra. Garrone visually and aesthetically represents a world that we can neither understand nor perceive completely.[36]

Like those of the Frazzi brothers, the specific aesthetic choices of Garrone's poetic camera are significant per se, as they highlight the film's visual content, which corresponds to its whole meaning and message. The movements of Garrone's poetic camera do not mimic the narrative's progression; rather, they work as singular objects to which the film's narrative is subjected and by way of which viewers' attention is focalized. Garrone's and the Frazzi brothers' aesthetic resistance, in this case directed against the Camorra, speaks with the power of the images—specifically, with their formal elements—rather than with strong explicit accusations. This resistance is truer to the neorealist aesthetic legacy than might initially seem to be the case. Their films enforce an aesthetic resistance toward more conventional and commercial narrative-based films while denouncing a troubled social reality and the popular oblivion that hides it and makes it possible. More than documenting, these new Italian directors interpret the reality of the Camorra, respecting its actuality but depicting it in the most apt way for the visual medium of cinema. In line with a creative cinema of poetry, these authors represent such a reality by re-creating it and transforming it through their artistic eye, in always surprising ways and according to modes of representation that succeed in their ultimate goal: emotionally affecting viewers and making them feel like part of the picture, its real subjects. The directors use cinematic narrative in its purely aesthetic form, an anticonventional aesthetic, proper to a poetic camera that models the film form to its narrative content.

Numerous other authors have similarly employed a poetic camera that goes beyond the visible. In Italian cinema, Pasolini, Antonioni, Franco Piavoli, Fellini, Pupi Avati, Carlo Mazzacurati, Carlo Piccioni, Paolo Virzì, and Ermanno Olmi, among others, have offered models of a cinema of poetry. More recent and international examples also come to mind. Young Italian filmmaker Giorgio Diritti has had international success with *L'uomo che verrà* (The Man Who Will Come, 2009), which has been rightly saluted as a "neorealist film in poetic form"; the film indeed continues the development of the cinema of poetry.[37] Once again, the cinema of poetry can hardly be framed as a national project. While this essay is not the place to further elaborate the point, elements of the cinema of poetry can be found in the cinema of Jean-Luc Godard as well as in other protagonists of global neorealism, such as Jafar Panahi's *Ayneh* (The Mirror, 1997). This resonant aesthetic position has a national and international value and renews the essence of neorealism.

Like Garrone and the Frazzi brothers, all of these auteurs are *poietes* (poets) of the camera, engaged in enhancing the cinematic, visual language of poetry as a means to capture deeper dimensions of reality. Truer to the philological meaning of the word *poetry*, rooted in the Greek word *poiesis* (ποήιω, "to create," "to make"), these poetic works are original creations, new realities brought into being by their authors, but do not necessarily depend on mimetic representation of nature. Like the historical neorealist filmmakers, contemporary *poietes* of the camera continue to experiment with cinematic form, re-creating the "real," never allowing its language to solidify into trope or to slip into a conventional mode that would freeze an otherwise fluid concept of reality. In so doing, they cannot avoid coming to terms with neorealism itself. The cinema of poetry created by these authors in fact represents cinema's capacity to avoid allowing historical neorealism to inoculate itself but rather to bring neorealism up to date. These films demonstrate how neorealism can still continue to speak to the international contemporary landscape with a common language: the language of the poetry of cinema. These *poietes* prove that the cinematic art can surpass the visible, showing how going beyond the logic of a cinema of narrative is the first step toward a more profound penetration of both image and reality. In this way, these auteurs achieve results of surprising critical resonance for both cinema and poetry.

Notes

1. Roland Barthes, *Mythologies*, trans. Annette Lavers (New York: Hill and Wang, 1972), 150.

2. Millicent Marcus, *Italian Film in the Light of Neorealism* (Princeton: Princeton University Press, 1986), 96.

3. Ibid., 9.

4. Between 2008 and 2009, *Gomorra* won twenty-three international prizes (among them the Grand Prize at the Cannes Film Festival 2008, the David di Donatello 2009, and the Silver Ribbon 2009) and was nominated for eighteen others (including the Golden Globe 2009 and the Critics Choice Award 2009). For a complete list, see http://www.imdb.com/title/tt0929425/awards (accessed January 26, 2011).

5. See Zagarrio, in this volume.

6. Marcus reads Fellini's cinema as a representation of a "metaphysical reality" (*Italian Film in the Light,* 146) and investigates how Michelangelo Antonioni wanted to "recreate neorealism" in his films (188–89). Critic Maurizio Viano speaks of Pasolini's cinema as imbued with "a certain realism" (*A Certain Realism: Making Use of Pasolini's Film Theory and Practice* [Berkeley: University of California Press, 1993]).

7. "Certain people still think neo-realism is fit to show only certain kinds of reality; and they insist that this is social reality. But in this way, it becomes mere propaganda. It is a program; to show only certain aspects of life" (Federico Fellini, "The Road Beyond Neorealism," in *La Strada: Federico Fellini, Director,* ed. Peter Bondanella and Manuela Gieri [New Brunswick: Rutgers University Press, 1987], 217).

8. "Not just social reality, but spiritual reality, metaphysical reality, all that there is within man" (Federico Fellini, *Fellini on Fellini,* trans. Isabel Quigley [New York: Dell, 1976], 152).

9. See Marcus, *Italian Film in the Light,* 144–63.

10. Ibid., 188.

11. Antonioni quoted in Hollis Alpert, "A Talk with Antonioni," *Saturday Review* 31.27 (October 1962): 65.

12. Viano, *Certain Realism,* 61–62.

13. The piece was published in 1972 in *Empirismo eretico,* the volume that collects his thoughts on language, literature, and cinema. It has been translated into English as Pier Paolo Pasolini, *Heretical Empiricism,* trans. Ben Lawton and Louise K. Barnett (Bloomington: Indiana University Press, 1988).

14. According to semiotic theory, linsigns delineate the words per se in the complex communicative system of linguistic signs. Im-signs are concrete images that are simultaneously abstract in that they are formed by objects, pictorial or actual events, emotions, or even sounds, coming directly from the unorganized, endless, and chaotic world of memory and dreams. As Pasolini explains, "The linguistic archetypes of the im-signs are the images of our memories and our dreams, that is, images of 'communication with ourselves' (and of only indirect communication with others in that the image that the other person has of a thing of which I speak to him is a reference we have in common). Those archetypes thus lay a direct base of 'subjectivity' for the im-signs, which consequently belong in the highest

degree to the world of poetry. Thus the tendency of film language should be expressively subjective and lyrical" (*Heretical Empiricism*, 173).

15. This approach should guarantee a subjective-lyric expression in the cinema, but in practice, on the contrary, cinema productions tend to favor the rationale of prose narrative, which works according to logical and illustrative proceedings. The metaphoric power of cinema struggles to reach the level of abstraction of poetry but remains partly linked to the communicative nature of prose. Pasolini nevertheless realizes that he witnessed new tendencies that led convincingly in the direction of an uncorrupted "cinema of poetry": "I have already stated that cinema, lacking a conceptual, abstract vocabulary, is powerfully metaphoric; as a matter of fact, *a fortiori*, it operates immediately on the metaphoric level. Particular, deliberately generated metaphors, however, always have some quality that is inevitably crude and conventional. . . . Whatever part of the poetically metaphoric which is sensationalistically possible in film, it is always in close osmosis with its other nature, the strictly communicative one of prose. The latter, in the end, is the one which has prevailed in the brief tradition of the history of cinema, embracing in a single linguistic convention art films and escapist films, the masterpieces and the serials" (*Heretical Empiricism*, 174). Despite this hurdle, the fundamental irrational element of the cinema of poetry and its images, says Pasolini, is an attribute that cannot be eliminated, and only the filmmakers who embrace it can highlight the profoundly poetic nature of cinema and of the im-signs. According to Pasolini, a "cinema of poetry" avails itself of the power of im-signs and in so doing suggests abstract, subjective, and often emblematic connotations of the camera object.

16. Pasolini, *Heretical Empiricism*, 174.

17. These theoretical ideas found practical examples in various films. In "Cinema of Poetry," Pasolini saluted Antonioni's re-creation of reality as an example of "cinema of poetry" and praised films by Bernardo Bertolucci. Before theorizing his ideas, the auteur had also put them into practice. "Cinema di poesia" came out four years after his first film, *Accattone* (1961).

18. The most straightforward examples of a "cinema of prose" are the classic Hollywood films as well as the more commercial films released internationally.

19. In this regard, see Sandro Bernardi, *Il paesaggio nel cinema italiano* (Venice: Marsilio, 2002).

20. Gilles Deleuze, *Cinema*, vol. 1, *The Movement-Image*, trans. Hugh Tomlinson and Barbara Habberjam (Minneapolis: University of Minnesota Press, 1986), 198–205.

21. Àine O'Healy, "Are the Children Watching Us? The Roman Films of Francesca Archibugi," *Annali d'italianistica* 17 (1999): 121.

22. A few examples include Gianni Amelio's *Il ladro di bambini* (The Stolen Children, 1992) and *Le chiavi di casa* (The Keys to the House, 2004); Andrea and Antonio Frazzi's *Il cielo cade* (The Sky Is Falling, 2000) and *Certi bambini*; Francesca Archibugi's *Il grande cocomero* (The Great Pumpkin, 1993); Antonio Capuano's *Pianese Nunzio, 14 anni a maggio*

(Pianese Nunzio, Fourteen in May, 1996) and *La guerra di Mario* (Mario's War, 2005); Emanuele Crialese's *Respiro* (Grazia's Island, 2002) and *Nuovomondo* (The Golden Door, 2006); Garrone's *Gomorra*; Marco Tullio Giordana's *Quando sei nato non puio più nascond-erti* (Once You're Born You Can No Longer Hide, 2005); Gabriele Salvatores's *Io non ho paura* (I'm Not Scared, 2003); and Costanza Quatriglio's *L'isola* (The Island, 2003).

23. See Nicoletta Marini-Maio, "The Children Are Still Watching Us: The 'Visual Psycho-Mimesis' of *Il cielo cade* and *Certi bambini*," in *Coming of Age on Film: Stories of Transformation in World Cinema*, ed. Anne Hardcastle, Roberta Morosini, and Kendall Tarte (Cambridge: Cambridge Scholars, 2009), 40–57.

24. Speaking about the condition of the child in neorealism, Gilles Deleuze explains that "in the adult world, the child is affected by a certain motor helplessness, but one which makes him all the more capable of seeing and hearing. Similarly, if everyday banality is so important, it is because, being subject to sensory-motor schemata which are automatic and preestablished, it is all the more liable, on the least disturbance of equilibrium between stimulus and response (as in the scene with the little maid in *Umberto D*), suddenly to free itself from the laws of this schema and reveal itself in a visual and sound nakedness, crudeness and brutality which make it unbearable, giving it the pace of a dream or a nightmare" (*Cinema*, vol. 2, *The Time-Image*, trans. Hugh Tomlinson and Barbara Habberjam [Minneapolis: University of Minnesota Press, 1989], 3).

25. The film is the visual representation of Diego De Silva's 2001 novel, *Certi bambini*.

26. The Steadicam, explains Marini-Maio, was "created in 1975 as a substitute for the hand-held camera in running shots over rough grounds" and "is comprised of a camera, an arm that carries the weight of the camera and isolates it from the jerking caused by the operator's movement, and a series of rings and bearings that provide support and connect the arm to a vest that the operator wears" ("Children Are Still Watching Us," 53).

27. Ibid.

28. For an analysis of this scene, see ibid., 51.

29. Ibid., 45. Marini-Maio notes that "the notion of the social transition between infancy and adulthood, namely, adolescence, was formulated as an anthropological category in the nineteenth century with the introduction of compulsory education and of labor legislation."

30. Ibid, 50.

31. Ibid, 53.

32. In 1974, Pasolini published in the Italian newspaper *Corriere della sera* a provocative article in which he declared that he knew who the perpetrators of recent terrorist acts were: "I know. I know the names of those responsible for what we called a military coup. . . . I know the names of those responsible for the massacres in Milan, Brescia and Bologna. . . . I know all these names and know all the facts (the attacks on the institutions, and the massacres) of which they are guilty. I know. But I do not have evidence. I do not even have clues. I know because I am an intellectual, a writer who tries to follow all that happens, to

imagine all that we do not know, or that is silenced" (Pier Paolo Pasolini, "Che cos'è questo golpe?" *Corriere della sera*, November 14, 1974; translation by author). The article offers a moral, political, and aesthetic statement and testament by the poet Pasolini, asserting his knowledge of the facts and his role as an intellectual who knows because he has the freedom of seeing and imagining the most hidden realities.

33. Ibid.

34. See Pierpaolo De Sanctis, "Il crepuscolo della bellezza: Lo sguardo e il metodo di Matteo Garrone," in *Non solo Gomorra: Tutto il cinema di Matteo Garrone* (Cantalupo in Sabina: Sabinae, 2008), 15.

35. De Sanctis, "Crepuscolo," 16.

36. The same strategy is used at other times in the film—for example, when the tailor, Pasquale, is introduced and teaches the large group of Chinese workers. He is a stranger in their world and does not realize in what he is becoming implicated.

37. Marcello Masnieri, "Giorgio Diritti: Cinema neorealista che sa di poesia," January 25, 2010, http://www.bergamonews.it/cultura_spettacolo/articolo.php?id=20891 (accessed January 26, 2011).

CONTRIBUTORS

NATHANIEL BRENNAN is a doctoral candidate in the Cinema Studies Department at New York University.

LUCA CAMINATI is associate professor of film studies in the Mel Hoppenheim School of Cinema at Concordia University in Montreal. He is the author of *Orientalismo eretico: Pasolini e il cinema del Terzo Mondo* (Milan: Mondadori, 2007) and is currently investigating Rossellini's nonfiction films from the early "backyard experiments" to his 1957 trip to India.

SILVIA CARLOROSI is assistant professor of Italian at the University of Maryland. She is the author of "Pier Paolo Pasolini's *La ricotta*: The Power of Cinepoiesis," *Italica* 86.2 (2009): 254–71, and "Neo-romanticismo in risposta al postmodernismo? L'influenza leopardiana nella poetica cinematografica felliniana di *La voce della luna*," in *Film e letterature: Paesaggi* (Bologna: Gedit, 2007), 89–111. She is currently working on *A Grammar of Cinepoiesis: Poetic Cameras of Italian Cinema*.

CAROLINE EADES is associate professor in the School of Languages, Literatures, and Cultures at the University of Maryland. She is the author of *Le cinéma post-colonial français* (Paris: Cerf, 2006) and is currently working on a book on classical reception in film.

SAVERIO GIOVACCHINI is associate professor of history at the University of Maryland. He is the author of *Hollywood Modernism* (Philadelphia: Temple University Press, 2001) and of several articles on American and European cinema. His current project is *The Rise of Atlantis: Cultural Coproduction and the Making of the Cinema of the West*.

PAULA HALPERIN is assistant professor of Latin American history at the State University of New York at Purchase.

NEEPA MAJUMDAR is associate professor of film studies in the English Department at the University of Pittsburgh. She is the author of *Wanted, Cultured Ladies Only! Female Stardom and Cinema in India, 1930s–1950s* (Urbana: University of Illinois Press, 2009).

MARIANO MESTMAN teaches film studies and communication sciences at the University of Buenos Aires and is a researcher at the CONICET on visual representations of labor. He is the coauthor, with Ana Longoni, of *Del di tella a tucumán arde: Vanguardia artística y política en el 68 argentino* (Buenos Aires: El Cielo por Asalto, 2000).

HAMID NAFICY is the Sheikh Hamad bin Khalifa Al Thani Professor of Communication at Northwestern University. He is the author of numerous works in Persian and English, including *An Accented Cinema: Exilic and Diasporic Filmmaking* (Princeton: Princeton University Press, 2001), *Home, Exile, Homeland: Film, Media, and the Politics of Place* (New York: Routledge, 1998), *The Making of Exile Cultures: Iranian Television in Los Angeles* (Minneapolis: University of Minnesota Press, 1993), and *A Social History of Iranian Cinema*, 4 vols. (Durham, N.C.: Duke University Press, forthcoming).

SADA NIANG teaches in the French department of the University of Victoria. He is the author of *Djibril Diop Mambéty: Un cinéaste à contre-courant* (Paris: Harmattan, 2001) and has edited several volumes on African cinema.

MASHA SALAZKINA is assistant professor in the Mel Hoppenheim School of Cinema at Concordia University in Montreal. She is the author of *In Excess: Sergei Eisenstein's Mexico* (Chicago: University of Chicago Press, 2009).

SARAH SARZYNSKI is an assistant professor/faculty fellow at the Center for Latin American and Caribbean Studies at New York University. Her main research areas are in modern Latin American history, visual culture, and gender and sexuality. Currently, she is working on a book about rural social activism and regional identity in Northeastern Brazil during the Cold War.

ROBERT SKLAR was professor emeritus of cinema at New York University. Among his books are *Movie-Made America: A Cultural History of American Movies* (New York: Vintage, 1994) and *City Boys: Cagney, Bogart, Garfield* (Princeton: Princeton University Press, 1992), as well as *A World History of Film* (New York: Abrams, 2003).

VITO ZAGARRIO is professor of cinema and television at the University of Rome. He has written and edited numerous volumes, including monographs on Francis Ford Coppola, Frank Capra, and John Waters. He has also directed documentaries, television programs, and three feature films. *Divine Waters,* his documentary on John Waters, has been distributed in the United States.

INDEX

111567740 (MH)